MY FIRST
EIGHTY-THREE YEARS
IN AMERICA

BOOKS BY JAMES W. GERARD

My First Eighty-three Years in America
Face to Face with Kaiserism
My Four Years in Germany

Photograph by Lotte Jacobi

JAMES W. GERARD

My First Eighty-three Years in America

THE MEMOIRS OF JAMES W. GERARD

BY

James W. Gerard

GARDEN CITY, N.Y.

Doubleday & Company, Inc.

1951

G
.G3124A

To the charming and devoted companion of nearly fifty years,
MY WIFE

FOREWORD

THERE IS A HAPPY PERIOD IN A MAN'S LIFE WHEN HE IS UN-
able to believe that he will ever be old—say as old as thirty.
His experience with time is so limited that even his maturity,
while perhaps admitted as a probability, is so remote as to
approach infinity. This conviction of semi-eternal youth stems
from a half-formulated belief that the death sentence upon
mankind will somehow be set aside, at least for him. He re-
jects the thought of age along with the thought of death because he notes half-consciously that death does not come
suddenly, but by degrees, as interests and faculties slip away.
His ancient history textbooks tell him that Alexander the
Great found nothing to live for at the age of thirty-two, thus
bolstering his notions with classical proof.

As a youth, I was not free from the universal human—and
how fortunate!—belief that things will be better next year,
but generally I was content to think that my happy, active,
golden days were *now*. The future, when I thought of it at
all, seemed a great blur of stodginess and responsibility. Now
that I am eighty-three, I still do not believe that I shall ever
be an old man. Perhaps I am arriving at a definition of old
age as that period when one has lost the zest for living to the
extent of one's physical and mental capacities.

Somewhere around my middle twenties I concluded that thirty was not actually the gateway to senility, or need not be, and thereafter I began to realize that a great deal of living was possible between the thirtieth year and the grave. It was then that the idea of writing my memoirs took root. I began to look forward, more and more as the years came and went, to the actual business of recording my experiences and observations. I recommend this resolution to all the multitudes who feel that someday they must combine their thoughts and potential literary skill into a Great Novel. Memoirs, being a summing up, are necessarily deferred. This gives the intending author every excuse for temporary inaction, and he avoids tormenting himself with the feeling of guilt and frustration that procrastination, literary or otherwise, ordinarily brings.

Just what prompted me so early to decide on autobiography as a literary endeavor I am not altogether sure. I do not think that I felt more strongly than most young men that my life was to be filled with exciting adventures and spectacular achievement. Perhaps it was that my enjoyment of living was such that I determined to enjoy it twice, once in reality and once in retrospect. At any rate, it is because of that early determination that these recollections are aided by a faithfully kept diary, as well as a long memory.

During my eighty-three years I have ranged widely over Europe and North America as schoolboy, lawyer, judge, ambassador, sportsman, traveler, and—that unctuous phrase—Man of Affairs. That last, being translated, means that I have striven to defend my personal fortunes against the stratagems of other Men of Affairs and the powers of Wall Street, and, whenever possible, to improve them.

My experience in practical politics began in the 1870s

when I sat on President Grant's lap and gave him some childish advice on labor problems which he didn't follow, his own
judgment being slightly better. Then, after the lapse of a
few years, I became active again, beginning with Bryan's
golden age of free silver and continuing down through the
years, Democrat by Democrat, through Wilson, Franklin
Roosevelt and his determined heir, and the Century of the
Common Man. The Common Man I take to be properly included among the Democrats, for I have never known a Republican who would admit to being common.

Except for a few short interludes I have been engaged in
business as well as law ever since I left college. My law practice and my term on the New York Supreme Court bench
both brought me into close and constant contact with almost
every conceivable kind of business enterprise.

Out of my experiences has come the strong belief that individual enterprise is a freedom to be fostered and protected
in this or any other country, if that country wants to promote
the happiness of the individual and wants to exploit the
earth's fruits for the common good. This implies the necessity for reasonable restraints and safeguards in the general
interest, and not—as seems to be the trend during the present
swing of the pendulum—a strait jacket upon the initiative of
the individual, in the supposed interest of those having
neither initiative nor energy. It is true that a large portion of
mankind is actually in his sorry state not from the lack of
opportunity but from the lack of capacity to seize and develop the opportunity that confronts him. He is no more to
be blamed for this condition than I am because I did not
become an operatic tenor, considering that the doors of the
Metropolitan are always open to superior talent. The thresh-
old of opportunity is fairly high, but the individuals who have

crossed it are so numerous that they cannot be dismissed as exceptions or freaks. To my mind it is both possible and desirable to improve the lot of the submerged faction of our people without, of necessity, emasculating the productiveness of that portion of the population that has made us the vital nation that we are, and to whom we must look for future progress and leadership.

The stock answer of the socialistic thinkers is that men can be made to accept incentives other than profit. They mention honors, and the inner satisfaction of serving one's fellow men. My observation has been that these are compensatory mantles which men wrap about themselves as a consolation for having failed in more sincere endeavors. I do not believe that men reared in the tradition of freedom could be happy as faceless drudges for the glory of the state, where the only reward was a livelihood and lapel button bestowed by the neighborhood commissar.

If we are ever subjected to some form of Socialism or Communism, ninety-nine out of every hundred Americans would resent it fiercely. Even the most avid American *aficionados* of the Russian way of life rarely elect to settle down in that country and live under the strictures that it imposes on the individual. When examined objectively, the communal life partakes of the nature of a hive of bees. Indeed, its proponent's arguments are largely a case for the many admittedly excellent virtues of beehive life. But what always escapes the beehive proponent is that in beehives—and in all communized societies—existence is invariably completely regulated. All members labor under inexorable laws of function. Those who have no function are killed in one way or another. When the drone has finished his arduous task for the state, he is eaten. When the worker has finished his allotted work, he gets no more food. It is rather terrifying to consider the fate of the submerged portion of our population if it were fed into the maw of such a system. It is difficult to believe that these people would suffer the same gruesome fate as their companions in Russia have, for we do not have the fatalistic, oriental indifference to individual suffering that the Russians have demonstrated for centuries. A communized society in America might well find that the ineffective members of our population would prove to be a more distressing problem than they are under our present system. My anxiety is not so much over Socialism per se—for it is fascinating on paper and sounds enthralling over the teacups—as over the loss of human values that it results in, and the animalistic and materialistic existence to which it must lead.

CHAPTER I

WE AMERICANS LIVE SO INTENSELY IN THE PRESENT THAT any indication of interest in one's forebears is likely to be looked upon as an eccentricity. Family histories, for the most part, are as out of date as a crayon portrait on an easel in the parlor. It has become a stock joke that Americans become concerned with their grandparents' lives only when some account of them becomes necessary to support a tenuous claim to social eminence. Such an anecdote is the one said to be original with Mark Twain, and probably correctly, since it combines devastating wit with that biting scorn of things foreign that marred some of his work so lamentably. The story relates that a Frenchman twitted him with the remark: "Whenever an American acquires a few thousand dollars and a little leisure, he spends them trying to find out who his grandfather was." To which Mark Twain replied: "Yes, and a Frenchman in the same circumstances spends them trying to find out who his father was!"

Like the newly emerging aristocracy, memoir writers tend to devote an unconscionable time to reviewing the merits and importance of their ancestors. I have no complaint about this in principle, for obviously some account of a man's forebears and background is not only a proper part of his personal history, but also provides useful clews to his actions and attitudes.

In my own case, I am a typical American with a predominate Scottish ancestral strain. The first of my ancestral Gerards in Scotland went there from France in the seventeenth century, fleeing the persecutions of the French Protestants following the revocation of the Edict of Nantes. My grandfather, James Watson Gerard, passed on his name intact to my father, who in turn gave it unchanged to me, thus setting up a modest, uniform dynasty of James I, James II, and James III. It will be more relaxing, however, to refer to my two immediate forebears simply as Father Gerard and Grandfather Gerard. When I go back three generations, to my immigrant ancestor, Great-grandfather Gerard, the identity problem is eased. His name was William.

William Gerard was a native of Aberdeen, Scotland, a city now known chiefly as the locale of bad Scotch jokes, although actually it is a seat of learning. William was the son of Robert and Elizabeth Gerard who in 1774 lived on the northeast coast of Banffshire, where Great-great-grandfather Robert was a Presbyterian minister.

To offer more than limited opportunities for its young men, a land must have either unexploited natural resources or a rapidly growing population. Scotland had neither, and great numbers of its most adventurous young men left to seek their fortunes in foreign lands. Since a minister's purse is traditionally thin, it is unlikely that William's father supplied him with much capital. Family letters of the time, however, indicate that he was able to enter business on his own in Gibraltar and Tangiers, one successful venture being the importation of mules from Africa. Apparently he was a canny trader, for when he came to New York about 1776 he was prepared to set up an importing and general merchandising business that soon became quite profitable.

Great-grandfather William was a Loyalist, a circumstance for which no apology need be offered, since, being newly arrived, he had no experience of the conditions that irritated the colonies. So, when the British evacuated New York in the fall of 1783, William, of prudent necessity, went with them. He went to New Brunswick, where he remained until things quieted down before returning to New York. In 1781 he had married Christina Glass, who was also a native of Scotland, the daughter of a merchant, Alexander Glass. One of our family records describes the bride as "an attractive young lady of but sixteen years."

Upon his return to New York, William Gerard and his wife's brother went into business as "Importers and General Merchants" at the southwest corner of Wall and Water streets in a building that is still standing. Great-grandfather William died in 1794, not very long after the birth of his son, James Watson Gerard, my grandfather.

I have no record of Grandfather Gerard's childhood. He went to Columbia College, however, and after his graduation in 1811 he was admitted to the bar. In 1820 he married Elizabeth Sumner, the daughter of Governor Increase Sumner of Massachusetts, and took a house at 26 Broadway. It was there, in 1823, that my father was born. A few years after his marriage, Grandfather moved to 499 Broadway, and in 1847 he built the most northerly stone mansion in New York at 17 Gramercy Park, a fact which is mentioned in *Philip Hone's Diary*. Hone also noted that on November 2, 1842, Grandfather attended a banquet for Daniel Webster and made a speech "in his usual good taste."

If you go back far enough into anyone's family history you frequently land in Boston. In my own ancestry this connection came with Grandfather's marriage to Elizabeth Sumner, who was heiress to a large part of a section of the city known as East Boston. Her father, Governor Sumner, was born in Roxbury, Massachusetts, in 1746. He was elected to Congress in 1782 but didn't take his seat because in August of that year he was made an associate judge of the Supreme Judicial Court, a position which he held for fourteen years. His choice of the state judgeship in preference to a seat in Congress shows how much more importance and prestige the states had in those days than the Federal Government.

Sumner was governor of Massachusetts in 1797 and was re-elected in 1798 and again in 1799. He died in June 1799 at the age of fifty-three. His funeral was attended by the President of the United States, John Adams, and is said to have been the most solemn and imposing burial that had been witnessed in the Commonwealth up to that time. His wife was Elizabeth Hyslop, daughter of William Hyslop of Boston. It was through her that the inheritance of one third of East Boston came into the family. Her father must have been a stern old Calvinist, for when the Brattle Church, of which he was a member, proposed to import an organ, he strenuously opposed the innovation as being both sacrilegious and frivolous. When the instrument arrived in Boston Harbor he proposed to pay the cost of it if the church authorities would have it thrown overboard. His offer was refused.

Getting back to Grandfather James, his law career and the War of 1812 began almost simultaneously. This circumstance provided what was to be the only interlude in his long law practice. He joined a military company of young men who called themselves the Iron Greys because they affected battle charges of that color.

Having hung up his sword, Grandfather Gerard returned to his profession, and despite occasional vicissitudes became the most successful lawyer in New York. He had an impressive courtroom presence and that gift for persuasive speech that makes for unusual success in jury cases. He took no partners, and even though his fees were not so large as they might have been, he prospered greatly. On the side he was something of a speculator. An article in *Harper's Weekly* for June 19, 1875, quotes Chief Justice Daly of the Common Pleas Court, who had pronounced a eulogy on the character of Grandfather before the New York Historical Society. In the grandiloquent, formal periods of the day Justice Daly summed up that side of Grandfather in part as follows:

. . . in 1826 he achieved great success in a cotton speculation but in the subsequent panic lost his own and his wife's fortune and was deeply in debt. Their fashionable house in Broadway was sold, the upper part of a house in Chambers Street was taken, and Mr. Gerard applied himself with assiduity to his profession. The success which followed his return to the bar was remarkable. Still, the struggle was severe. His debts were large, and . . . it was a long time before he was able to meet his pecuniary liabilities. The time, however, did come. In time a house was purchased in Broadway and Mr. Gerard came to enjoy professional success, the accumulation of wealth, and an age of affluence.

Even though it reads like the synopsis of a success novel, with just the right amount of punishment as a warning against speculation, Mr. Justice Daly's circumspect choice of words can't hide the fact that Grandfather took a hard fall and had a difficult time recouping his fortunes.

In 1825 he founded the "Society for the Reformation of

Juvenile Delinquents." The Society built a house of refuge
in which young offenders were placed to segregate them
from the adult criminals in the regular cells. At one time or
another Grandfather provided money for the education and
support of artists, both literary and musical, who lacked
money to pay for their professional training. In an unostentatious way he did a great deal for all sorts of people who
needed help. He took an active interest in the public schools.

Grandfather was not an Abolitionist, and was violently
opposed to those who would drag the North into war with
the slave-holding South. The general public of that day did
not realize—any more than the public of this day—that slavery
was only the ostensible issue that was leading toward a
civil war. But the slavery issue was easily understood by the
masses. It had a tremendous emotional impact, and was reason enough, in the popular mind, to justify radical action,
the excesses of which went far beyond those of any political
and economic struggle. Grandfather believed that the slaves
could be freed without bloodshed. In 1851 he spoke at a
great meeting in Castle Garden and took the position that
slavery might be abolished by purchase, as had been done in
the British West Indies. He also spoke against the repeal of
the Missouri Compromise. It is possible that if this advice had
been followed the slaves could have been freed for a small
fraction of the cost of the Civil War, and that the war and
all its agony in blood and suffering might have been avoided.

During the 1850s, as the issues that were to culminate in
the Civil War became more bitter and feeling became more
violent on each side, there were those who feared, and not
unreasonably, that the Abolitionists who were promoting
sectional hatred in their efforts to free the Negroes might
cause a breakup of the Union. It was to prevent this immi-

nent disaster that the National Union League came into being in 1860, and Grandfather was its first president.

The New York *World* for October 8, 1860, carried the following advertisement, which gives a good idea of his activities:

DOWN WITH SECTIONALISM: NATIONAL UNION LEAGUE.

Ratification of the Union Electoral Ticket. The National Union League, and all who are opposed to the dangerous sectional and fanatical doctrines of the black Republican Party, are requested to meet on this evening, October 8th at Thorp's Union Hotel, Union Square, at 7 o'clock, for the purpose of proceeding in a body to the great Union ratification meeting at the Cooper Institute. Members and others are requested to appear in plain citizen's dress—black coat and beaver hat. Cockades and badges will be furnished to all by the League. Torches will precede the lines. A Drum Corps will be in attendance. Friends of the Union attend!

JAMES W. GERARD, Pres't

COL. H. A. T. GRANBERY, 1st Vice Pres't

GILBERT M. PLATT, 2nd Vice Pres't

John C. Gunther, Treas.

W. S. Tisdale, Sec'ry.

Grandfather also interested himself actively in the New York police force, which was not even remotely comparable with New York's finest of today. The cop of the fifties was usually a worthy but ignorant Irishman, often overweight but always underpaid. In groups—with their diverse and tattered attire—they looked like Falstaff's army. The only distinguishing mark of a policeman's calling was a star-shaped badge. Most people then considered that any uniform, with the exception of the military, was the characteristic garment of servitude, and the average policeman, who considered himself as good as any man and a damned sight better than most, refused to wear one.

When Grandfather was in London he had seen the police uniform created by Sir Robert Peel, whose efforts in behalf of the London police had caused them to be referred to for a long time as "Peelers." Grandfather realized the effect of appearance on morale and efficiency, and wrote a typically denunciatory pamphlet advocating this and other reforms in New York's police administration. When a new uniform was finally designed for the police they refused to wear it. About 1853, however, a Mrs. Coventry Waddell, who lived at Fifth Avenue and Thirty-eighth Street, gave a grand fancy-dress ball. Grandfather had one of the new police uniforms made for himself and wore it to the ball. After that the police decided that if the uniform was good enough for "Jimmy" Gerard to wear to a ball, it would do for them to work in.

During the 1870s Grandfather took a prominent part in the fight against "Boss" Tweed and the notorious Tweed Ring which exploited the city so thoroughly and cynically during that period. He was chairman of the committee that opposed and finally defeated Tweed. Grandfather died on February 7, 1874, when I was seven, and the sorrow at his passing was city-wide and shared by all classes.

My father was born, as I said, in 1823. He didn't marry until 1866, and during those first forty-three years he seems to have led something of a butterfly existence. For a while he was an attaché at the American Legation in London, and was presented at Court in 1851. Later he found time to make a trip on horseback through Spain. It never occurred to him, however, to venture any farther west in the United States than Buffalo, a town that still marks the last western frontier of civilization to many New Yorkers. But after his marriage, to Jenny Jones Angel, of Geneseo, New York, he settled down to hard work in the law and produced a standard work on real-estate law, called *Gerard's Titles to Real Estate,* which is still re-edited and re-published from time to time.

When Father was just over fifty and had practically retired from active law practice, he was elected to the State Senate, which made it necessary for the family to spend the winter of 1876–77 in Albany. Later he ran for Congress, but was defeated by Levi P. Morton. Thereafter he turned to writing, and produced a political history called *The Peace of Utrecht,* a good, solid work on the subject which was published by Putnam's.

Father was given the degree of Doctor of Laws by Columbia University in 1890, a degree which had also been awarded to his father in 1863. When I received the same degree from Columbia in 1927, Dr. Nicholas Murray Butler said he thought it unique for father, son, and grandson to have received a LL.D. from the same university.

In 1893 a crisis occurred in our household which I have always remembered. The revolution had just taken place in Hawaii. President Cleveland offered to send Father to Hawaii as United States Commissioner. His task would be to determine whether the revolutionaries should be recognized and Hawaii brought into the United States, or whether the restoration of Queen Liliuokalani should be encouraged and the Hawaiian royal dynasty continued. We were in Bar Harbor when this offer was made. I was twenty-six at the time, and for a full day I had visions of marrying the beautiful princess, niece of the Queen, and reigning as king of the islands. Unfortunately, Father also had a dream. When he came down to breakfast the following morning, he said that he had dreamed all night of natives climbing over his bed, and he had decided to decline the offer. He undoubtedly had a better reason than this, which seems rather frivolous, but I have never heard what it was. When I grew older, I wondered whether Hawaii's unfortunate location well west of Buffalo might not have been a significant factor in his refusal.

Whenever I go to Forest Hills nowadays and watch the young girls cavorting about the tennis courts like Diana's handmaidens, my mind goes back about fifty years to a conversation I had had with my father. The subject was the old-fashioned girl versus the modern girl. The modern girl of this discussion was the one of the nineties, and the old-fashioned girl was she of the 1840s, when Father was in his salad days. To Father, the "modern girl" was an emancipated and startling creature. He dwelt on the young females of the 1840s with unabashed nostalgia. It was the fashion during the forties, he said, for young females to be demure—a far cry from the boldly fetching hussies of the nineties—and they went to some pains to achieve that state. He described, for example, the hoopskirts that ladies wore, and how these affairs had a tendency to swing. In consequence, long pantalets were worn lest swinging hoopskirts reveal the lower limbs. (Ladies did not have "legs" in those days.) Finally, he revealed, the lace-frilled pantalets twinkling beneath the skirts became a more provocative sight than the ankles they were intended to hide.

Father was also partial to their fragility (still speaking of the girls of the 1840s). This was manifested by their ability to faint—an utterly captivating maneuver which they carried out in the Delsartean tradition of calisthenics. He cited the Sunday-morning services at fashionable Grace Church at

Broadway and Tenth Street, where, one after another, at decent intervals, the belles of the town would punctuate Dr. Wainwright's sermon with their swoonings. Their agitated swains would promptly carry them out to the vestibule for resuscitation. There the departing congregation would see them, gracefully recumbent, while their escorts fanned them with quiet concern.

Father had two sisters, Juliet, who married father's partner, Thomas C. T. Buckley, and Ida, who was married twice—first to an English banker named Wiggin, and, when he died, to Sir Buckley Matthew, another Englishman. Sir Buckley was British Minister to Brazil and later became governor of the Bahamas. A daughter of my aunt Ida married Charles Lawrence, younger son of Lord Lawrence, savior of the Punjab in the Indian Mutiny who was afterward raised to the peerage and made Viceroy of India. Charles died in 1927. When my cousin, Lady Lawrence of Kingsgate (her husband had been raised to the peerage), died in 1934, she willed me a beautiful house on the corner of Eton Square in London, which they had made the center of a charming intellectual and artistic society. I sold it before World War II.

My mother, Jenny Jones Angel, was a celebrated beauty of the sixties and seventies. She was the daughter of Judge Benjamin E. Angel, of Geneseo, who was surrogate of Livingston County from 1838 to 1847. In 1853 President Pierce appointed him consul to the Sandwich Islands, as the Hawaiian Islands were then called. A journey to the islands in those days involved a long, comfortless sailing-ship expedition to the Isthmus of Panama. Then came an arduous trek on muleback over jungle and mountain trails, with malaria and yellow fever constant threats, and the final long sea voyage. My mother, then a young girl, made this difficult trip with her mother and Grandfather Angel. They reached the islands, and after a delay of months learned that the United States Senate, in a fit of unexplained pique, had refused to confirm his appointment. There was nothing to do but come home. Reluctant to risk the dangers of the Isthmus crossing, they sailed around Cape Horn. The monotony of this voyage was relieved by a riot among the Chinese passengers—an affair which Grandfather was in just the mood to help quell.

In 1855 President Pierce appointed him Special Commissioner to go to China to settle a dispute between the Chinese Government and certain American merchants over customs duties. His mission accomplished, he returned by way of India, Egypt, and Europe. When he got back to New York in 1856, President Buchanan appointed him Minister Plenipotentiary to Norway and Sweden. Having gone to Hawaii on an exhausting wild-goose chase because of some senatorial whim, Grandfather Angel sat grimly on his front porch until his new appointment was confirmed. He served as Minister until 1862, when President Lincoln and the Republicans came into office.

One of Judge Angel's sons was my uncle Charles Angel, who as a young man made a large fortune in trade in China, which he promptly lost in Wall Street upon his return to America. He was in China when the Taiping rebellion occurred. The defense force was reassuringly called—long before it had seen any action—"The Ever-Victorious Army." Uncle Charles served with the Ever-Victorious, under an American commander named Ward and later under the British officer famous thereafter as "Chinese" Gordon. The Chinese soldiers won the admiration of Uncle Charles, who considered them excellent fighting men when properly equipped and led. It was interesting to hear Generals Stilwell and Chennault reach the same conclusion during the last war.

My maternal great-grandfather was Captain Horatio Jones, whose frontier career rivaled that of his famous contemporary, Daniel Boone. In 1781, when he was eighteen, he was captured by a war party of Seneca Indians, who were allies of the British during the Revolution. Horatio was one of Bedford's Rangers, and his company had set out with the hope of ambushing part of a British-Indian expedition that was raiding and pillaging white settlements as far west as the Juniata River in Pennsylvania. Unfortunately the defenders were themselves ambushed. Most of them were killed, but Horatio and a few others were taken to the Indian village which occupied the present site of Caneadea on the banks of the Genesee in New York.

A full account of Horatio's stirring career, written by the Rev. George H. Harris, was published in the papers of the Buffalo Historical Society (Vol. VI, 1903). His journey as a captive in tight thongs to the Seneca village was filled with torture and other horrible incidents. Each night his feet were bound, and he was secured to the ground by stakes driven slantwise across his body. When the painful march to the village was over, Horatio and the others were forced to run the gantlet. Few of them survived, but Horatio came through alive, although beaten to shreds. His fortitude and physical prowess won the admiration of the Indians. They kept him with the tribe when they handed over to the British as prisoners the few other whites who remained alive after the repeated tortures they had undergone. When it is remembered that these Indian war parties were under the command of British officers, who stood by unwilling or unable to halt the torturing and killing of prisoners, it is no wonder that for years after the Revolution the very name "Englishman" was anathema to the frontier settlers.

The Senecas who had spared Horatio adopted him into the Hawk Clan of their tribe and gave him the name of "Hocsa-gowah" (which means "Handsome Boy" and which I hope made him blush). At some unknown period the North American Indians had discovered that the marriage of cousins did not always produce normal children. To avoid this, each tribe was divided into clans, each bearing the name of some bird, animal, or fish. An Indian lad became a member of his mother's clan and was obliged to marry outside it. Horatio learned their language, and eventually became the sachem, or chief, of the Hawk Clan. How he then found a white mate is a story that sounds almost as improbable as the similar circumstances under which the fictional Tarzan found a mate of *his* own kind in darkest Africa. In Horatio's case, however, the facts are well authenticated.

In March 1780 a Seneca war party attacked a white settlement at Fishing Creek Valley near the Susquehanna. On Easter morning they descended on the farm home of a German immigrant family named Whitmoyer. As Whitmoyer jumped out of bed, the savages shot him. They tomahawked his wife and took the scalps of both. Sarah, aged seventeen, her three younger brothers and a baby sister were placed upon horses and started toward the Indian country. The infant, carried by Sarah, so enraged one Indian by its incessant crying that he snatched it from her arms and brained it against a tree.

The captives eventually reached the village where Horatio lived, and Sarah had no choice but to adopt the life of the Indians. Inevitably, one of them wanted her as his squaw. Horatio had taken an Indian wife, but she had died. So he married Sarah according to the customs of the Senecas. Eventually they were married by a missionary minister, the Rev. Sam Kirkland, at Schenectady in 1784, and theirs was the first white child born in the state of New York west of Utica.

The Senecas surrendered all their prisoners at the conclusion of the Revolutionary War. Freed, Horatio and Sarah settled near Seneca Lake, where he engaged in the fur trade. John Jacob Astor, on one of his fur-buying expeditions, stayed at their home, and made an agreement whereby for many years Horatio purchased furs for the house of Astor. When Horatio gave up his sojourn with the Senecas, they gave him a square mile of land where the city of Buffalo now stands. With a total lack of prescience he sold it before it became valuable. They also gave him some beautiful rich land which he called Sweet Briar Farm, on the hills sloping down to the Genesee River, and it was in this valley that he buried his wife Sarah, where he could always see her grave. His tomahawk is in the museum in beautiful Letchworth Park, at Portage, New York.

By Sarah Whitmoyer, Horatio Jones had four children, all boys, two of whom were killed by Indians in Lewiston, New York, in 1813. By a third wife, Elizabeth Starr, daughter of Elijah and Rebecca Hewett Starr, Horatio had twelve children. One of these children, Jenny, married Benjamin Angel, who became my grandfather. In 1938 another descendant of Horatio Jones, by his Indian wife, called on me in New York, and we spent a pleasant hour or two exchanging family lore. He is a gardener on the Seneca Reservation in western New York.

CHAPTER II

My LIFE BEGAN ON AUGUST 25, 1867, AT THE HOME OF Grandfather Angel in Geneseo, New York. Except for a handful of violin prodigies with difficult names, little boys between the ages of one and ten are not customarily active in the arts, nor in science or statecraft; neither was there much of anything else on my childish mind that would be of interest to posterity. Those years are, of course, the age at which the little twig is bent into a shape that its elders hope will grace it in maturity. I do not know all the traits my parents sought to inculcate during this bending period. But since I have spent most of my life giving advice—either legal advice to clients for a fee or diplomatic advice to the State Department for pigeonholing—it seems probable that my critical faculties were encouraged.

With my parents and my brothers, Franklin, Julian, and Sumner, I usually arrived at Long Branch on the New Jersey coast for the summer on about June 15. Our house faced the ocean and was flanked on one side by that of Harris Fahnestock, vice-president of the First National Bank, and on the other by the cottage of Moses Taylor, the importer and merchant prince. Next to the Fahnestocks was the house of General Grant, and next to it the home of George W. Childs of the Philadelphia *Public Ledger*. These and most of the other summer residents were well-to-do if not downright wealthy. Yet their mode of living was simple and quite unostentatious when compared to the standards of today.

Each morning the men, including my father, took an eight-o'clock train to New York. They returned by train, arriving at five-thirty, and were met by their wives in well-turned-out victorias—but without footmen on the box—and were taken for a refreshing drive along Ocean Avenue. The fine Morgan horses and equipages were the only real extravagances at Long Branch. The houses were large but unpretentious, and three hundred dollars would have covered the value of the furnishings. We rose early because the departing fathers had to have time to consume oatmeal or other cereal, then eggs, followed by fish, steak or chops, and topped off, if the weather were cool, by buckwheat cakes, but always by hot biscuits and marmalade.

The inventiveness of childhood never allowed life to grow dull except perhaps on Sunday. After Sunday school we were permitted only a dull walk in the afternoon, the use of our ponies being forbidden. If it rained, we were allowed to improve our spiritual lives by reading our choice of three moral books. One was entitled *Line upon Line,* and another *Precept upon Precept.* The title of the third escapes me, but I recall without relish that it followed the careers of two English boys, a poisonous fellow called Sandford and a sniveling youth named Merton. They left their mark, though, for I always had a distaste for rainy Sunday afternoons. I was also compelled on occasions to read Miss Edgeworth's *Moral Tales.* This book's only effect on me, moral or otherwise, was to make me save string all my life. One tale concerned the perennial story of the lad who saved string and was thereby able to "have a second string to his bow" and come through in an archery contest against some very unsportsmanlike competitors. I heartily recommend this book to any parent who thinks his child will benefit from the habit of saving string.

We would vary the summers by going for a short time to Newport or to Saratoga. The routine at Saratoga included a stroll to one of the various springs about seven in the morning. Then, after a large breakfast, the colonists sat in the courtyard of the hotel listening to the band and anticipating the enormous dinner that was to be served in the middle of the day. Perspiring colored servants brought all the delicacies of the season in an astonishing array of plates, platters, boats, cups, and glasses, with about three times as much silver as is customary today.

We spent the winters of this period at my grandfather Gerard's stone house at 17 Gramercy Park. The New York of those days was something more than a town, but not quite a city. The horse cars and the Broadway stages of the 1870s and the 1880s jingled slowly through the city. Straw was scattered on the floor to keep passengers' feet warm, while the drivers huddled in their old military overcoats, relics of the Civil War. At every street corner, in snowy weather, pitifully poor boys and girls, or old men, would sweep the crossings, for which they expected a fee. Whenever I was taken out to walk in the winter I was given a few nickels to give to the crossing sweepers. It is something to remember when I hear complaints that this country has lagged in social progress.

Before 1870 there were practically no apartment houses except a few two- or three-family houses, or "flats," in the poorer sections. The apartment house built by my father and his cousin, Benjamin Welles, grandfather of Sumner Welles, was, I believe, the first to contain really luxurious apartments, although there was no elevator. It was at Park Avenue and Fortieth Street. From childhood I remember that on Fifth Avenue, above Forty-ninth Street, there was only one house, that of Ruppert, the brewer. There were high cliffs on the blocks along the Avenue on which were perched wooden shanties occupied by Irish immigrants with countless children and always a dog. The term "shanty Irish" thus began as a description as well as snobbish derision.

Several parts of the city were made so dangerous by gangs of hoodlums that a well-dressed person dared not walk through them for fear of assault and robbery. The number and violence of these gangs are almost unbelievable today, and their ferocity toward the police, the citizenry, and each other was epic. They flourished as a result of several things: a large, ignorant, and poverty-stricken immigrant population, and the depression and unsettled conditions that followed the Civil War.

A more charming aspect of the New York of my childhood was the militia. Even companies in the same regiment chose the distinctive uniform that fancy dictated. Highland dress and the regalia of the Prussian Guards and French Hussars could be seen side by side on parade. The same touch of light opera was noticeable in their behavior. On holidays the "target companies" marched to some bosky dell where they might practice musketry. Accompanying them would be a proud Negro bearing a two-foot target garlanded with flowers. More important even than this dignitary was another bearing a keg of liquid possibly called Old Rip Van Winkle.

After the period that has been called the Age of Innocence and before the arrival of the great fortunes from the West, New Yorkers of the old stripe were very conservative, as evidenced by their houses and the contents thereof. The brownstone front housed little in the way of art or furniture that was worth anything.

With the influx of the western fortunes came a period when the wealthy vied with one another in many ways. In my childhood the dinner hour had advanced to half-past six. Gradually it crept forward, until "really smart" people were dining at eight—an hour that Old New Yorkers outspokenly termed sinful. The Vanderbilt house on Fifth Avenue on the block from Fifty-first to Fifty-second Street was a notable example of extravagance in housing. This lavishness was especially in evidence at Newport. In a resort where wooden cottages had satisfied the first comers there appeared great palaces such as "The Breakers," built by Cornelius Vanderbilt, Sr., and the house of Ogden Goelet, an imitation of a French château. Stanford White designed for Mrs. Herman Oelrichs a reproduction of the Grand Trianon at Versailles, constructed of shining white terra cotta. On Bellevue Avenue was the great white palace of E. J. Berwind, whose friendship I valued. I was often a guest, both before and after my marriage, of this splendid sailor who left the Navy to become a great magnate of coal. All these houses that should have been set in parks of a thousand acres were plunked down in lots scarcely wide enough to contain them. Their owners still referred to them as "cottages."

In 1879, when I was almost eleven years old, my parents took me to England and put me in school. My arrival in Liverpool brought experiences that have never been erased from my mind. I could not get accustomed to the abysmal poverty on all sides. The streets were filled with men and women in the last degree of poverty and degradation. Barefoot men and women walked the streets with the unwashed skin showing through their torn rags, and everywhere our cab was followed by people begging for a penny. In London it was a horrible thing to see crowds standing outside the gin mills avidly watching the ejection of those who had been allowed to drink until they were stupefied.

The "preparatory" school which was chosen for me was in the pretty village of Southboro, in the county of Kent. It kept a Spartan schedule. On arising in the morning we were given a large piece of cake, containing raisins but little sugar, and were supervised at an hour of study. Then we had breakfast and more study, relieved at regular intervals when we were driven out into the yard to play prisoner's base, doubtless to keep our circulation active in the cold, damp English climate. The main repast of the day was dinner, served at one o'clock. It always consisted of a joint, boiled potatoes, Brussels sprouts, and a tart. With this we were given a mild beer to drink. These meals laid the groundwork for my understanding of what a British visitor to the United States during the postwar food shortage in England meant when he told me: "Here things seem to taste all right; perhaps England needs cooks as badly as it needs food."

The afternoons, until four o'clock, were devoted to compulsory exercise—football in winter and cricket in the spring and summer. Once when I failed to catch a ball at cricket my offense was so serious that the headmaster felt it advisable to defend me apologetically before the entire school. He reminded them of what they had obviously forgotten in the Turmoil—that *foreigners should not be held to the same standard as the English.*

On Sundays, clad in the Eton suit, Eton collar, and topper, we went to church, and during the afternoon walked solemnly about the common that adjoined the school.

During my first vacation I was left at the school, despite my tears and complaints, with the family of the headmaster. One of his sons taught me the rudiments of Greek and started me in Sanskrit. To my delight, my parents took me with them when they returned to America in the last weeks of 1879. I felt more comfortable attending the normal school at Geneseo.

When we resumed the simple life at 17 Gramercy Park I had a number of tutors, but was finally enrolled in the Wilson and Kellog Day School. In addition to rifle drills in the school, I went every afternoon to the Woods Gymnasium on Twenty-eighth Street, a trip that was repaid not only in pleasure and muscle, but in forming what proved to be a life-long friendship with a fellow athlete, Frederic R. Coudert, Sr., the distinguished international lawyer. In the fall of 1881, when I was thirteen, we went to Europe for the winter, staying first at Biarritz, where I attended a French day school. Here the principal sport of the small boys was a mock bullfight. As I was the largest boy in the school, I was detailed to be the bull. For realism and protection a bull's head of wickerwork was fixed on my shoulders. The teachers sat upon tall chairs and applauded excitedly while the boys, with cheesecloth capes, enacted the entrance of the matador and gave a small boy's version of a bullfight. Later in the winter we moved to Pau. I was permitted to ride every day, often to the hounds, for Pau had celebrated packs for many years under the grand old sportsman, Frederick H. Prince.

In the course of the winter of 1881–82 our family visited many parts of Europe—London, Paris, Cannes, Nice, and Montreux, Switzerland. It was at Cannes that we were saddened by the death of my brother, Franklin, who died of scarlet fever. He was two years my junior.

At Montreux, in addition to work with my tutors, I first took up the study of fencing, a sport in which I remained active for years after. At that time dueling was the accepted medium for settling serious differences, and the fencing masters were kept busy perfecting the gentlemen of Europe in this important skill. I was only fourteen when in 1881 I became a pupil of Don Anziano in his *salle* at Montreux. Later I studied in Paris at the Salle Pons. These salles were the equivalent of men's fashionable clubs, where gentlemen would meet in the afternoon to fence and gossip.

I suppose that World War II finished dueling completely in France; it had almost disappeared by the close of World War I. Once I looked up the last duel on record in New York and found that it had been between James Gordon Bennett and Frederick May, in 1877. They used pistols, but neither was hit. My wife's brother-in-law, Count Sigray, fought several duels in his native Hungary, where they fight with sabers. In the German universities dueling was a sport. The contestants held their arms extended in the manner of a Nazi salute and hacked at each other's face by swift movements of the wrist. Student duelists are covered with leather, and iron goggles protect their eyes. They take pride in facial scars from these matches and used to keep the cuts open for a time so that the scar would be more conspicuous. The military never went in for this sport, and it was curious to see the doctors of philosophy looking ferocious with their saber-marked faces, while the army officers had smooth faces and philosophical brows.

I added boxing to my sports with lessons from Billy Edwards, an ex-champion lightweight and chief bouncer at the Hoffman House.

In the fall of '83 I was sent to St. Paul's boarding school in

Garden City, Long Island, which was connected with the Episcopal Cathedral there, and was at that time a military school. Fortified by my instruction from the redoubtable Billy Edwards, I arrived at St. Paul's with two sets of boxing gloves. Immediately I set to work to establish myself by challenging each of the older boys, in succession, to a boxing bout. It was unnecessary for the headmaster to apologize for me there as had been the case with cricket.

Two years at St. Paul's gave me a respect for military schools that has not been diminished by the criticisms in the series of propaganda plays—plays which were nobly financed by pacifists of the type who believed, prior to Pearl Harbor, that we should disarm as a means of preventing wars. St. Paul's was run on the West Point pattern, and we were drilled by a government-detailed West Pointer, Lieutenant C. A. L. Totten. It is my observation that such schools have given their graduates a high degree of personal discipline, both mental and physical, and inculcated a fine sense of honor.

When I was about eighteen my love for horsemanship was so greatly stimulated by a visit to the circus that I determined to learn the trick of bareback riding. An ex-circus rider named Sam had had a school for this purpose at Fordham. I practiced the rudiments, standing on the back of an old white retired circus horse. I wasn't a successful pupil, though. Sam said my knees were too stiff to bend and sway successfully with the horses. So I had to console myself with another career.

It was about this time, also, that I was permitted to attend my first theatrical performance. It was a matinee, carefully chosen for me, and was so dull and unsuccessful that when the sole other customer fell asleep I remained the only auditor. Its chief effect on me was to confirm my taste for athletics.

In the fall of 1885 I entered Columbia College. It is interesting to note that since that day the opinions of college educators have described a full circle and returned to the belief of my college days that the number of elective courses permitted students should be limited. We were obliged to take all of the basic liberal arts studies offered—Latin, Greek, mathematics, science (then called natural philosophy) and, of course, English. Great emphasis was placed on the classics. At Columbia one commonly learned to read Greek and Latin at sight. The idea was that the young mind needed hard exercise and discipline. Latin has been of vast assistance in helping me learn the Romance languages—and English. We were compelled to attend chapel in the morning, an example of the religious atmosphere in the last century, when failure to attend services regularly was to invite the extreme disapproval of society.

My professor of philosophy at Columbia was a young man named Nicholas Murray Butler. I don't know whether this course bored me or him the more, for Dr. Butler was a practical philosopher rather than a contemplative one, and I sensed that he squirmed when the metaphysics became too involved. It is because of him that the little Columbia College of my day has become the enormous, influential institution that it is today. I am sorry that Nicholas Murray Butler confined himself to the university, for I have often felt that he would have made an excellent president of the United States, and, in times of national stress, even a great one.

At that time in Columbia there was a barbarous practice in vogue known as the "cane rush"—a contest between freshmen and sophomores for the possession of a stout cane. It was a variation of a kind of battle that has brought bloody noses to many a campus. Being heavily built, I was one of the freshmen charged with defending the cane. We were all stripped to the waist, and, since we freshmen didn't know one another, red figures were painted on our backs. In the struggle that ensued a likely young freshman named William Snowden, son of the rector of St. John's Episcopal Church at Fort Hamilton, was injured so severely that he died.

CHAPTER III

I WAS SPARED THE UGLY FATE OF BEING AN ONLY CHILD—A MIS-
fortune that must rank high among life's handicaps—by having three brothers to grow up with. I am sure that every man
suffers from a sense of loneliness, and craves more understanding and devotion than he ever gets, but this isolation is
certainly mitigated in large families. The psychologists who
seek a healthy-minded race do well to join the geneticists,
who seek a sturdier one, in deploring the tendency toward
fewer children among the prosperous and better educated.

My brother Julian's early experiences included participa-
tion in the celebrated mystery involving a character known
as "Death Valley Scotty." Immediately after graduation
Julian went to Colorado and with another young engineer
opened an assay office. Julian was a great horseman, and
eventually he deserted assaying to work as a horse wrangler
with a cowboy outfit in the Southwest. He never lost his delight in these associations, and when he was a bank official
in New York he used to enjoy reunions with the cowboys in
Buffalo Bill's Wild West show when it came to town.

One of the cowboys with whom Julian was very friendly
was named Walter Scott. Scott had ambition to prospect for
gold, and at his urging my brother staked him for such a ven-

ture in California. I also supplied some cash for a small interest. Suddenly, in the summer of 1905, the country was startled by news that "Death Valley Scotty" had chartered a special train and was heading East on it, all by himself, to confer with his partner, Julian Gerard. The New York *Tribune* printed this account of the trip:

LOS ANGELES, *July 9.*—In a special train consisting of a Pullman sleeper, a diner and baggage car, Walter Scott, the once poor mining prospector, left Los Angeles on the Sante Fe Railroad at one o'clock this afternoon and to the cheers of two thousand onlookers started on a record-breaking trip to Chicago and New York.

The Sante Fe road has agreed to land "Scotty" in Chicago in forty-five hours or forfeit $500 of the $5,500 in gold paid in advance for the train, which made the first 141 miles in 141 minutes. The miner is trying to arrange by telegraph to continue his journey to New York at a record-breaking speed and he talks of chartering an ocean steamer to make a sensational voyage to England.

The railroad trip with all its champagne and accessories will cost him about $10,000. The larder was stocked like that of a prince. He took along his wife, two boon companions, representatives of all the local newspapers, and last, but not least, a mangy yellow dog, picked out of the streets, for which "Scotty" bought a $1,000 diamond collar. "Scotty" says he is going to give the dog the time of his life. "I am going to feed him until he almost bursts," said this latest Monte Cristo, "for I was a yellow dog once myself."

Scott has discovered a bona-fide gold mine in the Mojave Desert—an almost inaccessible place—just where, nobody knows. He disappears for two months at a time, and comes out loaded with gold which he spends as fast as he can.

When Scotty arrived in New York, Julian and I had several interviews with him. It was a frustrating experience, like talking back to the radio. All he would say, waving his arms and shouting with enthusiasm, was, "She's a whale! She's rich! She's great!" He would not yield the slightest clew to the location of his golden bonanza.

In the years that followed, Scotty used to make excursions into the desert and come out with nuggets of gold, but he would never tell where he found them. Once, motivated as much by curiosity as in a return on our investment, we hired an enormous one-hundred-and-eighty-proof Indian named Apache Joe to follow Scotty into the desert. After several trials the Apache gave up the job of shadowing him as hopeless. Later, a Chicago insurance man named Albert M. Johnson took up with Scotty, and together they built an extraordinary mansion in Death Valley that became known as Scotty's Castle. There were rumors that the lode of gold was beneath the castle. A particularly fantastic tale was that Scotty and Johnson worked the lode while a great pipe organ played fortissimo to drown out the sound of their picks.

Various individuals came to Julian and me and professed to know for certain just where Scotty's mine was, but all these helpful people proved to be frauds. Finally, Julian brought action in the California courts, and claimed that the castle, at least, had been located as a mining property, and that he was entitled to an interest in it. A lawyer was sent out to Death Valley to serve papers on Scott, and found him living in a small hut near the castle, title to which was apparently in the name of Johnson. Scotty was surrounded by cocked pistols, Bowie knives, and other instruments of death. These rather distracted the lawyer, who was of a nervous type, but he proceeded with the details of his legal mission. The court denied Julian's claim.

The solution to the mystery was hardly less fantastic than

the story itself. Scotty's "gold mine" proved to be his partner, Johnson. The denouement came in 1937 when Scotty's wife sued him for divorce, claiming half of the desert castle and his holeful of gold nuggets, wherever they might be. Johnson decided that the time was ripe to disclose the fact that he had paid the bills for what was certainly among the most expensive practical jokes in history. He had made millions from the ownership of zinc properties and as president of the National Life Insurance Company of Chicago. When Scotty's wife grew exigent in her dreams of luxury without Scotty, Johnson revealed that he had supplied the ancient prospector with money much as one feeds caramels to a dog, to enjoy his antics. His motive seems to have been solely his puckish sense of humor, and a very rich vein indeed. "Scotty repaid me in full—in laughs," said Johnson.

There were, as if further to strip the romance from the legend of Scotty's modern Golconda, reports that the frantic cross-country trip by special train was mostly a publicity stunt arranged by an astute railroad press agent.

Intimates of Johnson disclosed after his death early in 1948 that he felt a warm friendship for Scotty because the latter had persuaded him to come to Death Valley for his health after he had suffered a partial paralysis from injuries sustained in a railway wreck. The climate proved beneficial, and Scotty shared the credit.

Johnson's final laugh seems to have been at the expense of Scotty himself. He left all his money to the Gospel Foundation, a non-denominational evangelical society which he had founded. The Foundation also inherited the desert castle, but Scotty kept his nearby shack. He said, though, that he would never have been comfortable in that great baronial hall, which required many Indians to staff it. "Too many gadgets," said Scotty.

Sumner, my only surviving brother, went to Yale, where he was a good student and captain of the track team. He married Helen Coster, a daughter of Charles Coster, who was a Morgan partner. Sumner and his wife, who are now divorced, have three sons, all of whom served well in the armed forces during World War II. Their eldest son, James W. Gerard IV, was a major in the Army; Sumner, Jr., was a captain in the Marine Corps, and Coster, the youngest, was a lieutenant in the Navy. Most of my brother Sumner's activities have been in real estate, in which he has been unusually successful. In recent years Sumner has been treasurer of the Committee for Constitutional Government, an organization which has been a thorn in the side of many free-spending, power-hungry politicians.

Although my brothers and I were given a free choice in deciding upon our careers, I wavered only once in my determination to enter the law. That was in 1888, when I was twenty. The previous December I had developed such a bad cough that my parents took me out of Columbia and sent me to Colorado, where I spent an enjoyable and health-restoring six months. I learned something of the boundless hospitality of the West when I tarried in Denver until an epidemic of typhoid fever should subside in Colorado Springs, my destination. James Bush, proprietor of the Windsor Hotel, and his partner, Mr. Goulding, were unusually kind to me. They gave me a beautiful saddle horse to ride and often took me to Mr. Goulding's ranch near by and to the Tabor Opera House where Tabor, the Silver King, sat in his box in state, accompanied by his wife—who died in poverty a few years ago. A gentleman named Ward who came from Geneseo and who owned a ranch in Colorado drove into town and invited me to be his guest for as long as I chose to stay.

Before I left for Colorado Springs, Bush and Goulding offered me a partnership in their stockyards business. This my parents vetoed. I still think it was a wonderful business. When ranchers sent cattle and horses in for sale, the stockyard company boarded them while they were awaiting sale, advanced money on them to their owners at high rates of interest, and, finally, charged a commission when they were sold. I have never since discovered a business, even in precrash Wall Street, where the profits seemed as sure as this.

When I returned East in May 1888, I brought with me my fastest quarter horse to use in the polo games at Westchester Country Club. On him I managed to win the Pair Cups for polo that spring, playing with Edward C. Potter in the matches. I had hopes for my pony in the spring race meeting at the club, but muddy going handicapped him. I had also entered a beautiful thoroughbred named Glenban in another race. He was such a splendid animal that when I came out on him the crowd at once made him the favorite. But as I galloped down the stretch, painfully last, a friend of mine, who had lunched mostly out of a glass, rose in the grandstand and bellowed, "Here comes Jimmy, driving them all before him." When you are twenty such an occasion is uncomfortably deflating.

A regrettable result of my half-year in Colorado was the drop back from the class of '89 to the class of '90 at Columbia. This caused me real regret, for I was fond of my classmates of '89. Among the lasting friendships I made in that group were those with the late Benjamin Cardozo, who was to become a justice of the United States Supreme Court, and with the future Judge Bondy of the United States District Court.

I was graduated from Columbia in June 1890. The following fall I entered the Columbia School of Law and also attended the School of Political Science of Columbia University, which awarded me a master's degree in June 1891. The next year I sat in the Lectures at the New York Law School and commenced my apprenticeship in the law, going in the mornings to the old office established by my grandfather in 1812, which had become Platt, Bowers and Sands. I am sure that we worked much harder than law clerks do today. I spent many nights in the Bar Association, searching for opinions, and broke many dinner engagements to chase recalcitrant witnesses through the wilds of Westchester or East New York. I felt fully rewarded for this industry when the combination of afternoon law course and apprentice clerk the rest of the day enabled me to pass the examinations and be admitted to the Bar in 1892.

Our law offices in those days would seem to today's readers like a stage setting for *A Christmas Carol.* We did have one of the first telephones, installed in a hallway wall between two offices. But the most impressive sight in the office must have been the two scriveners who, before the days of typewriters and lovely typists, engrossed in a bold, round hand and embellished with red ink all the deeds, wills, and the like which are made in a law office. They were Englishmen, and invariably wore cutaway coats and an air of dignity and rectitude that outshone any of the partners. At that period women were an unusual sight south of Fulton Street, and office boys followed with insolent curiosity any woman who ventured into Wall Street.

My grandfather Gerard's law office, which was celebrated as a school for lawyers, was then at William and Pine streets. Later we moved to the corner of Nassau and Cedar streets, then to Cedar and Williams, and finally around the corner to 40 Wall Street. It is indicative of the stability of that part of the city that during all those years our offices remained within a radius of a block.

It was shortly after I had turned twenty-one that my father told me that a great mistake of his life had been not aligning himself with a political organization. To keep aloof from partisanship is an advertisement of independence, but the merest glance at the United States Congress is a demonstration that there is room within party ranks for the most diverse opinions. My father advised me, therefore, to join the regular Democratic organization in New York City, which is known as Tammany Hall. On the eve of an election he took me down to visit Richard Croker, the boss of Tammany, to whom I handed a $200 check as a campaign contribution.

Tammany Hall is not fully understood, either in this country or abroad. Although the very name has been used as a synonym for corruption to frighten members of ladies' aid societies, Tammany as a body has nothing to do with the politics of New York. It is true that those who have become leaders of the Democratic party in New York City have been by custom elected sachems, or officers, of the Tammany Society. But the society itself does not engage in political activity, and, as a matter of fact, is kept alive by a few old members devoted to ancient traditions. The Society of Tammany or Columbian Order was organized after the end of the War of the Revolution as a protest, or perhaps antidote, to the supposedly aristocratic Society of the Cincinnati. Aaron Burr wrote the beautiful ritual, which is read when a member is admitted and given the secret password.

In any event, I joined the Society, paid my two dollars' dues, and have not been to a meeting since, although once a month I receive a notice that on the fifth day of the month of

Blossoms, or some other Indian month, there will be a meeting of the Society in the Great Wigwam at Tammany Hall.

The power of the Tammany Democratic organization lies in the fact that it held something of the old Roman client system and something of the Irish and Scotch clan system. A change of boundaries shifted our house in Gramercy Park from the Hour Glass District, which extended along the Bowery, to the Gas House District, of which the Tammany leader was Charles F. Murphy. I had my first assignment during the 1892 presidential election, as a poll watcher. We met at dawn outside the Anawanda Club at Twentieth Street and Second Avenue, and were given steaks to eat as we stood in the street. Later I used to go to the Tombs Police Court or other courts to defend any good Tammany voters who had been accused of illegal or faulty registration. It is by being assiduous in such political chores that a young lawyer attains merit in the eyes of a political organization.

CHAPTER IV

BRIGHT IN MY EARLY MEMORIES IS THE SOCIAL LIFE OF NEW York in the 1890s. Society was a closely organized and tightly controlled enterprise governed by strict rules. From the end of the Civil War until the end of World War I it was ruled by a succession of dictatorships, and, as under all successful dictatorships, the ruler's power was unquestioned. There was no competing group. Either you belonged to Society, or you didn't. The first of the hierarchy was the elder August Belmont. Despite the fact that he spoke with a thick German accent, he ruled as absolute social arbiter. He had come to America about 1837, when he was twenty-one, as the representative of the Rothschilds, whose riches and interests in Europe were all-embracing. In addition to his wealth, he had great charm and intelligence, and these attributes, together with his marriage to the beautiful niece of Commodore Perry, the naval hero, led him swiftly and easily to the dominant social position that he held so long. He had fought a duel in 1841—some fifty years before I met him—with one William Heyward of South Carolina, a close friend with whom he had quarreled at the theater. He got a bullet wound in his hip which caused him to limp for the rest of his life. In town, the Belmonts occupied a large house on the northeast

corner of Fifth Avenue and Eighteenth Street, and owned a
still larger place in Newport, called "By-the-Sea," where they
went in summer. In both establishments they lived in baronial style. I still cherish the memory of Mrs. Belmont sallying
forth in her almost regal equipage. It was the sort of open
carriage known as a modified *"attelage à la Daumont."* There
was a rumble on which sat two footmen in the Belmont livery, maroon and scarlet. There was no box seat; liveried
postillions wearing caps with gold tassels rode the horses. It
was something the town looked forward to seeing: the gaily-
clad postillions astride the horses, the footmen behind, and
between them the beautiful Mrs. Belmont posed gracefully in
the carriage.

August Belmont was more, however, than just a social
leader. Both he and his sons, August, Oliver, and Perry, took
an active part in politics. He was the American minister to
The Hague, and was once treasurer of the Democratic National Committee, a post in which I succeeded him years
later. He was also first president of the Jockey Club, and
Belmont Park gets its name from his son August.

A number of prominent and wealthy women contested
keenly, if politely, to succeed old August Belmont as leader
of New York Society. The foremost contenders were Mrs.
Stuyvesant Fish, Mrs. Oliver Belmont, Mrs. Herman Oelrichs, the more conservative Mrs. Ogden Mills, and, finally,
the still more conservative Mrs. William Astor, who, with
her lieutenant, Ward McAllister, finally stood at the top. Mrs.
Fish, nee Anthon, was of an old New York family, and her
husband was a son of the Secretary of State and descended
from a long line of Hudson Valley Dutch ancestors. Mrs.
Oliver Belmont was a southern woman who was married first
to William K. Vanderbilt, whom she divorced. Mrs. Herman

Oelrichs inherited a large fortune as the daughter of Senator Fair, one of the Big Four of the miraculous Comstock Lode, which was among the richest mines ever discovered.

Ward McAllister, though quite a different type from August Belmont, shared with him a combination of qualities that enabled each of them, in his way, to dominate the social life of a rich and sophisticated city. Sam Ward of glorious memory was his uncle, and his nephew is the energetic Ralph Ingersoll, founder and former editor of a curious, and now-defunct political pamphlet which was called the Newspaper PM. A fair appraisal seems to be that McAllister was a civilizing influence on both the native rich and on the more tough-fibered oil, steel, and railroad millionaires who began to gravitate to New York during this period. He might be compared, with certain obvious reservations, to Beau Nash, the celebrated master of ceremonies in eighteenth-century Bath, whose many innovations in rules of conduct constituted a distinct advance in manners. When he died in 1895, it was the beginning of the end for the closely restricted organization he had built up. The steel, oil, and industrial magnates of the country were descending on New York like wolves on the fold, and the impact of this onslaught broke down the resistance of the local noblesse completely. Today there is no "New York Society" but only a score or more of large groups in which practically anybody can find a place. The growth of the city was probably a contributing factor in this, indicating the point at which New York changed from a parochial small town to a cosmopolitan city.

So much has been said about the gargantuan appetites of our fathers' day, and the startling amount of food that was served at their dinners, that I exhumed a menu of a fashionable meal of sixty years ago in New York.

In the centennial history of the Union Club, which called itself the Mother of Clubs, is printed the menu of a dinner given by Ward McAllister at the club on October 9, 1880. Here it is:

GREEN TURTLE SOUP, CLEAR

OYSTER TIDBITS

BOILED SHEEPSHEAD FISH, HOLLANDAISE SAUCE

POTATOES   CUCUMBERS

YOUNG TURKEY   STRING BEANS

LAMB CUTLETS WITH PUREE OF

CHESTNUTS

SWEETBREADS WITH PERIGORD SAUCE

ARTICHOKES WITH ITALIAN SAUCE

KIRSH SHERBET

ROAST WOODCOCK

LETTUCE SALAD

ICE CREAM

COFFEE

Of the four ladies who, together with Ward McAllister, dominated Society in the nineties, Mrs. William Astor was not only the most powerful but also the most interesting. The invitation lists for her annual balls were vital factors in deciding just who was, or was not, "in Society." In a period when everything imaginable about a fashionable house was festooned with drapery of one sort or another, Mrs. Astor's drawing rooms, in her house at Thirty-fourth Street and Fifth Avenue, were notable for their petticoated mantels, their tasseled valances, and the opulence of the *décor* in general. This elegance extended to Mrs. Astor's costume as well. It was customary for ladies, on occasion, to wear a great deal of heavy gold jewelry, with large stones and great strings of pearls. However, even the most heavily laden matron at a ball seemed conservatively jeweled when Mrs. Astor made her entrance, and every feminine eye, following her progress to her box, was hardly able to catalogue and evaluate the flashing, tinkling armor of diamond rings, emerald pendants, brooches, and necklaces with which she was bedecked. These might be supplemented with jeweled sunbursts, butterflies, a tiara, as well as with that most uncompromisingly named adornment—the diamond stomacher. I recall particularly one occasion when she attended some public ball held in the Metropolitan Opera House. A dance floor had been built over the orchestra seats almost at the level of the lower tier of boxes. In one of these boxes sat Mrs. Astor and her party, of whom I was one, and throughout the evening hundreds of people who ordinarily wouldn't have had an opportunity to see her in full rig crowded around the box and paid her the tribute of rapt, open-mouthed scrutiny—a tribute which she seemed to enjoy.

One of my best friends was Mrs. William Astor's son, John Jacob Astor IV, who in 1912 met his death so bravely in the sinking of the *Titanic*. He was tall and charming in a quiet way, and unassuming to the point of being actually bashful. On many evenings we would share a hansom cab when returning from a party, and as we drew up before his house, he would suddenly put what he judged to be the total cab fare on the seat, jump to the sidewalk, and run up his steps despite my protests. His son, Vincent, is a fine young man and quite devoted to the sea. During the early years of Franklin Roosevelt's regime, the President was a frequent guest on Vincent's yacht, the *Nourmahal*. He was a naval officer in the recent war.

William Waldorf Astor III had political ambitions, was elected to the State Legislature, and was made minister to

Italy. However, for some reason he became disgusted with life in America, moved to England, became a British subject, and was eventually given a title.

It would be a serious omission not to mention the role of Harry Lehr during this era of New York social life. He was the son of the German consul in Baltimore, was a clever piano player, and was credited with having a great sense of humor. Although he was somewhat porcine in appearance and had a high falsetto voice, he became, nevertheless, the darling of the dowagers. Old Mrs. Astor had him constantly at her house. He picked and seated the guests at her great dinners and held in her house a position that came somewhere between that of a court jester and a major-domo. He became an agent for a brand of champagne and used his social popularity to push that particular wine. Finally, backed by a coterie of dowagers, he married a widow, Mrs. Dahlgren, who had been born a Drexel and an heiress. After his death she wrote, or mothered, an extraordinary book in which she relates the events of her wedding night.

However, my social life was not confined to old Mrs. William Astor's circle. I remember being at a party given by the then Tammany mayor, Mayor Gilroy, where I sat next to an attractive young lady who impressed me with her stories about Father's yacht and country place and horses. When I saw Miss Gilroy after dinner I asked her who the lovely heiress was who seemed to have everything. "Why, don't you know?" she answered. "Her father is a police captain." In those days it often happened that a policeman's lot was a happy one.

These activities of mine in the ten years between college and marriage represent the typical life of the well-to-do, God-fearing young man during the 1890s. I spent long, hard hours at the office satisfying the demands of "that stern mistress," as the law is still rather fatuously called by its practitioners. Golf had not been taken up generally, and thus had not had time to undermine that strict Sabbath observance to which my generation was reared. Lawn tennis, based on an old game in France and England, was just becoming popular during my twenties. Masculine players wore short, tight flannel knickers, red silk stockings, a white Norfolk jacket, and a little skullcap of white and red. Women, of course, wore ground-sweeping skirts, and thus attired the contestants would pat a squashy ball back and forth. These genteel athletes would have been shocked and horrified if by some magic of time and space Alice Marble could have strode onto the court with her fine bare legs and driven across a few forehands.

New York has always been comparatively sophisticated, and, moreover, it has an inheritance of indulgence from its Dutch founders. The powerful thumb of the Methodist Church, *et al.*, particularly with regard to such matters as drinking, dancing, card-playing, and theater-going, never pressed so hard on New York as on the rest of the country. Nevertheless, in the New York of fifty years ago this tolerance went hand in hand with an ironclad family discipline and a great many strictures on youthful behavior, some sound and some silly. Strict rules governed most social activity. This conception of what was "proper" was quite rigid. Even when I was thirty years old, if I had asked a girl to dine with me alone, I would have been kicked down her front steps. If I had offered her a cocktail, I would have been tossed out of Society for my boorish effrontery. It remained for Prohibition to teach the women of America how to drink.

It may seem somewhat frivolous to write so much about

so-called "Society," but I am trying to give a picture of manners and customs in the gay nineties. That period had distinct advantages for the young man. Though he could not invite the girl he admired to sup and dance in a night club, at least he was spared the expense. Today a young man who takes the girl of his dreams to dine, the theater and a night club after, must break the back of a fifty- or even a hundred-dollar bill; in those departed days he was entertained at splendid dinners and balls, his only expense being an occasional bunch of flowers.

Then, too, he made useful acquaintances—even clients, if he was a lawyer or broker. He met the most charming and eligible girls, and the magnate whose daughter or wife he had saved from going home alone from a ball or rescued when partnerless for the cotillion or supper, gave him, when he made a business call next day, a warm and kindly reception.

A young man who neglected to win, if possible, entrance to Society missed a great opportunity. As my father once said, "If you have a box ticket you can go all over the house."

The formalities of that day extended to dress. Women, for example, did not wear evening gowns to the theater, but wore high-necked dresses and such enormous hats that several states legislated against this obstruction to the view of those behind. An exception to that style was the opera, especially on Monday nights, when the boxholders appeared in full evening regalia, the women vying with one another in the number of their jewels. Many wore enormous tiaras, and I remember that Mrs. W. K. Vanderbilt, Jr., was considered very daring when she appeared with a closed crown, as if she were royalty.

For daytime occasions of any formality, men wore a Prince Albert, or frock coat. This garment persisted well into the present century. In 1910, when I was one of a presidential commission to Mexico, my fellow members and I sported these dignified garments, like professional pallbearers, all over that steaming country. In 1916, when I lunched with Kaiser Wilhelm in German-occupied France, I wore this costume and a high silk hat. The Kaiser, a lover of colorful uniforms, made tired little jokes about the unimaginativeness of American diplomats who dressed always as if they were in mourning. Male evening dress called for white gloves, particularly at dances, and it would have been a gross breach of etiquette to ask a girl to dance if one's moist palms were exposed. One of the first breaks in men's fashions was the introduction of the informal dinner jacket by Edward VII when he was Prince of Wales. William Waldorf Astor, who was an attentive and sedulous Anglophile, immediately ordered a jacket like the Prince's, and began to wear it at the clubhouse at Tuxedo Park. There were many other imitators, and soon it became known as the "Tuxedo coat."

The 1890s marked the end of a century, but they also marked the end of an era of thousands of years during which the horse had been man's chief means of land travel. Many people kept extensive stables in town, and I remember being told by the old groom of the Belmont family that they kept twenty-six horses at Newport. Of course wages and feed were very much lower than they are today. Most people can visualize to some extent the changes wrought in urban living by the motorcar. But all may not realize that the removal of the thousands of stables from the city had other effects. Manhattan smells better, it supports a much smaller rat population, and escapes the billions of flies formerly spawned in the stables.

Horses are decorative animals, as well as noble ones, and make a fine display when they pull a smart equipage. Many people had attractive turnouts that achieved more individuality and color than is possible with the rather somber motorcars of today. After my marriage, for example, my wife drove in a very smart-looking victoria of miniature build, with two small, high-stepping chestnut horses and a small coachman and footman (who were brothers and almost twins). At night she drove in a miniature brougham with a single large gray trotting horse.

Even the well-to-do looked upon the hansom cab, which had only recently been introduced, as an extravagant innovation, and any young man who hired one was likely to be branded a spendthrift. I recall going by cab one afternoon in the nineties to call on Polly Brewster, the daughter of a quite wealthy Standard Oil official, at her home on Fifth Avenue. She happened to glance out the window at the moment of my arrival and her horrified greeting was, "Why, you have come in a cab!"

When the automobile was developed in the late nineties, it was taken up enthusiastically by the Newport "cottagers," and they played an important part in introducing motoring in America, for they made it fashionable and gave it much valuable publicity. In a recent book on the automobile called *Combustion on Wheels*, the author, David L. Cohn, describes the first "automobile flower parade"—an event in which I was a participant—held in Newport in September 1899. It was quite a gala event, and Bellevue Avenue was crowded with traps and victorias whose occupants had come to see the flower-decked horseless carriages pass in review. Mr. Cohn writes:

All of Mrs. Belmont's servants had poured out of her house and were engaged in transforming the smooth green lawns of her estate—Belcourt—into an "obstacle park." Wooden horses hitched to carriages, dummy figures representing policemen, nursemaids, and loafers (presumably Democrats) were scattered strategically, and through them a devious course was staked out with golf flags.

Leading the procession came Mr. Belmont, riding with Mrs. Stuyvesant Fish in a runabout decorated with yellow field flowers surmounted by an arbor of cat-o'-nine-tails bearing a stuffed eagle. . . .

Behind him was Mr. J. W. Gerard, with Mrs. Belmont as his partner, driving her car known as a golf rig. They were almost lost to view amid blue hydrangeas ("In a cowslip's bell I lie"), while Mrs. Belmont, symbolically spurring on their mechanical steed, carried a whip made of hydrangeas and daisies.

Next came Mr. Harry Lehr, one of the famous playboys of the day, riding with Mrs. Astor. . . . Mr. Lehr, however, who achieved fame and fortune among the Newport set by burlesquing their overstuffed manners, now filled with champagne and a fine frenzy, wove dizzily in and out of the course, hurling over all of the obstacles and demolishing a straw figure.

As a matter of fact, my car was being pulled by a pair of blue butterflies—each with a wingspread of about three feet —which were harnessed to a miniature wagon tongue which projected about six feet from the front of the car. Mrs. Belmont controlled these airy steeds with flower-entwined reins and belabored them with her whip of hydrangeas and daisies.

Actually, few of the cars in this event ran by internal-combustion engines; they were mostly electric autos, rented for the season. One of the gasoline-burning cars in the parade was a Winton belonging to H. Rogers Winthrop, but its engine was recalcitrant, and he spent the entire time futilely cranking it and tinkering.

A stern-minded wayfarer at Newport, seeing me sweep by with Mrs. Belmont in a motor apparently drawn by giant butterflies, might have said there goes a frivolous young man who might better be reading in a library or seeking health in the Maine woods. But it was not so. Mrs. Belmont projected me into a law affair involving millions. This in turn led to my becoming a partner in my grandfather's old firm, toward which no influence would have helped.

In legal circles in the relentless city of New York a partner is defined as one who brings in business.

Mrs. Belmont was a woman of strong personality and great ability. At the request of her son I was an usher at her funeral, an occasion made impressive by the suffragettes and their banners, for she had been a strong fighter in the cause of female suffrage.

The motoring that I have described had a long way to go before it would alter social habits and become an adjunct to romance as well as utility. The young men and women of the 1890s were not given much opportunity to be otherwise than decorous in their behavior. The conventions, moral standards, and chaperons practically breathed on the necks of a young couple, and this continued relentlessly right up to the moment they plighted their troth at the altar. Mamma, or some other respectable female, accompanied daughter and daughter's intended to dances, and a groom usually rode discreetly behind couples cantering in Central Park. Long Branch and Newport were only slightly less strict in these matters. But for some reason I never discovered the strictures and customs were greatly relaxed at Bar Harbor. The same mothers and chaperons who had been eagle-eyed in town or at Newport relaxed their vigilance in Bar Harbor. There it was quite proper, for example, to ask a girl to walk in the woods à deux, or to go canoeing, or even to land from a rowboat on one of the small islands that dot Frenchman's Bay.

The canoes, delicate birchbark affairs rented from the natives and local Indians, were especially favored by the mothers. The young man sat balanced with a paddle and the girl lay on the bottom of the canoe on deerskins with her back against a rest. Great skill was required in the management of the canoe and the slightest movement would upset it—hence its popularity with the chaperons. The rowboats were less favored by the mothers.

At Bar Harbor there were no cocktails or informal parties, and the height of dissipation was a buckboard drive to the neighboring village of Somesville to eat popovers, washed down with a little champagne. The buckboards had about six or seven seats, each seat holding three, with two men and a girl on one seat and two girls and a man on the next, and so on.

James G. Blaine had a cottage at Bar Harbor. When I was introduced to him, I was quite interested in the method by which he remembered names, a faculty for which he was famous. He held my hand in both of his, breathed deeply, and repeated my name four or five times, looking fixedly at me all the while. Although I was an inconsequential youth, whenever I met him afterward he remembered my name.

On the whole, I think that the young women of the nineties, bearing themselves, as it were, so very carefully, were induced to do so in order to improve their chances for the only career that was open to them. There was no alternative to marriage except a rather unexciting spinsterhood. Those few women who could and did enter business were rare exceptions and not representative of women of well-to-do families. The mystery and aloofness that womankind cultivated, and which greatly enhanced their value in the marriage market, were partially achieved by women's fashions. The concealment of the female form divine was so successfully carried out that my father, whose slightly cynical judgment in these matters was acute, once advised me either to observe any young lady toward whom I might have matrimonial intentions in her bathing dress, or to stand outside her house and yell "Fire!" in order to see what sort of spectacle she presented without the benefit of her false hair, orris-root pads, and bustles. I think that the modern freedom of dress and manners is a contributing factor in the present high percentage of divorces—which were almost non-existent in the nineties—but I also think that other things in modern life are probably more to blame in this, and that all in all the modern freedom is best. The entire subject was once summed up interestingly, if incorrectly, by a German diplomat who had a post in this country before World War I. He said to me, "You have a most beautiful system in America. Your young people marry early from pure passion and have lovely children, and then they get a divorce and make a marriage of reason."

CHAPTER V

I KNOW THAT IT DID ME A GREAT DEAL OF GOOD TO BE schooled in the law by John M. Bowers, for he set a standard of industry that seems to be no longer endurable either in the professions or in business. It was the rule in our office that no one might go home until Bowers had left, which meant eight o'clock on many evenings, and his idea of a profitable holiday was to summon me to his home to help write a brief. After I had spent six years on the Supreme Court bench and four years in Germany and returned to the practice of law, nothing surprised me more than that everyone seemed to live with far less labor. I suppose it is the increased productivity of our agricultural and industrial machinery that enables us to prosper with progressively fewer hours of work, and yet I think it is unfortunate that men should still want so many things and be unwilling to expend the work necessary to get them.

A venerable law firm like ours becomes an accepted institution, enjoying, to the exasperation of competent newcomers, the benefits of that inequitable but inexorable rule: "To him that hath shall be given." Several clients had been with us a long time. The Corn Exchange Bank had engaged our firm since 1853. Many families in New York, such as the

Rhinelanders and the Stewarts, left their legal affairs with us for generations. The fabulous P. T. Barnum was at one time a client of my father. As a very small boy I remember being taken by Father to the circus in the old Madison Square Garden and occupying a box with Barnum. I remember the beautiful lady who put her horse through its paces of the *haute école*, but not one word of any stray wisdom that may have been uttered by the great Barnum. Barnum said that this lady was a friend of the Empress of Austria and I think she wrote the book *The Tribulations of an Empress*.

A memorable client of my father was a Russian princess, the Princess Fraloff. Once she sued the New York Central Railroad for the loss of some trunks which she said contained laces of enormous value. The railroad was represented by Eliot F. Sheppard, son-in-law of W. H. Vanderbilt. The princess won a substantial verdict despite the fact that during cross-examination whenever Sheppard asked her a troublesome question she would look at him with flashing eyes and spit contemptuously.

Another interesting client was Canfield the gambler. His place on Forty-fourth Street with its great raid-proof steel door was the constant target of William Travers Jerome, the crusading district attorney. I have somewhere a letter from Canfield thanking me for the successful outcome of his dispute with a brokerage house and telling me that I was the only honest lawyer he had ever known. Canfield was a patron of the arts and owned a notable collection of paintings by Whistler.

I was detailed by the firm to take care of the legal interests of the celebrated Hetty Green, that super-rich woman, who, because she devoted her surplus income (and it was large) to the development of the country rather than to frivolous expenditures, attracted the constant attention of the Press.

She was always accompanied by her charming daughter, Sylvia. Mrs. Green was not stingy, as the reporters would have it. I was once invited to spend an evening playing cards with Sylvia and Mr. and Mrs. Philip Livingston. When the game was over Mrs. Green gave me a silver calendar. I objected, saying that I was not the winner. "Never mind," said Mrs. Green, "I bought it for you." A supper, with all the delicacies of the season and a bottle of vintage champagne, followed.

One day in her office in the Park Bank she showed me a little black book. "That," she said, "is the record of my fortune when I first inherited it, and now look at it," and she pointed to a great row of enormous ledgers lining the wall.

After I was married and living at 725 Fifth Avenue, Mrs. Green and Sylvia, who were at the nearby Plaza Hotel, came over on several occasions to spend the evening with us. She talked most amusingly about old New York. Once she told us that when her father sent her for a season to Saratoga, the fact that her father had made a fortune in sending out whaling ships led to her becoming known as the "Princess of Whales."

Sylvia married a rich man, a descendant of the original Astor, Matthew Astor Wilks, a great gentleman, with whom I often rode in Central Park. Sylvia, now a widow, lives quietly in New York. In June 1948 she gave the magnificent Massachusetts estate inherited from her brother to the Massachusetts Institute of Technology.

Rudolph Valentino, whose image on the screen set up romantic physiochemical reactions in so many women, once dealt with our office. A motion-picture company had obtained an injunction restraining him from any activity, contending that he had violated the negative covenant of his contract with them. At his request, we were able to get this injunction modified. Conversation with him and his handsome wife, who had taken the name of Natacha Rambova, revealed him as a most agreeable young gentleman. He made quite a point of telling me that he had attended the University of Perugia. He seemed most intelligent and well informed and without the overweening vanity which makes so many actors insufferable.

It happened that I argued the case which established the right to enforce a negative covenant in a contract of employment. Musicians or actors, in their contracts with producers or managers, frequently agree not only to work for the employer but also, in the so-called negative covenant, not to work for anyone else in a similar capacity. Such covenants have been found an effective way to compel temperamental artists to keep contracts.

In the late eighties or the early nineties there was a craze in London which might have been compared to the tulip craze in Holland in the previous century. That was the professional beauty craze. The whole nation seemed to take the same interest in the ladies in British society who were acclaimed as professional beauties as the Americans take in Hollywood stars. Among them and pre-eminent was Mrs. Langtry, daughter of the dean on the Island of Jersey; a Mrs. Wheeler, Mrs. Cornwallis West, and Countess of Lonsdale.

Later Mrs. Langtry, much and publicly admired by the Prince of Wales, later Edward VII, capitalized her beauty and renown by going on the stage. In the course of her career she came to America where her cavalier was a young New Yorker named Frederick Gebhardt. He had a large income and owned race horses and was the man-about-town of the day. A tall, handsome, Irish-looking man, he used to walk up and down Fifth Avenue between four and six every afternoon. He followed the Jersey Lily, as Mrs. Langtry was called, across the continent. As he and his family had been clients of our office for years, the Jersey Lily naturally came to us with her various troubles with her managers, contracts, and so forth.

As she was a client, I naturally cannot tell all the extraordinary stories of her career told to me by her manager. She was tall, strongly built, with very broad shoulders and large beautiful violet eyes.

Years later, when we were in Berlin, we entertained her daughter at lunch or dinner in our embassy. The daughter was married to a young man named Ian Malcolm, who was very popular in England and who had something to do with moving seriously wounded British prisoners to Switzerland during World War I. He and his wife were guests of Sir Edward Goshen in the British Embassy in Berlin.

The deaths of Mr. and Mrs. Charles Fair, in an automobile accident in France about 1900, involved me in a most unusual case. At stake was the proper disposition of Mr. Fair's fortune of more than six million. Under Fair's will, if he died first his money went to his wife and then to her relatives. But if Mr. Fair survived his wife, the money went to Mr. Fair's two sisters, Mrs. Herman Oelrichs and then Mrs. W. K. Vanderbilt, Jr., whom I represented.

Obviously it was essential to know whether Mr. Fair or his wife had died first, even though their deaths had occurred within a few seconds of each other. On behalf of Mrs. Fair's relatives, two Frenchmen, named Maas and Moranne, came to America and testified that while on a bicycle tour they had witnessed the accident and had seen Mr. Fair succumb first.

But Edmond Kelly, an American lawyer in Paris whose help we had engaged, found proof that Maas and Moranne had not witnessed the fatal accident. When these two plotters returned to France, they were convicted of giving false testimony in the United States—an unlikely sounding procedure but permitted under French law. After that it was easy for us to arrange a settlement with the heirs of Mrs. Charles Fair, for, since no one had witnessed their deaths, the order in which Mr. and Mrs. Fair died had, of necessity, to be relegated—in the felicitous words of a learned judge—to the realm of moot.

An unforgettable case grew out of the death of Washington Irving Bishop, a mind reader. Bishop was celebrated for his apparent ability to identify hidden objects by merely holding the hand of another person who concentrated his thoughts upon the object. One night while giving an exhibition at the Lambs Club, he was stricken with some sort of attack and fell lifeless. Several well-known New York physicians were present. After the body had been removed, these physicians, with more scientific enthusiasm than sober judgment, proceeded to open the skull of Bishop to discover whether his seemingly uncanny power was owing to some unusual structure of his brain.

The next day the mother of the victim appeared and said that her son was subject, especially when giving exhibitions, to sudden trances in which for long periods he had the appearance of death. She charged that he had been murdered by the doctors, who had neither moral nor legal support for their ill-judged zeal in conducting the post-mortem examination. The physicians were indicted, and our firm represented one of them.

I went to court with my doctor-client, and we sat in the

back of the room. It was a day for sentences, and before our case was called, the clerk would summon one or another Joe Felon to the Bar of Justice. After a tongue-lashing from the judge, Joe would hear his sentence of twenty years, or life, while Joe's wife and children near us shrieked and wailed. A little of this reduced my client to a state of nerves verging on collapse. When his case was finally called, and the district attorney consented to a motion to quash the indictment, his relief was almost pitiful. The state had recognized its inability to prove murder when a number of qualified physicians were prepared to testify that Bishop was dead before their exploratory operation was performed.

One of my favorite cases involved the Coney Island Jockey Club, a client which was then constantly embroiled with bookmakers. Many a day I was sent to the races carrying lawbooks under my arm, an assignment which I didn't view with disfavor. By sitting on the lawbooks, I got a better view of the track. On the occasion of the Futurity of 1891, the Jockey Club rejected the entry of a horse named Huron. However, through an injunction obtained by its owner, the horse was permitted to race on the theory that if he didn't run—and if his owner's right to enter him was sustained—there would be no way of ascertaining the damages because no one could tell whether the horse would have won or not. Thus protected under the shield of the Supreme Court, Huron ran. Although I was watching the Jockey Club's legal interests, and even had developed a fatherly interest in Huron's success, I had fortunately taken the precaution of not betting on him. He didn't win.

Just as I was getting well settled in my law work, a violent streetcar strike occurred in Brooklyn, and the resulting turmoil required the National Guard to restore peace. On a bitterly cold Sunday night I was enjoying myself thoroughly at a large dinner party at the home of P. F. Collier, publisher of *Collier's Weekly,* when a sergeant from the Twelfth Regiment appeared with a summons to the armory. Early the next morning we marched bravely across the Brooklyn Bridge to the district in which we were to keep order, a fife and drum playing to keep us in step and in courage.

No headquarters had been prepared for us, but a private home on Dean Street had just been completed, so I took possession. The gas fitters, plumbers, and electricians in my company soon had the house in working order. I was quite comfortable for a few days, until a superior officer came along. Seeing how snug I had made myself and my company, he took possession for himself, and dispatched my company to another section of the city. As we marched along, bemoaning our ill luck and expecting to bivouac in some rat-infested warehouse, I saw an electric sign blazoned against the sky, "The Long Island Brewery." So, the public safety and our comfort requiring it, I marched in and took possession. For this act of bold and shrewd leadership my company accorded me honors worthy of Hannibal or Napoleon. My chest expanded visibly, as did the girth of my men after a protracted stay in the brewery.

Mayor Hugh J. Grant was a client of our office, and when he served as mayor of New York—which he did most acceptably—John Bowers was his unofficial adviser. I have always felt grateful to him because he insisted in those early days that Bowers give me full charge of certain litigations, in order, as it were, to flesh my maiden sword.

When John F. Hylan was elected Mayor, it was arranged that I was to serve as unofficial adviser to him as Bowers had to Grant. But at my first interview with Mayor Hylan we disagreed so thoroughly and completely that I found it impossible to work with him as counselor. He was an honest but thick-headed man of extreme obstinacy. It was his intention, he said, to devote himself primarily to the perfection of the police department, for which he considered himself somehow peculiarly qualified. He desired that I should become his adviser on matters of finance, under guiding principles which I found unacceptable. Mayor Hylan clung tenaciously to any proposition he advanced, even though it was the height of the preposterous. Once, for instance, a movement was initiated limiting the height of the buildings on Fifth Avenue, which, of course, would have prevented the erection of apartment houses there. It was undoubtedly backed by the Park Avenue apartment owners. As I had some property on Fifth Avenue, I attended the hearing at which Mayor Hylan made the absurd contention that the Fifth Avenue interests sought to erect a Chinese wall to keep the west wind from blowing on the poor people on the East Side. This was as silly a piece of rank demagoguery as I have ever heard in my life. Fifth Avenue, of course, is west of Park, but he declined to acknowledge that the Park Avenue apartment houses had already shut off the East Side from the beneficent wind.

One widely circulated story about Mayor Hylan was his reported comment when Albert, King of the Belgians, and his Queen made their successful American tour after World War I. The story went that when the Queen remarked on the beauty of the skyline, Hylan replied, "You said a mouthful, Queen."

The Belgian royal tour was managed by a clever diplomat, later the Belgian Ambassador in London, Cartier de Marchienne. One night I was guest at a dinner given by De Marchienne in the course of which King Albert presented me with the Grand Cross of one of the Belgian orders for my work on behalf of prisoners of war when I was Ambassador to Germany. During the evening I asked one of the King's aides if Mayor Hylan's remark to the Queen had been accurately quoted. He told me that when Hylan was walking with the Queen what he actually had said was, "Say, Queen, you're the only queen I'd be seen walking with." Surely a very pretty compliment.

CHAPTER VI

For about ten years it was my particular job to defend the New York *World* in the numerous libel suits brought against that newspaper when Joseph Pulitzer, its founder, was building its circulation and influence by violent articles and crusading vigor. Over the years this brought me into contact with as strange and varied an assortment of people as any novelist could imagine. Chorus girls and politicians, tycoons and playboys, reformers and curmudgeons—all in consuming fury and with outstretched palms over some alleged hurt to their virtue or business reputations.

Newspapers rarely have serious trouble with libel suits when the danger is foreseen and the risk accepted. A forthright attack is almost invariably bolstered by facts that will make truth a defense against charges of libel. It is inadvertent twisting of fact, or careless use of unsubstantiated report, that most frequently leads to payment of damages.

Fairly typical of the sort of litigation that engages a newspaper libel lawyer was a suit against the *World* by a certain actress. She objected to an article referring to an affair of hers with Buffalo Bill Cody. I obtained a court order to take the testimony of Buffalo Bill. Rarely have I been so sorry for anyone as I was for him on that occasion. Here was a fine-looking plainsman with his long hair and striking costume, miserably uncomfortable in the unaccustomed atmosphere of a New York lawyer's office, and in a touching state of mortification as a circle of sharp-nosed lawyers probed into his love life. It was apparent that he was an easy mark for any designing young woman. The libel case gave us no further trouble.

Joseph Pulitzer was a man of consuming energy, and he drove his associates at the same strenuous pace he set for himself. It was not only as defense against libel suits that the crusading Pulitzer found use for his legal aides. Our firm was more than once enlisted in one of the Pulitzer campaigns to eradicate sin and corruption. He devoted himself particularly to the matter of regulating public utilities and to fighting for franchises fair to the public. The first charter for Greater New York, which went into effect January 1, 1898, provided that no franchise might thereafter be granted for longer than twenty-five years. In the short interval between the legislative adoption of this charter and its effective date there was a concerted rush to obtain long-term or perpetual charters from the city. The aldermen were actually about to grant one, known as the Kingsbridge franchise, when Pulitzer, through his able lieutenant, Bradford Merrill, editor of the *World*, told me that I must get an injunction to stop it. When I replied that I knew no legal way to block the franchise, Pulitzer sent word, "Lock yourself in the Bar Association Library until you find a way."

Thus driven, I restudied the charter, and noted that the provision limiting franchises to twenty-five years read: "After *the approval* of this act . . ." et cetera. Since the act had been signed by the governor, I went to court with the claim that this approval of the act was sufficient to prohibit long franchises, even though the act itself was not effective until

January 1. The Court of Appeals sustained this view, the franchises were blocked, and Pulitzer was pleased.

This incident was typical of the way Pulitzer got results by simply refusing to tolerate the idea of failure. I was in the newspaper offices almost every day, conferring with Merrill, S. S. Carvalho, Don Seitz, or Florence White, who were business managers at various times. All of them were able marshals of Pulitzer in building the paper to be the great civic force that it became.

When libel suits were brought against the *World* in counties outside Manhattan I always engaged local counsel for the trial. In one serious case the local lawyer I employed had, it later developed, been educated at Heidelberg and spoke excellent German. At first I was puzzled by his apparent anxiety to get Germans on the jury. "Never mind, never mind. Wait and see," was the only explanation he would give me.

When the evidence was all in, and he was summing up the case, he told the jury, "As the great Goethe remarked in his wonderful poem of Faust," and then he recited some German phrases. The judge, who was soon to run for re-election, nodded and smiled approval, to signify that he, too, was familiar with the works of the German poet. The opposing counsel likewise smiled and nodded, as if to show that he was also a cultured man. What my counsel actually said was, "Don't give this man a cent. He not only hates Germans but last week he swindled an old German woman in South Brooklyn out of thirty-seven dollars."

The result was a verdict, in a dangerous and difficult case, of a nominal six cents for the plaintiff. As I knew no German at that time, I had joined the judge and plaintiff's lawyer in their knowing nods, but my discomfiture, when he told me the truth, was amply salved by the legal victory.

Pulitzer was keenness itself about little things. Once at Bar Harbor I was riding with him, for he rode horses despite his blindness, and I was whistling idly as we slowed to a walk. "What is that you are trying to whistle?" he asked. "It's the popular song of the day called 'Sweet Marie,' " I answered. He asked me about its composer, its background, and its popularity in such detail that I was not surprised to learn within a few weeks that the composer of "Sweet Marie" had written another song called "Dear Louise" especially for the New York *World*.

Often he would ask me the most irrelevant questions. If we were discussing politics he would suddenly demand the totals of the vote in Nevada for the previous year. He seemed to think that I should have the answers ready. After a while I formed the habit of giving him a bold guess for an answer, and he seemed satisfied.

Of the many notable crusades undertaken by the *World*, none was more memorable than the achievement of destroying the bond syndicate of which J. Pierpont Morgan was sole manager and director. The expression "Wall Street" is still bandied about a good deal as a synonym for financial power, but few know on how solid a base this conception rested. The operation of this bond syndicate was a characteristic Wall Street maneuver.

In 1896 the United States Treasury was trying to get gold to deposit as a reserve against a new issue of currency. The great value of gold held by our government today and the enormous increase in currency make the figures of 1896 seem insignificant, but they were of awesome size at the time. To get the gold for the treasury vaults, the government was in the habit of exchanging bonds for gold. Most people did not care to handle gold, which was inconveniently heavy in any quantity. Since paper currency was preferred by the public, it was the banks and bankers who were able to accumulate gold and to whom the Treasury had to turn for it.

An article in the World Almanac of January 1896, written, of course, under the eye of Pulitzer, shows how this system worked.

During the year the *World* steadfastly continued its advocacy of sound national finance. It urged upon Congress the necessity of authorizing the Treasury to issue low rate bonds when the necessity of bond sales to keep the currency at par should arise. It urged that such bonds should be issued in small denominations as a popular loan, thereby ensuring a full price and interesting the people in the integrity of our national debt. The *World* warned the Administration that the crisis of February last was approaching and strongly urged that measures should be taken to prevent that "hold up" of the Treasury which, in fact, occurred. When the Bond Syndicate, by reason of the neglect of this warning, secured the power to exact what terms it pleased, The *World* pointed out the fact that the Government 4 per cents, which were sold to the Syndicate at 104½, were actually worth 120 or more in the open market. Later, as soon as the public had a chance to buy the bonds, they advanced at once to the figures named by the *World,* but the profit which should have been given into the Treasury went instead into the strong boxes of the Syndicate bankers.

It is said that J. Pierpont Morgan I, who headed the bond syndicate, was a proud descendant of Sir Henry Morgan who was known as Morgan the Pirate. Whether this is true or not, it is true that he named his yacht the *Corsair,* and the *Corsair Morgan,* when he invaded the Spanish-American town of

Porto Bello, exacted no such ransom from the inhabitants as the J. Pierpont Morgan syndicate took from the pockets of the American public.

Joseph Pulitzer undertook a campaign to compel the Treasury to offer the bonds for public subscription and finally succeeded in accomplishing this. The following is quoted from the World Almanac of January 1, 1897, to show how successful the *World* was in breaking the monopoly of the Morgan Syndicate, a monopoly which put millions of dollars in the pocket of Morgan for managing the deal as well as giving him and his firm enormous profit in the operation of the Syndicate.

The smashing of the "bond ring" in the first month of the year was a crowning triumph for "Publicity, the greatest moral force and factor in the universe." New Year's day, 1896, it was announced from Washington that there would be an issue of 30-year 4 per cent bonds, and that the government had negotiated with the Morgan Syndicate for the sale of the bonds at about the same price paid in February 1895 for an issue of $62,300,000 worth of the same kind of bonds, the new issue being made necessary by the depletion of the gold reserve. The country was shocked, for the *World* had pointed out that the bonds of the previous issue sold to the Syndicate for 104¾ were quoted on the market at 118 or more, and the new bonds should surely bring as much. The sale as planned would not only involve an immense loss to the Treasury but the very suggestion of it impaired the nation's credit at home and abroad. On January 3, 1893 the *World* addressed an Appeal to the President. The appeal of the *World* was heeded. On January 7 the *World* was able to announce that the bankers of the country, alone, were ready to subscribe for double the amount of the issue, and reluctantly the Administration yielded. The battle was won. The head of the smashed Syndicate bid $6,000,000 more than his syndicate would have paid had not the *World* knocked the bottom out of the secret deal and secured a public sale for and to the people. The whole issue was finally disposed of at an average price of nearly 112, netting $6,888,836 more to the Treasury than would have come in had the secret sale been consummated. If the interest on the saving for 30 years, the life of the bonds, is added, the saving to the Treasury was over $20,000,000. But more important than all this was the restoration of the credit of the nation.

Aside from anything else, the foregoing should indicate that to be a lawyer for a Pulitzer newspaper was to be a busy, busy man.

When the bylaws and organization of the Associated Press were revamped, I attended the sessions on behalf of the New York *World*. These took place, as I recollect, in the old Astoria Hotel on the corner of Fifth Avenue and Thirty-fourth Street. Melville Stone, the founder of the Associated Press, was a most charming and talented man, and a great friend of ours.

The city of New York has been fortunate in the independence of those who own its newspapers. Joseph Pulitzer used the *World* consistently for the public good. Later, Adolph Ochs came up from Tennessee, purchased the old New York *Times,* and built it up into the great organization it is today. He gave me a standing invitation to come at any time to the lunches of the editors of the *Times,* at which interesting guests were usually present. Dr. John Finley was another of the editors of the *Times* for whom I had a great admiration. His sudden death occurred only an hour and a half after he left our house where he had attended a reception that we gave for young Otto, the present pretender to the throne of the Hapsburgs. That death was a great loss not only to the *Times* but to the community as a whole.

In the same period Whitelaw Reid was the editor of the *Tribune*. He was not only a brilliant writer and a great journalist but the man who did most of any of our diplomats to establish the friendly relations which now exist between Great Britain and the United States. For years after the War of the Revolution and the War of 1812 the country still smarted from Indian barbarities of the Revolution which were carried out under British officers. The anti-British feeling was fed by the burning of the Capitol in the War of 1812, and, in our Civil War, by the threats of Great Britain and the sinkings of northern ships by the *Alabama*, fitted out in a British port. Even as late as President Cleveland's time a war between the United States and Great Britain seemed imminent over the boundary dispute in Venezuela.

William Randolph Hearst looms large in any account of American journalism. In character, with his imperious daring, he was a throwback to the feudal barons. I have always admired his courage and ability. He is absolutely fearless, a great crusader, and a great writer.

My wife's father and Hearst's father were partners. Each owned a fourth in the great Anaconda mine. Mrs. Gerard remembers Senator George Hearst on his visits to Butte rolling gold pieces across the table to her and her sister. Mrs. George Hearst was a remarkable and splendid woman, and often invited my wife to visit her in Washington.

There are innumerable stories concerning Hearst's minute interest in the great newspaper organization he built and his despotic control over its operation. A typical one is illustrative of his custom of dismissing his employees by telegram, and the dread of these missives that even the mighty were not always able to dismiss. It relates that an executive of one of the Hearst papers, returning from lunch, passed by the row of glass-enclosed offices of his colleagues and noted on the desk of each the yellow envelope of a waiting telegram. His alarm grew as he progressed toward his own office, and, sure enough, as he entered he found a similar envelope awaiting him. With trembling hands he opened it. Seconds later his excited gurgles brought his secretary running into the room. "What is it, sir?" she inquired solicitously. "Oh," said the Hearstling happily, "my father is dead!"

During the fights between Pulitzer and Hearst I was, of course, legally on the Pulitzer side. When I ran for justice of the New York Supreme Court in 1907, the Hearst papers attacked me violently. After I had won the election, I met Hearst in the street one day. I said to him, "I want to thank you. You might have made a stronger attack on me." Afterward, when I was appointed Ambassador to Berlin, and when I ran for the United States Senate in 1914 without being in the country, he supported me just as violently as he had previously opposed me.

After I returned to America from my post in Germany, Hearst and his newspapers were fiercely attacked on the ground that he was pro-German. Towns such as Mt. Vernon passed ordinances forbidding the sale of Hearst papers in the streets. I was asked to take up this fight in his behalf, and before 10 P.M. of the day I was engaged I obtained an injunction halting enforcement of the Mt. Vernon ordinance. Later my office represented Hearst throughout the country wherever he was similarly attacked. Of course he never wavered in his devotion to what he considered the best interests of his own country.

Another rich man who entered the journalistic lists was Marshall Field. I am very fond of him, and often shot with him on the Long Island place where he used to raise pheasants before he became interested in bigger game. It is my judgment he has not yet exactly found himself, and that eventually, ably seconded by his capable and charming wife, he will be credited with solid achievement. At present he is too modest and retiring.

We often met Frank Munsey, owner of many newspapers who left his fortune to the Metropolitan Museum, and Mrs. Gerard and I used to dine with him in Paris in the gay days before World War I. He was a great speculator and increased his fortune many times by his operations in the stock of United States Steel. At one time he owned a string of stores in which soap and like commodities were sold, and overwhelmed Mrs. Gerard with presents of these useful articles.

Whitelaw Reid married the daughter of D. O. Mills, who made a great fortune in California. They had two children, a daughter who became Lady Ward, wife of a distinguished Englishman of a great family, and a son, Ogden Mills Reid, who, while he lived, managed the New York *Herald Tribune* with the aid of his super-capable and attractive wife.

As a molder of public opinion the newspaper today has to compete to some degree with the radio. Usually only a few thousand people read the most successful book, although there are occasional exceptions as, for instance, when Wendell Willkie's pamphlet account of his travels without binding reached a circulation of more than a million and the book which I wrote on my return from Germany (and which sold for four times the price of Willkie's book) reached a sale of more than half a million. It seems patent to me that in recent elections radio was far more effective in swaying people by bringing them into direct contact with the candidates than were the newspapers, with their indirect and journalistically styled offerings.

Millions of people are reached by the radio, and the use of this medium involves the traditional freedom of speech. In Great Britain, for example, the authorities were quick to seize the radio for the government. Those owning receiving sets pay an annual tax, and this tax is used partly for the programs sent out by the government over the air. There is no advertising on the radio and no one can speak except with the permission of the radio officials who, of course, are the representatives of the government of the day.

In a political campaign the radio is the most effective—as well as the most expensive—instrument for molding public opinion. The general practice has been that if the President, for example, wants to give a fireside chat on the radio, he is not charged for the time, but once a political campaign has commenced, then the President, like anyone else, if he speaks politically, must pay. In the 1928 campaign as treasurer of the Democratic party I spent about $740,000 for radio time, and in subsequent campaigns that sum has been nearly equaled by both of the political parties.

Today, of course, no campaign intended to mold men's thoughts and actions could very well be undertaken without adequate radio time being used. Radio and its lusty offspring, television, will eventually become—if they have not already— a greater force for good or for evil than the Press has ever been, and the leaders in this field must of necessity measure up to the high standards set by the great independent editors who have been responsible for the integrity of the Press.

CHAPTER VII

FOR THE MOST PART THE RICH NEW YORKERS OF MY PARENTS'
day were cleverer at avoiding unfavorable publicity than
those of the present. Cloistered behind their protective, uniform, brownstone-front houses, they avoided ostentation,
knowing well that the newspapers and sensation-seeking
preachers would seize on any excess of display and make a
moral issue of it. The Bradley Martin ball was a famous example.

Mr. and Mrs. Bradley Martin returned from Europe for a
short visit in 1897 and decided to give a fancy-dress ball in
the Waldorf to greet their New York friends. It was the
climax of the season, and invitations were eagerly sought.
There was nothing extraordinary in the party plans, however.
Every town has an occasional "dress-up" party, but in a great
city the party is larger and more expensive—that is the only
difference. In any event, at the news of this ball the newspapers and preachers vied in denouncing its wickedness and
in quoting pertinent passages from the Old Testament about
the folly of great riches.

The ball was very colorful. It happened that Count Fes-
tetics, a Hungarian, had just married Miss Eila Haggin, a
granddaughter of James B. Haggin, and at the wedding he

wore the uniform of his Hungarian regiment, the Red Hussars. I had this uniform copied in white and gold as my costume for the ball, and added a white wig with the traditional Hussar locks of Napoleon's time, which hung down in front of the ears. To complete the effect, I carried a saber which had been worn by my great-uncle, General William Sumner, when he was adjutant general of Massachusetts in the War of 1812. Apparently this costume made a hit, for in the current *Harper's Weekly*, in a full-page picture of the event, I appeared prominently in the center of the picture.

I went to supper twice, being able to eat and drink more in those days, the first time taking in Mrs. Oliver Belmont, who was dressed as La Tosca, and the second time the very beautiful daughter of General Sickles. She was dressed as Queen Louise of Prussia and was certainly one of the most beautiful girls I ever met in my life. She afterward married the British diplomat Crackenthorpe. Old General Sickles, who had lost a leg in the Civil War, had a front-row seat at the opera, and used to make an impressive entrance on crutches after the audience had been seated and the aisles were clear.

For a long time after the event the Bradley Martin ball was regularly cited in the Press and from the pulpits as evidence of the rotting of the social structure, and in some quarters it became synonymous with Sodom and Gomorrah and the wild orgies of the decadent Roman emperors.

It was only a few years after this, in 1904, that James Hazen Hyde gave the celebrated ball at Sherry's to introduce to Society his niece Miss Ripley. This was the ball which led to so much scandalmongering and silliness that he finally became disgusted and went to live in France, where he had had a house for some time. Actually the ball, which Mrs. Gerard and I attended and remained at until breakfast, was the height of respectability and good taste. The public indignation and the moral outcry that followed the stories that it was an orgy were part of a carefully planned campaign by certain Wall Street interests, certain lawyers who wanted business, and George W. Perkins, a vice-president of the New York Life Insurance Company and a partner of the Morgan firm. These people wanted to force Hyde to give them control of the stock of the Equitable Life Assurance Company. This is not generally known and it sounds fantastic, but it is true. Having failed to get him to sell stock, which would have given them control of the company's half-billion-dollar assets, this ruthless group took advantage of the public's antipathy to excessive displays of wealth—an antipathy that had been demonstrated in the still-recent Bradley Martin case—and saw to it that the worst sort of rumors and stories about Hyde were started and kept alive.

The costumes at the ball were magnificent and the whole thing was beautifully done. I remember that Mrs. Clarence Mackay's dress was copied from a picture of the mistress of Louis XIV, La Vallière, and her long train was carried by two little Negro pages throughout the entire evening. The French actress, Réjane, appeared in a one-act play and during supper she stood on a chair and, possibly to maintain her balance, as she was rather fat, put one foot on the table and recited a charming poem in French. This was seized upon by the detractors, who claimed that the French actress had danced on the table in the middle of a fifteenth-century orgy. Even the *Sun,* which up to then had never published a picture, had one on the front page representing a young woman, dressed as Folly, wildly dancing at the Hyde ball. So it went.

Among the people at large in the country there was a feeling of suspicion toward foreigners in general and a special feeling that the French, in particular, were a sin-loving race. This feeling was exploited to the hilt by stories that Hyde was a Francophile, that he affected French manners and dress, and, what was worse, that he actually preferred to speak French rather than English. In a completely harmless way Hyde did admire France and was, indeed, a Francophile, which at other times in history might have been cited to his credit. But it was made to appear terrible then, and his life was made unbearable in many distressing ways.

The Equitable was an unusual company and understandably was quite a plum in the eyes of Wall Street. Hyde's father, Henry Baldwin Hyde, had founded the insurance company with a capital of $100,000, and owned a majority of the stock which, on his death, he left to his son. Under the company's charter it could not earn more than 7 per cent on its $100,000 capital stock—or only $7,000. However, so competent was the elder Hyde's management that an enormous fund of assets and surplus was built up which, by 1904, amounted to well over $500,000,000—all controlled by whoever owned at least 51 per cent of the original capital stock.

On this the corsairs of Wall Street cast envious eyes. That a young man, not a member of the gang, should control this seemed monstrous to them. Aided by certain faults of management brought out by Charles E. Hughes in his investigation of insurance companies, they endeavored to shake young Hyde out of his control. That this control was a prize is evident by the fact that before the Hughes investigation Mutual Life, through Morgan's Perkins, offered James Hazen Hyde $10,000,000 for his majority of the stock of a $100,000 corporation which could never pay more than 7 per cent.

When the fancy-dress ball was pictured as an orgy, young

Hyde, disgusted with the whole situation, sold the control to Thomas Fortune Ryan for $2,500,000. It was said that when Ryan made this purchase, James H. Harriman, who had been quite active in trying to purchase the stock for himself, went in a rage to Ryan and said, "I shook that plum tree!" Forced by public opinion, which had become dubious of the deal, Ryan turned over the control to three trustees, Morgan J. O'Brien, Grover Cleveland, and George Westinghouse.

In Paris, Hyde became a member of the French Institute and was given the Grand Cross of the Legion of Honor. During World War I he turned his house into a French Red Cross hospital and was assistant to the High Commissioner of the American Red Cross.

It was at Hyde's house in Paris on our way out of Germany in 1917 that I met the celebrated authors Marcel Prévost and Jules Huret, who both, in a discussion about America, agreed without irony that the one thing that had impressed them about America was the absence of that bitter hate which so often impaired the usefulness of the statesmen of France.

In the litigation growing out of the Hughes insurance investigation our law firm defended some directors of one of the companies involved. That accounts for my particular interest in the Equitable Company matter which started the chain of inquiry and litigations involving a majority of the great insurance organizations.

In the light of history it is now clear that the Spanish-American War was a necessary undertaking, despite the fact that we were thrust into it by an emotional surge, and despite its bitterly unnecessary cost in lives and needless suffering from wounds, bad food, and disease.

I was present at Delmonico's in 1898 when William Randolph Hearst gave his famous reception to Evangelina Cisneros and her mother. These two had been rescued by the enterprising Hearst reporter, Karl Decker, from a Spanish-Cuban prison and allegedly brutal treatment. The pro-interventionist Hearst press exploited the señorita's plight to the hilt. This and similar propaganda, climaxed by the blowing up of the U.S.S. *Maine,* projected us into war.

The newspapers played up the formation of the Rough Riders, of which Theodore Roosevelt was lieutenant colonel. I wrote a letter to Roosevelt describing my qualifications and offering my services. On the way to post this letter I ran into my brother Sumner, who informed me that he had just joined the Rough Riders. On the spot I decided that one Gerard in that outfit was enough, and tore up my letter.

A month or so later General Butt and his staff, of which I was a member, were summoned with the first brigade of the New York National Guard to Camp Black, which was situated on the Hempstead Plains about two miles east of Garden City, Long Island.

When the Federal Government accepted volunteers from the National Guard, it called on them by regiments and not by brigades, so that our staff gradually lost its command and was left suspended in the air. General Gillespie of the regular Army finally offered me a place on his staff, but as the war was practically over, I did not accept.

My brother Sumner went off with the Rough Riders. One day in the autumn, after the close of the war, I was sitting in the Gramercy Park house when the doorbell rang and a yellow shape was admitted. It was my brother, suffering from malaria and looking like a jaundiced ghost. When he recovered, he was entrusted by Teddy Roosevelt with the task of

getting the Rough Riders out of town. I invited him one night
to bring some friends to dinner and a play. He brought with
him as his most intimate friends in the regiment a lawyer
from Arizona, two gamblers from Yuma, a house painter from
St. Louis, and a bicycle policeman from Buffalo. We all dined
at Rector's. When I asked the gamblers what they would like
to drink, they said they would like sherry as they'd heard a
song about "Sherry Wine" in their cowboy days. It symbolized high life to them, even if it *was* weaker than rye
whisky.

I performed my final chore in the Spanish-American War
when Admiral Dewey returned from having beaten the
Spaniards at Manila Bay. He was given a magnificent reception in New York. As one of the staff of General Butt, I rode
in the Dewey parade at the head of the first brigade of New
York troops.

In the few months between the end of the Spanish War
and my marriage in 1901, I worked hard at the law, and it
was during that period that I became involved in one of the
most extraordinary litigations of my career. It grew out of
the murder of the Texas millionaire, William Hamilton Rice,
founder of Rice Institute. He had made his millions in business in Texas and at his death he owned a great estate in
securities and thousands of acres of valuable Louisiana tim-
berlands. His New York bankers were the distinguished firm
of S. M. Swenson Sons, who were clients of our office.

Rice was murdered in New York on September 23, 1900.
Several months before the murder Eric Swenson and his
brother came to our office. He told us that their chief clerk,
one Weatherbee, had been approached by Mr. Rice's valet
Jones with the proposition that he, Jones, could get Rice to
name Weatherbee as one of the executors of Rice's will. Jones

proposed that Weatherbee should agree to split whatever fee he received with him.

Late in the afternoon of September 24, the day after Rice's death, the Swensons came to our office in great perturbation. They told me that a man giving his name as Albert S. Patrick —a lawyer—had come to their banking office and had presented for certification a check for $250,000 drawn to the order of Albert S. Patrick by Rice. For some reason or other Swenson Sons' cashier became suspicious and asked Patrick to write his name across the back of the check. The difference between the words "Albert" and "Abert" which Patrick wrote gave the cashier an excuse to say that he would not certify the check until he had first spoken with Mr. Rice. He telephoned Rice's apartment and was told by the valet Jones that he knew all about the check, and that it was all right for the Swenson bank to certify it. The cashier insisted that Mr. Rice himself come to the telephone. To this the valet replied that Rice could not come to the phone, as he had died the night before. The cashier then refused, of course, to certify the check. A short time later Patrick came to the Swenson office and said that he had a paper entitling him to the contents of Rice's safe-deposit box, and also exhibited a letter signed by Rice in which Rice asked that his body be cremated. Patrick thoughtfully invited the Swensons to attend this cremation.

When all this has been told to me, I said that I thought it was a case for the district attorney. The Swensons said that they would not go to the district attorney as they might be sued for malicious prosecution. I said that I would go on my own responsibility, and I hurried immediately to the office of Asa Bird Gardiner, the district attorney, to whom I told these happenings. He agreed that the case looked highly suspicious and had the chief of detectives detail to me a detective named Vallely.

Vallely and I first went to the office of the cremation company and inquired whether the cremation of Rice's body had been ordered. There we found that Patrick had ordered the cremation for the following morning. We countermanded this. Then, as it was late in the afternoon, we went to Patrick's boarding house on Fifty-eighth Street west of Eighth Avenue. Patrick was not at home, so Vallely and I waited across the street until about ten o'clock that night when he returned. We followed him to his room and I introduced Vallely as one of my clerks, although his very detective air and thick shoes would have proclaimed his calling to a child. Patrick said Rice had died from indigestion caused by eating bananas. I asked him what he was going to do with the body, and he said it would be taken to Milwaukee where relatives of Rice were buried and would be there interred. As Vallely and I knew that Patrick had ordered the cremation for the following morning I think there was enough evidence at the time to have justified the arrest of Patrick. Vallely and I learned later that after we left, Patrick went down to his office and spent the rest of the night destroying papers.

At this point Captain James A. Baker, a lawyer from Texas, arrived in New York. He had in his possession a will made sometime before by Rice in which, after various legacies to relatives, he left the bulk of his fortune to found a college in Texas to be called the Rice Institute. It was arranged that my firm should join with Captain Baker's New York lawyers in protecting the interests of Captain Baker as executor of the true will.

At this point Patrick produced what he claimed to be Rice's will, with Rice's signature not only at the end, but on each page. In this will the legacies to all the relatives named in the Baker will were increased and the balance of the estate was left to Patrick for an alleged secret trust. It was then arranged that Rice's safe-deposit box should be opened in the presence of Patrick and those representing the Baker will. Patrick, who had become particularly hostile to me, said that he wouldn't consent to the box's being opened if I were present, but he finally agreed. I remember telling Patrick that it soon would not make much difference to him whether I was present or not. I knew that after the box had been opened the police were going to arrest him, for an autopsy had disclosed that Rice had been chloroformed.

Jones and Patrick were arrested and taken to the Tombs, where by accident, they were placed in cells that were in view of each other. Immediately Patrick's cell was crowded with lawyers he had engaged, but no one came near the unfortunate valet. Observing the crowd of people going to Patrick's cell, Jones concluded that his confederate was planning to turn state's evidence, and he quickly decided that his best course was to turn state's witness himself. In the middle of the night he sent for Assistant District Attorney James W. Osborne, to whom he confessed.

It appeared that Patrick had never seen Rice, but had learned about Rice when he had been attorney for some relatives of Rice's divorced wife. She had died leaving whatever property she possessed to her own relatives. Patrick had raised the point that under the Texas community property statute, although Rice was alive, his divorced wife still had a claim to half of his property and that on her death this had vested in her relatives.

It was in the hope of avoiding this claim that Rice had left Texas and was living in New York unknown and lonely. At the criminal trial I testified to my conversation with Patrick on the night when Vallely and I visited him. He was convicted and sentenced to die in the electric chair, but his sentence was later commuted to life imprisonment and later he was scandalously pardoned by Governor Dix.

In the civil suit that remained after the criminal suit was settled, we encountered one great difficulty. The two witnesses to the will produced by Patrick, both young law students, stuck tenaciously to their story that Rice had executed the will in their presence. Here, however, was where the clever Patrick failed in his perfect crime. Only one signature at the end of a will is necessary, but on the will produced by Patrick, Rice's signature was on each page. When these signatures had been enlarged by photography to two feet or more in height, we found that each one fitted exactly over the other. The Appellate Division set aside the Patrick will on the ground of its inherent evidence of forgery, since no person can write a signature two or more times exactly alike, and obviously the signatures of Rice on the false will had all been traced from one genuine signature.

Many years after the pardon of Patrick I heard that a small oil company in Oklahoma was in difficulties and that its property might be sold. I sent a man to Tulsa to see if there were any bargains to be had, and when he came back I asked him how he had made out. "Made out, nothing! When I met the lawyer from the oil company, one Patrick, and told him I came from you, he put both hands over his face, let out a sort of scream, and left the room saying, 'That man kept me for years in state's prison—most of the time in the death house!' " Patrick died a few years ago. He had been practicing law in Oklahoma—rather a sad commentary on our judicial system.

When I attended the Houston convention of the Democratic party in 1928, Captain James A. Baker, before his death perhaps the most distinguished lawyer in Texas, gave me a dinner and took me to see the beautiful buildings of the Rice Institute. It occupies more than three hundred acres in the city of Houston and has an endowment of more than $22,-000,000—a great tribute to the skill of Captain Baker and his fellow trustees. The captain asked for my photograph to hang in the office of the Rice Institute. This, he said, was fitting, as the Institute might not have existed if I had not gone to see the district attorney in New York twenty-eight years before.

CHAPTER VIII

MY MARRIAGE TO MOLLY DALY, DAUGHTER OF MARCUS
Daly of Montana, took place in 1901 as a climax to the two
rather stormy years of our engagement. For the most part,
our friends regarded us as an "idyllic couple." But just as your
friends may admire your shoes without guessing where they
pinch, the fact is that we were individually strong-minded
and our idyll was punctuated from time to time by spirited
disagreement. In retrospect, this long engagement was beneficial as well as interesting. We apparently worked all the
scrapping out of our systems and made the psychic adjust-
ments that the marriage counselors write about so earnestly
in a period when it was possible to sulk at a distance without
the wrenching of faith and promise that that implies after
marriage. In any event, we have lived together most happily
ever since, and while this feat is not unique, sometimes I have
sorrowful fears that if we live much longer, it may become so.

The circumstance of having no children has had the compensating effect of making us closer together than might
otherwise have been the case. Molly has been not only a devoted helpmate, but also a charming companion, a skillful
hostess, and a great aid to my career. Both government and
business concerns are beginning to appreciate the value to a

man of these possessions in appraising his fitness for important positions. I know one executive in a great publishing concern who never hires a man without getting a convincing affirmative to the question: "Do you and your wife love each other?"

During our days in Germany in World War I Molly's diplomatic skill was largely responsible for the peace that reigned in our embassy, with its large staff of wartime secretaries and employees, throughout a period when nerves were on edge in a tense little community isolated in a foreign and hostile land. Devotion to family responsibility is placed high on her list of virtues. Her mother lived to the ripe age of eighty-six, and to the end Molly was her constant companion, saw her three times a day, and stayed with her during the summer at her estate in the Bitter Root Valley of Montana, which her mother loved, but which was hardly a substitute for the stimulating social life of Europe or Newport.

Because of the still recent death of Molly's father in 1900, our wedding in 1901 was a quiet one, and because my law work in New York was particularly heavy, we had to take only a brief four-day honeymoon at Atlantic City. After a stay with my mother in Bar Harbor, at the end of August, we went to the Bitter Root Valley for a delayed honeymoon. Theodore Roosevelt, then Vice-President, was on the train, and I went back to his car to pay my respects. In the course of a long talk my wife and I told him that we hoped some day to see him President of the United States. A few hours after voicing this hope, we arrived at Hamilton, Montana, and were startled to learn that President McKinley had been assassinated.

In 1902 I played a part in one of the most celebrated chapters in the municipal annals of New York. Mr. Pulitzer decided that the *World* would investigate the activities and ramifications of the so-called Ice Trust of New York, with which Mayor Van Wyck was supposed to be connected. The assignment fell to me, and I found an obscure provision of the city charter under which any taxpayer could demand an investigation. The inquiry centered on the renting of city piers by the ice company—which is a still tip for crusading editors in cities owning diverse properties. Mayor Van Wyck was ultimately shown to be innocent of grafting, and although Tammany had a finger in the pie, Charles F. Murphy was cleared of all charges of chicanery. As a result of the investigation, Murphy was enabled to oust the Richard Croker-Carroll forces from control of Tammany Hall, a victory historic in New York politics. Shortly thereafter, in 1903, I was made chairman of the County Committee of Tammany Hall, and later chairman of the Campaign Committee of Tammany, which supplanted the Finance Committee of which Richard Croker had been chairman.

At this time in New York, we made our home at 725 Fifth Avenue with my wife's mother, her brother, Marcus Daly II, and her sister, Harriot. These three had inherited from Marcus Daly large mining properties throughout the West, and I have since devoted a large share of my time and energy in watching and furthering these interests.

Marcus Daly was a colorful man, and his career was a rainbow. He was born in 1841, the son of a small farmer at Ballyjamesduff, in County Cavan, Ireland. As a young man of twenty he landed in New York with only fifty cents left of his slender capital. Daly toiled energetically at odd jobs in Brooklyn until he had saved enough money to go to California. Working for farmers and others, he eventually drifted to Virginia City, where he became superintendent of a mine.

Later he became general superintendent of a mine at Ophir, a small mining town in Utah, where my wife was born.

Daly married Margaret Evans, daughter of a western pioneer, whom he had met in a way romantic enough to satisfy even Hollywood. One day, as he stood at the bottom of an inclined crosscut, his future wife, who was visiting the mine with her father, lost her balance in walking down the steep passageway, and ran against her will down the incline. At the end stood Marcus Daly, who caught her in his arms. They were married in 1872. It is an authentic case of the irony of fate that his wife's sister married Ross Clark, brother of Senator William A. Clark, who became the violent enemy of Marcus Daly in a celebrated political feud.

About 1878 Daly went to Butte, Montana, where James B. Haggin, George Hearst, the father of William Randolph Hearst, and Lloyd Tevis of California had taken over a silver prospect. Daly acquired a quarter interest. As the shaft went down on this silver prospect, one of the greatest bodies of copper ore in the world was laid bare, and the great Anaconda Mine came into being.

Daly developed an 18,000-acre estate in the beautiful Bitter Root Valley. There he raised blooded horses and achieved a success only slightly less than his enthusiasm as a race-horse owner. He once told me that he thought horse racing was the greatest sport ever devised, and on several occasions he gave the men in his mines holidays so they could attend the races. Among his successful race horses were Montana, Senator Grady, Tammany, Hamburg, Scottish Chieftain, and Ogden.

Tammany was Daly's favorite. This genuinely great horse won the Eclipse and Criterion stakes as a two-year-old, and the Withers, Realization, Jerome and Lorillard Stakes as a three-year-old. Ridden by the celebrated jockey Garrison, Tammany also won a great match against Pierre Lorillard's horse Lamplighter. Garrison was well known for his sensational finishes in which he would dramatically come from behind to win, and the expression "a Garrison finish" crept into our colloquial talk. Hamburg, another of Daly's horses, won the Swift Stakes, Realization Stakes, and Brighton Cup. Scottish Chieftain won the Belmont Stakes, beating his stable companion, Ogden, winner of the Futurity of 1898.

At Mr. Daly's breeding establishment at Aperfield Court in England one of Mr. Daly's mares, Optime, was bred to the stallion Melton, and brought in foal to this country and, after Mr. Daly's death, sold at the great sale of his English horses held at Madison Square Garden. Optime was bought by James Keene and the foal by Melton was the celebrated race horse Sysonby.

Dr. Edward W. Hagyard was the chief veterinarian for Mr. Daly and for a time was the manager of the Bitter Root Stock Farm. He had many interesting adventures in buying race horses for Mr. Daly. One year in England John Huggins, a trainer, recommended a horse called Diamond Jubilee, then a two-year-old. Huggins was training the horses of Lord William Beresford. The latter's brother, Lord Marcus Beresford, was representative for the then Prince of Wales, later King Edward VII, who owned Diamond Jubilee. Huggins told Dr. Hagyard that he was sure that Diamond Jubilee could win the English Derby. Lord Marcus placed a price of $100,000 (20,000 guineas) on Diamond Jubilee. Dr. Hagyard took a twenty-four-hour option on the colt and then cabled Mr. Daly, who instructed him to close the sale. But when Dr. Hagyard returned to Lord Beresford to accept the colt, the latter declared he had overlooked mention of one condition.

That was that the new owners must not race the colt in England. Naturally that killed the sale. Diamond Jubilee afterward did win the English Derby. At the Aperfield Court breeding farm in England near London, Mr. Daly had a great collection of mares. In the Bitter Root Valley he had a breeding establishment for thoroughbreds, another for trotters, and a racing stable of trotters. There was also a racing stable of runners in the West, another in the East, and another in England, so that the family, after his death in 1900, sold hundreds of trotting and running horses. His racing colors, approximately, were copper, silver, and Irish green.

Within certain obvious limits, the height to which a man climbs provides a rough measure of his capacity. How he behaves after reaching the heights is the yardstick of his character. For one who had worked his way from penniless immigrant to riches and power, Marcus Daly was remarkable for his unfeigned modesty and consideration for others. Possibly the only subject on which he was really vain was the fact that the great financial interests of the country were always ready to back him in any venture of whatever magnitude. They had absolute faith in his judgment and integrity. The fact that his associates and the miners who worked for him shared this good opinion was a constant source of pleasure to him.

His inexhaustible energy and quick imagination led him frequently into ventures far afield from mining. He was almost inordinately proud of his home state of Montana, and this patriotism prompted him to seek to develop it into a better place in which to live. His zeal found expression in initiating banks, waterworks, irrigation systems, electric plants, hotels, and many other constructive projects. The Montana miners, with good sense, liked and admired him. He was familiar with the routine of their hazardous toil, he understood their wants, and becoming an "industrial giant" never robbed him of the common touch. In a day when the comfort, even the subsistence, of the workingman was frequently at the mercy of the whims of absentee owners and distant capitalists, Daly fought the miners' battles for fair wages and better working conditions. This fight was often conducted in directors' meetings thousands of miles from Montana. The intelligent miners understood and appreciated this championship of their interests, and rallied to him in his political fights with a temper and a loyalty rarely equaled since.

Although he was a conservative—few men attain great wealth without desiring to hang onto it—he waged no war on radicals. Indeed he went farther than merely to tolerate them. Among the thousands of men in his employ were many political radicals, a fact of which he was well aware. In one authenticated instance, when another mining company fired a man for promoting labor bills in the Montana legislature, of which he was a member, Daly—after agreeing that the man was a "damned radical"—proceeded to find a job for him.

Senator Clark of Montana was once engaged in business with Marcus Daly, but they quarreled, and their subsequent political feud became classic in its bitterness. My mother-in-law told me that the quarrel originated when Clark, during the absence of Daly, acquired a water right necessary to the operation of one of Daly's mining enterprises. Later, Daly wanted his town of Anaconda made the capital of Montana. Clark was opposed, and won the contest. When the Montana legislature elected Clark to the United States Senate, Daly descended on Washington with a swarm of witnesses to accuse him of bribery. Clark was rejected, but subsequently

managed, by a shrewd device, to recapture his seat in the
Senate. Pending an election, the vacancy left by his unseating
could be filled by appointment of the governor. But the governor was a Daly supporter. Clark's ruse was to promise the
governor a large fee to argue a lawsuit in California. In the
governor's absence, the lieutenant governor, a Clark man, appointed him to fill his own unexpired term as senator. Since
the legality of means by which he thus obtained his seat could
not be questioned, he was accepted in the Senate.

After Daly's death, his family declined to include the feud
among their inheritances, and the two families became
friends. During World War I, when I happened to be at
Bitter Root Ranch, a delegation of citizens from Butte asked
me to speak to the Butte miners, among whom there had been
considerable anti-war feeling. Clark and I addressed them
from the same platform in the baseball park. The next day I
called on him at his office. There were three great piles of
letters on his desk, and I asked if he intended to answer them
all. He said he did, and launched into a description of the
virtues of sober industry, early rising, et cetera, interrupted
suddenly by an engaging laugh, and he added: "But I admit
I have been a pretty bad boy sometimes." One of his sons,
Charles Clark, was at school with me in Garden City, and we
were friends until he died.

A statue of Mr. Daly, subscribed for by the people of Montana and executed by Saint-Gaudens, was erected on the
main street in the city of Butte, on the slope of the great
Treasure Hill. With the years this neighborhood deteriorated.
At the suggestion of Dr. Francis Thomson of the Montana
School of Mines, Mr. Daly's widow provided funds to move
the statue to the campus of the School of Mines in Butte,
overlooking the city brought into being by his energy.

Dr. Thomson has built the Montana School of Mines into one of the finest and most practical technical schools in the country, where students get firsthand knowledge of the operation of great mines. In the spring of 1938 I addressed the students and was given the honorary degree of doctor of laws—my fourth incidentally—by the University of Montana.

Butte, known as "the richest hill on earth," has amply borne out that name. The value of ore taken from that extraordinary deposit can be totaled in the billions. There have been a number of books written about Butte, some fiction, like *Glittering Hill,* and *The War of the Copper Kings,* and *Devil's Footstool.* All of them stressed the picturesque and unruly side of this great mining town. I have had many contacts with the citizens of Butte, and I know no other city in the United States where the mass of the people are more well-behaved, more cultured, or have a broader, more progressive outlook than those of Butte.

To encourage the miners of Butte who were ambitious to advance themselves, Mrs. Gerard created scholarships in the School of Mines at Columbia University open to Butte miners or their sons. A number of men availed themselves of the opportunity, but I believe the only one of them to follow mining engineering as a career was John Norton. He held a high position with the minerals division of the Reconstruction Finance Corporation in Washington, and now is with the Anaconda Company.

Of late years no one came forward to seek this scholarship, so we finally abandoned it. I regard the indifference toward this opportunity as indicative of one of the unfortunate trends of the times.

No account of Marcus Daly's life would be complete without noting his association with William Jennings Bryan. Daly was the principal backer of Bryan in the 1896 presidential campaign, contributing more than $300,000. Bryan's election, of course, would have been a boon to the silver-mining industry.

The most remarkable trait of Bryan was the depth and tenacity of his convictions. On small matters he may have had mere opinions, but on monumental subjects he had unshakable beliefs—the literal truth of Holy Writ, the curse of gold, the benefits of free silver. Some of his arguments seemed naïve in the mouths of other men, but his oratorical skill and the magic of his voice made them intensely convincing when they came from him. Not even all skeptics could stay unpersuaded after two hours of his oratory, and many came away from his serene presence converted to bimetalism—especially the very poor and those connected in any way with silver mining.

He visited Montana during the presidential campaign of 1896 and made a point of stopping overnight at the homes of both Senator Clark and Marcus Daly, whose support he needed. Mrs. Bryan and the two small Bryan children accompanied him. During their stay at the Clarks' even the Bryan youngsters contrived to picket the gold standard. Shortly after they had been sent up to bed, loud weeping was heard from their room. The combined Bryan and Clark families rushed up to see what was wrong. The small Bryans pointed tearfully to the brass bed. "We won't sleep in that room," they sobbed. "It has a gold bed in it." Clearly they had been thoroughly indoctrinated.

With what the cynical might suspect was suspicious impartiality, during their stay with the Dalys the Bryans provided them with an equally good anecdote. While out for a walk, Bryan plucked a dandelion and placed it in his lapel. Without warning Mrs. Bryan snatched the flower from his buttonhole and threw it on the ground. Everyone, including Bryan, was a little startled. But her explanation was quite reasonable. "It's yellow," she said.

I did not agree with Bryan's monetary ideas, and in 1898, the year of the Free Silver campaign, I led a battalion of lawyers in the Sound Money Parade up Broadway. Bryan's Free Silver campaign had a basis in reason. That is to say there *was* a shortage of gold, creating a condition of monetary scarcity which required a remedy. But the remedy that he proposed would have been the financial ruin of the country—particularly the farmers. Had Bryan succeeded in obtaining the free coinage of silver, at the ratio of 16 to 1 in relation to gold, we would have seen immediately in operation the axiom of political economy that "bad money drives out good." The gold would have been taken from our country by foreign traders, and we would have been left with nothing but silver and scant power in foreign exchange. The serious monetary situation was eventually corrected by discovery of the cyanide process which enabled profitable treatment of low-grade gold ores in South Africa. Later the flotation process further increased the world production of gold.

With Norman Mack, Buffalo publisher and stanch backer of Bryan, I motored several times to Miami to call on Bryan at his lovely little villa which he called "Villa Serena" on the shores of Biscayne Bay, where he spent his declining years. In his semi-retirement, Bryan was indulgent toward all the world except anyone who bought, sold, or drank alcoholic beverages. The Great Commoner took a strictly Old Testament view of sin, and once he said to me, during Prohibition, that people who smuggled liquor should be treated as pirates, and hanged.

It was a great pity that he permitted himself to get involved in the ridiculous Scopes case, the "monkey trial" at Dayton, Tennessee, in his last days. His efforts to prove the literal truth of every word of the Bible against the merciless jibes of Clarence Darrow made a fantastic spectacle from which common sense should have saved him.

It seems improbable that Bryan and Marcus Daly could have had much more in common than their interest in silver. Bryan could hardly have approved of Daly's absorbed interest in horse racing. It is a hobby that I understand fully, however. My own long interest in racing led me at length to become a director of United Hunts for some years in the 1930s. That organization kept racing alive in the state of New York when it was under the dark cloud of the prohibition of legal betting. I gave several trophies of silver—which might have pleased Bryan—one of them being won by Mrs. William Wright of Philadelphia, a beautiful rider. She was born Charlotte Dorrance, one of the four sisters who inherited the enormous fortune made in Campbell's soup. I noticed that her racing colors were half red and half white and remarked, "Why, those are the colors of a can of Campbell's soup!" "Of course they are," she answered gaily, "and I don't care whether anyone likes them or not." From which I gathered there were those in Philadelphia who were upset at this injection of the canned-soup motif into the Sport of Kings. Marcus Daly would have approved.

Mr. Daly had three daughters and one son. One daughter, Mary—or Molly as she prefers to be called—married me. The eldest daughter married H. Carol Brown of Baltimore. She died in 1911, leaving two daughters. The youngest Daly daughter, Harriot, married Count Sigray of Hungary. The son, Marcus Daly II, was an able businessman and engaged with me in various mining enterprises. To my deep regret he died in 1930. He had married a very pretty Viennese.

CHAPTER IX

Before his death Marcus Daly had taken up a prospective gold claim in the valley of the Similkameen River in British Columbia, and I planned a trip to examine this prospect at firsthand and decide whether it would be worth while to continue spending money on it. As it happened, Mrs. Daly bought an option on some copper prospects near Goose Bay on Observatory Inlet, a fjord forming part of the boundary between Alaska and British Columbia, so I planned to visit it, too, since it was in the same corner of the world.

Alaska and the interior of British Columbia in the summer of 1902 were just as primitive as the gold-rush miners had found them four years before, so I set out upon this business trip with considerable zest and anticipation. I went first to Seattle, where I was joined by Horace V. Winchell, one of the greatest economic geologists in the country, and John Toole of Montana, to whom Daly had given an interest in the gold property.

From Seattle we three set forth to Vancouver on a small ship called the *Tees*. This craft had been fitted out to carry miners to the Yukon during the gold rush of 1898. It was only two hundred feet long, and yet there were nearly three hundred people on board. The stateroom that I shared with

Toole had just enough space to turn around in between the three-decker bunks and the bulkhead.

We finally arrived at Port Essington (now called Prince Rupert), which was then only a little trading post, and with a large fee persuaded the *Tees'* skipper to go up Observatory Inlet and land us at Goose Bay, where we were met by M. K. Rodgers, the resident engineer in charge of the prospect. Winchell, Toole, and I lived in a tent which we shared most of the time with thousands of ravenous mosquitoes.

Recent government-sponsored attempts to colonize Alaska with families from the States have not been conspicuously successful, and I feel sure that the mosquito plague is one of the reasons. The only satisfactory way to live with such mosquitoes is the formula of the hard-drinking Kentuckian, who never seemed to mind them. "The first part of the night," he explained, "I am so full I don't pay any attention to them. The rest of the night they're so full they don't pay any attention to me."

Rodgers took us to the copper prospect which was at the top of a small hill about seven hundred feet high, and showed us an outcropping of native copper, about forty feet across, gleaming in the sun. Rodgers had tunneled horizontally into this and in twenty feet had run out of ore. He had repeated this process at about thirty-foot intervals for some distance down the steep hillside, but in each instance the copper ran out after a few feet and the tunnel ended in solid rock.

This discouraging evidence made us decide that the prospect was not worth developing. Actually, because of geologic idiosyncrasies too complicated to explain here, our explorations had missed the great body of rich copper that lay in the hill. The prospect was later successfully developed by the Granby Company and was known as their Anyox property.

We left Goose Bay on Observatory Inlet in Rodgers's launch, intending to go to Ketchikan on Prince of Wales Island, where we could catch a boat for Seattle or Vancouver. As we chugged down the inlet—a narrow fjord with mountains on each side—on a dark rainy night, the launch engine suddenly coughed and stopped. We were left rolling silently around in an unknown country with no settlement that we knew of for hundreds of miles. However, to our prayerful relief we spied a light on shore, and so the lightest member of the party got into a skiff that the launch carried and made for the light. The light came from the house of Archdeacon Collison, a British missionary to the Indian village of Kincolith. The sons of the archdeacon rowed out to us in a whaleboat and towed us ashore. We spent the next three or four days there while waiting to flag a passing steamer that could get us to Vancouver.

I spent the nights on the sofa in the archdeacon's sitting room and soon came to know about and admire the work of these British missionaries among the Indians. Not far away was the settlement of Metlakatla, where a young missionary named Duncan held sway. The law strictly prohibited the sale of liquor to the Indians. Duncan felt it impossible to explain to the Indians that it was all right to take wine at the sacrament of Communion on Sunday but all wrong to drink anything containing alcohol on weekdays. He appealed to the Archbishop of Canterbury for permission to omit the wine from Communion service. When his request was refused, he enlisted the aid of the Woman's Christian Temperance Union in the United States. Finally from Grover Cleveland's administration he obtained permission to make use of an island on the American side of the line. He called this island New Metlakatla and moved his mission and his Indians there.

Being technically outside the archbishop's jurisdiction, he then, with a clear conscience, omitted wine from the Communion service.

On the boat trip up I met a huge Indian called Big Albert, and found that he was a resident of Kincolith. I went to call on him at his wooden house, situated on the boardwalk, which was the main village street. Big Albert's squaw put her head out of the window and informed me that Big Albert was not well. He had managed the day before to get hold of several bottles of Florida Water and had consumed them with almost fatal effect.

Big Albert was a very progressive Indian and earned sometimes as much as forty or fifty dollars a day during the salmon-fishing season. He had seen pictures in the *Illustrated London News* of the Prince of Wales (afterward Edward VII) and the royal family in Highland dress, so nothing would satisfy Big Albert until he had sent to Vancouver and bought a complete Highland dress for himself. Following his progressive inclinations, he also sent to Vancouver for a bicycle, which he painfully mastered. On holidays, such as the royal birthday, he would put on his Highland dress, mount his bicycle, and ride up and down the hundred yards of boardwalk, the only practicable place for bicycling in the settlement.

The archdeacon told me of one Indian who came in to see him and said he wanted to be baptized and have a new name. The archdeacon demurred, saying, "You have been baptized; I can't baptize you again." But his caller was so insistent that the archdeacon probed for his reasons. It developed that the Indian had a vague knowledge of bankruptcy proceedings. He was somehow of the belief that if he could be baptized with a new name, he could drop all the debts contracted in his previous identity.

From Victoria, Winchell and I went to Penticton at the foot of Okanagan Lake. Rodgers and Toole joined us again, and we drove fifty miles from the foot of the lake to Nickel Plate Mountain, where the prospect owned by the Daly Estate was located. The mining prospect was on the top of a mountain about 4,000 feet above the valley of the Similkameen. The ascent from the valley below, on horseback over a zigzag trail, was spectacular and dizzying. At each turn we seemed to hang over the edge of a precipice. At the prospect, on top of the mountain, there were only a few log cabins, and at the foot of the mountain only a log stable. Three or four years afterward, when I again visited the place, the mine was in full blast, and at the foot of the mountain there was a little town called Hedley, with two churches, a newspaper, hotels, stores, and homes—a good example of how a large community can be supported by one industry.

The Nickel Plate Mine was very successful. My brother-in-law, Marcus Daly II, was president and I was vice-president, and during our administration we took out a substantial profit in gold, greatly to the advantage of Rodgers and Toole, each of whom had been given an interest in the property by Marcus Daly, Sr. Mr. Toole, a most pleasant traveling companion, is now dead, but his fine sons are living in Missoula, Montana, where I had the pleasure of meeting one of them recently.

It was not long after my safari to the wilds of British Columbia that I became involved in an interesting—and expensive—adventure in what might be called president-making. A journalist with impressive selling ability named Maurice Minton, once editor of the New York *Herald*, came to see me early in 1903 and pointed out that since Bryan had been badly defeated in 1896 and 1900, the time seemed ripe to select a conservative as the presidential candidate of the Democratic party. He had cast himself in the role of catalyst to this reaction. It developed that his description of the qualities necessary in the candidate was embodied in the person of Judge Alton B. Parker, a jurist from upstate Esopus, and at that time presiding judge of the New York State Court of Appeals. As he freely admitted, Minton had the enthusiasm and the publicity skill to advance the cause of Judge Parker. All that he required was money and someone of apparent political influence in New York to advocate the nomination.

Alton Parker had a pontifical manner. He had a good reputation as a judge. He was respectable, and he was conservative. Indeed, he had everything needed in a candidate for that particular race except the colorful personality that would get him elected. The dynamic Theodore Roosevelt, Parker's Republican opponent, had more color than a painter's overalls, and by comparison Parker was as stodgy as a Quaker meeting. All this was revealed to me, however, only by hindsight, and I began immediately to devote considerable money and energy to promoting Parker's nomination. Taking advantage of my position as chairman of a Tammany committee that sounded important to outsiders, I gave numerous interviews to the Press explaining the superior qualifications of Judge Parker. With Minton's help, we saw to it that country newspapers received appropriate half-tone cuts in boiler plate, all ready to be inserted at no cost to the newspaper.

They represented Parker in his library with his dog; Parker playing lovingly with his grandchild; Parker (dressed in a cutaway) raking hay at his country place in Esopus. He was chastely portrayed in all the stock situations that the voters seem to desire—or have been led by long custom to expect— of their candidate.

After a while the expenses became so great that I began to fret under the lonely burden and persuaded Francis Burton Harrison (of whom more later) to join with me. We used to call Minton the "money eater" because of his insatiable demands for campaign funds. Minton's manner was so exquisitely impressive that I think we were more than a little awed by him. In any event, despite our knowledge of the inner machinery, we were duly impressed when we were first taken to dinner at the home of the Sage of Esopus. He did not fail to produce champagne for the two city slickers who had taken such a kind interest in his political fortunes.

The campaign for Parker went swimmingly. Perhaps from reading our own campaign material, it seemed to us that he had a good chance. But as the time for the convention approached, Minton informed us that he needed an immediate twenty-five thousand dollars for expenses. By that time the dip in morale that comes from signing endless checks prompted us to reappraise Parker's prospects more realistically, particularly as an opponent of Theodore Roosevelt, with the result that we decided to retire. Minton immediately carried out a plan with which he had threatened us; viz., he sold Parker to August Belmont, and we accepted minority stock, as it were, for our efforts to date. To guard this interest, Harrison and I went as delegates to the Democratic convention at St. Louis.

Harrison and I were surprised but pleased to learn that Parker had won the nomination. Having financed the campaign up to the opening of the convention, we felt full of merit and acumen. August Belmont had taken over the burden at the convention, and was, therefore, a genuine deserving supporter. At this point, however, the nimble-footed "Blue-eyed Billy" Sheehan, who had risked little or nothing on the candidate's chances, appeared on the scene. He proceeded to snatch Parker from Belmont's bosom by the simple device of hiring a house in Esopus next door to Parker's and assuming the exclusive possession of the candidate's person, time, thoughts, and plans. It was a sort of political kidnaping. I don't know what reward Belmont got for his pains. Harrison, in consideration of his support, was nominated for Lieutenant Governor of New York and subsequently went down in defeat with the rest of the Democratic ticket. Since it seemed unlikely to me that Parker would become President, and would thus be unable to reward my support with anything except personal gratitude, I decided to accept my compensation in the form of treasure in heaven—a sort of political due bill—a credit obligation in the party's books.

Mild-mannered though he was, Judge Parker during his campaign strongly attacked Roosevelt's appointment of his former Secretary of Commerce, George B. Cortelyou, to manage his campaign. Parker charged that this arrangement enabled Cortelyou to extract large campaign contributions from corporations concerning which he had acquired secret information. It was intimated to me that William Travers Jerome, the district attorney, was ready either to indict someone for criminal libel or to investigate the charge that corporations were blackmailed. By appointment I met Jerome at his favorite stamping ground, Jack's Restaurant, and he confirmed to me his readiness to investigate. But the Parker camp, timid and uncertain, decided not to pursue the charge.

In Irving Stone's book *They Also Ran,* page 96, he writes:

. . . In 1907 it was disclosed that the insurance companies had contributed rather too heavily to the Roosevelt campaign; that Roosevelt himself, only a week before election, had called E. H. Harriman, the railroad king, to Washington to ask him to raise funds to carry New York State. . . .

If my account of the preconvention campaign for Alton Parker makes politics seem like a somewhat haphazard business, that impression will be strengthened by a recital of the manner in which I introduced Harrison to politics. In 1903, a few days before the deadline for filing nominating petitions, I was dining with Tammany Hall's Charles Murphy and his intimate, J. Sergeant Cram. Murphy told me that the local party was at a loss for an appealing candidate for Congress in a rock-ribbed Republican congressional district. In conclusion, he said, "You've *got* to find me a candidate." Lacking any inspiration, I took a volume of the Social Register over to a corner and began to scan its pages. When I reached the name of Harrison, I exclaimed happily that he was just the man. When I described him, Murphy ratified my selection.

Harrison was in California, but I telegraphed an offer of the nomination. I told him there seemed little chance of election but that it was a good opportunity for a debut in politics if he cared for it. He wired an acceptance while the convention was in session, and Murphy told me to go quickly to the convention hall and nominate Harrison. Some of the delegates demurred. "Aren't we going to even *see* him?"

they demanded. "He's in California and can't get here in time," I replied.

To which they said, "Can't you just show us a photograph?"

Perforce, I answered, "No, you'll just have to take him on trust." After that I made a short speech nominating Harrison, and he was as quickly accepted as the nominee.

When Harrison arrived in New York, I engaged the services of an astute old political campaigner, Willis Holly. Holly managed the campaign so successfully, with some small help from me, that Harrison was triumphantly elected and began a career in Congress, interrupted only, as I have said, when he ran for Lieutenant Governor in 1904. After that he was returned to Congress from a safe district and later, while still a congressman, was appointed Governor General of the Philippines by President Wilson.

By a curious coincidence, some years after Harrison's election I happened again to be dining with Murphy and Cram when again they told me they were desperate for a candidate in the same Republican district. That afternoon I had been riding in the park with a lawyer named Edward R. Swan, and his name immediately suggested itself. Murphy said that if he liked Swan's looks, Swan would be the man. I telephoned Swan, who came at once to Cram's house, passed inspection, and consented to make the race. He was beaten in the election, but soon afterward, and as a reward, he was named a judge of the Court of General Sessions. Still later he became district attorney, and ultimately was nominated, but defeated, for the Supreme Court.

These early experiences gave me useful instruction in the fact that politics is much less of a science than it is an art. When, about 1903, Murphy had me named chairman of the campaign committee, which is supposed to raise money for

New York City campaigns, I learned that even the minor cogs in a political machine come to a creaking halt unless greased with money. One or two days before election I would go to Tammany Hall with little bags of cash which I distributed to district leaders to pay the workers on election day. This day of reception was known to the faithful as "Dough Day."

Doubtless a man is wise to consult his own taste in these matters, for the perfume of the political ring is not equally pleasant to all nostrils, any more than that of the circus, which some find so enchanting. I am reminded of my last meeting with Richard Croker, whom I first saw as a stripling youth. In the mid-twenties Norman Mack and I called on Croker at his home near Palm Beach. Dressed comfortably in old clothes, he was hoeing the garden on his estate. We sought to discuss politics, but he refused to stay on that subject, interrupting continually to show us the items in his garden. In the midst of another attempt he shoved a handful of some herb under my nose and said, "Smell that. Doesn't it have a pleasant odor?"

CHAPTER X

THERE HAS BEEN A GREAT CHANGE, SINCE THE DAYS I HAVE been describing, in the impact of politics on everyday life. It used to be considered that the function of government was to create conditions favorable to prosperity. Now government is expected to create prosperity. That conception involves the intrusion of government into fields of business and social activity, control, assistance, and regulation undreamed of at the turn of the century.

I have many of the same complaints about business, as it has been carried on, that the latter-day prophets of Utopia denounce so bitterly. But I complain in turn that these economic reformers lack understanding of the nature of what they observe, and confuse symptoms with actual maladies. My brief for fostering private enterprise is made in spite of, and not because of, my observations of the blind stupidity and arrogance of many of those who manage our great corporations.

My experience has included a score or more of the most unlikely sounding incidents, a few of which will serve to illustrate what has been wrong with the business mind. In the late 1890s, when Marcus Daly was president of the Amalgamated Corporation Mines—the parent company of the Anaconda and other properties in Butte—the local company officers advised that Anaconda buy a large property called the South Ground, which was adjacent to the Anaconda holdings. The purchase was suggested because the geological peculiarities of the South Ground were such that any smart speculator who acquired it might start litigation which could be extremely damaging to Anaconda. This was possible because of technicalities in the badly framed mining laws. They were particularly afraid of a young engineer named F. Augustus Heinze. Under the peculiar so-called Apex Law of the United States, Heinze was able to strike at the Anaconda companies and claim some of the richest mineral deposits in the super-rich Butte hill.

When a prospector discovers a vein containing metal, he stakes a claim. This claim is fifteen hundred feet long and seven hundred and fifty feet wide. Since a vein almost always slants off at an angle, some of it may be under property adjoining the claim originally staked. By the Apex Law, if that claim staked by the prospector is the discovery lode, so-called, its vein may be followed by the owner of the claim outside of his side lines but not outside of his end lines. As the vein has many branches, this has led to many litigations. Corrupt judges have taken away a vein or part of it from the original discoverer on the ground that a vein outside of the original claim went to the surface, and was therefore an independent vein which did not give its original discoverer any right to its continuation. Canada has taken a wiser view of this problem and made claims twice the size of those in the United States. The Canadian claim is fifteen hundred feet by fifteen hundred feet, and no excursion in a vein is allowed outside the lines of the claim projected perpendicularly downward.

The involved and expensive litigation in Butte was based on claims of this kind. Heinze, through his control of certain judges, was a real threat to the Anaconda and Amalgamated companies, and it was because of dangers of this kind that Mr. Daly was urged, as I have described, to buy the so-called South Ground. As Anaconda didn't have the five hundred thousand dollars needed for the purchase, Daly bought the South Ground with his own money, with the understanding that the company would reimburse him when it could. At the time of Daly's death, in 1900, this money was still owed him.

After his death, the Amalgamated Company—of which H. H. Rogers, the Standard Oil magnate, was the head—delayed and delayed and postponed, and finally declined to take over the properties, knowing very well that the Daly family would do nothing hostile to Anaconda. Sometime in 1904 I was walking up Wall Street when I met a friend who casually asked whether the Daly estate had any mining properties for sale in Butte. When I told him of the South Ground property and the string to it, he said, "Well, if there were no string, I think I could sell these properties for you." So I wrote a letter to H. H. Rogers and told him that the Daly estate had a chance to sell this property. I referred to the circumstances under which Daly had acquired the property and asked the company to take it over. When this letter went unanswered, I sent a telegram and a registered letter. These were also ignored. I then sold the property, not for $500,000, but for $750,000. This transaction stirred Rogers from his aloof silence, and he all but ordered me hanged in the Bowling Green in front of the Standard Oil Building at 26 Broadway.

It turned out that the property had been bought by the wily Heinze. Eventually Anaconda and Amalgamated were

forced to buy it back at a much greater price than the $500,-
000 for which Mr. Daly had originally bought it. It probably cost several million dollars. This incident gave me an
insight into the arrogance of big business. It became clear
to me from similar cases that this arrogance usually cost a
business a great deal of money in the long run.

Another example was the case of the Cunard wharf, a very
large wharf in East Boston which had been built by Great-
uncle General Sumner, and in which we owned shares. The
Boston and Albany Railroad acquired the shares of some
Boston families and then informed the remaining sharehold-
ers that if we refused to sell our shares to the railroad on its
own terms, it would commence a partition suit and take the
property at what price it pleased. The railroad officials knew
very well that none of the owners were able either to bid in
the whole property or to operate it. I managed to get a few
thousand dollars more than I had been originally offered,
but the interest was sold for a mere $110,000 despite the fact
that in past years it paid an income of $50,000 a year.

One of my brothers had had banking experience, and I
thought that it would be an excellent venture to establish
a French-American bank. We found that a Swiss from California with French connections had the same idea, so we
joined forces and organized a bank called the Banque Franco-
Américaine. We had a splendid banking office on the Place
Vendôme in Paris, and, as most of the French provincial
banks became stockholders, the bank seemed to offer a great
opportunity for the placing of American securities. We had
a French board of directors who knew the ins and outs of
French banking, and an impressive American advisory board
who were experts on American stocks and bonds. Between
these two bodies we should have had the benefit of excellent

guidance. I soon discovered, however, that the American advisory board, instead of being patient and building up a good business, wanted to unload every stale bond that they had on their shelves on the innocent French. The situation became even more dubious when the French directors said that they were going to declare a dividend at the end of the first year. I said, "How can you declare a dividend when you haven't made any money?" But they insistently pointed out that if a French bank doesn't declare a dividend at the end of its first year, it is considered a failure. My reply to this— and my last word to all of them—was, "If it does that in the United States, the directors go to jail. So give me par and interest for my stock, and I will kiss you good-by on both sides of the Atlantic." Shortly thereafter the Banque Franco-Américaine quietly failed.

In the two most striking examples in my experience of early twentieth-century financial "wizardry" the large shadow of the elder J. P. Morgan was present. Morgan always stayed in the background, and so great was the awe and fear in which he was held by those who carried out his will that his operations often had an aura of mystery about them. When the hand of Morgan was laid on any company or stock, the little men quickly ran to cover and the big men made haste to discover what was expected of them, and to do it. My first insight into the workings of the Morgan Company came about as a result of the financial collapse in 1907 of the strong, safe New York, New Haven and Hartford Railroad. Although I was not involved in the events leading to its debacle, I had had a disillusioning experience with that railroad a short time before, and was therefore a keenly interested observer of what befell.

My interest in the New Haven came about as a result of

a real-estate venture in Boston in 1903. From the time of Governor Increase Sumner my family had owned rights to certain land under water, as the phrase is, in the harbor area between Boston proper and what is known as South Boston. With other property owners, we formed a company under the presidency of John C. Cobb, a pleasant and competent gentleman, to fill in the area and provide sites for new factories. All went well until we asked the New York, New Haven and Hartford Railroad, whose tracks adjoined our land, to install the spurs and sidings necessary to give our factory sites an outlet. The New Haven refused to provide an outlet to their tracks with the obvious purpose of forcing us to sell the land cheaply to the New Haven, which could then develop the sites in unrestrained monopoly of the entire project.

This crude form of "shakedown" was scotched by Mr. Cobb. He went to the legislature and obtained passage of a law that compelled the New Haven to give us access to its tracks. He was so successful that my mother and I gave him a loving cup inscribed "To one corporation president who looks out for the interests of his stockholders."

Thereafter our venture went forward, and in the next couple of years it prospered to such an extent that the New Haven offered to buy it for a fair price. We sold it to them and accepted payment in stock of the New Haven railroad. It had been as high as $255 a share. It was not long after this that the New Haven road became a victim of a group of New York financiers, who milked it so thoroughly that it collapsed financially with a loud bang, the stock falling as low as $2.00 a share. Many New Englanders up to then had considered the stock of the sound, well-run New Haven as an investment on a par with the bonds of the United States.

When the collapse came, there were many ruined institutions and individuals in that section, as well as weeping and wailing and gnashing of teeth throughout the country. It took an investigation by the Interstate Commerce Commission, a stockholders' suit against the management, and several years' time for the details of the collapse to become fully known. These facts demonstrate the nature of the blight that was responsible for the disastrous business and banking collapse of 1907.

The New York, New Haven and Hartford was absolutely dominated by the elder Morgan, and it is some sort of tribute to his domination to note that none of the victims of the railroad's financial troubles had the nerve to bring up the matter of blame and restitution until after Morgan's death in 1913. The whole story of the investigation is long and involved, but it revolved mainly around the testimony of Charles S. Mellen, who had been president of the railroad and who was admittedly one of Morgan's humble and obedient servants to command.

The trouble, in brief, began in 1906 when the New Haven decided to buy up and absorb two small railroads that operated mostly in Westchester County—namely, the New Haven and Port Chester, and the New York, Westchester and Boston railroads. Mellen had never considered these roads as being of any value to the New Haven and, on the several occasions when they were offered for sale to the New Haven, he had refused even to bother his board of directors with the notion. In 1906, however, he was given a broad hint by one Oakleigh Thorne, president of the Trust Company of America, that maybe the purchase of the two small roads was more important than he thought. So he laid the proposal before his board, and was considerably surprised when the chairman of the board—J. P. Morgan himself—moved that the purchase be made. Mellen named Morgan as head of a committee of three to handle the purchase and authorized his treasurer to pay whatever money the purchase required into a special account in J. P. Morgan and Company.

After about a year of mysterious and silent activity, the Morgan committee announced to the other directors that it had made the purchase and had spent $11,000,000. Morgan then presented his committee's report of the transaction. The directors were puzzled and pained to note that the report merely noted that two railroads had been bought for $11,000,000. But none of them had the courage to ask Morgan to itemize the costs or explain why these two practically worthless properties had cost so much. When Mellen softly broached the subject with Morgan in private, the great man showed his displeasure and gave Mellen a tongue-lashing. It was in this fashion, then, that the New Haven's finances came to their eventual low estate.

The foregoing résumé of what transpired doesn't give the flavor of the personalities involved, nor does it show the pettiness, the fears, and the lack of courage of those who, by virtue of their positions of trust, controlled the fortunes and happiness of so many people. I therefore quote some selections from the testimony of Mr. Mellen before the Interstate Commerce Commission, as reported in the New York *Times* for May 20, 1914. It makes rare reading: a naïve, obsequious, and obedient little group of men—apparently chosen for these very qualities—trying desperately to keep out from under the feet of a ruthless, tough-fibered man who was bigger than all of them put together. After thirty-six years the following selections from Mellen's testimony are even wryly amusing:

Q. "Were you Morgan's man as president of the New

Haven?" A. "I have been called by the newspapers his office boy. I was very proud of his confidence. I desired to acquit myself to meet his approval. I regarded (the remark) that I was his man as a compliment."

Q. "Who dominated the Board of Directors of the New Haven?" A. "They used to vote as a rule pretty near where Mr. Morgan voted. I regarded Mr. Morgan, and I think we all did on the Board, as a man of very great experience, very great energy, very great capacity and naturally looked up to him. I think I was no different from the rest in that respect. There were strong men on the New Haven Board other than Mr. Morgan, but I do not recall anything where Mr. Morgan was determined, emphatic, insistent—I recall no case in which he did not have his way."

Q. "When this committee reported that it had spent more than eleven million dollars in this transaction, did you see Mr. Morgan in reference to it?" A. "I objected—I demurred."

Q. "To whom did you demur?" A. "I asked Mr. Morgan after the meeting if he would stop a moment and see me in my office. He did, and I told him that I thought that report was not in detail so much as it should be, that there was nothing to indicate to me how much had been spent in the different items that are enumerated. 'You have a report,' I said, 'and you will see that there are a number of items enumerated and the whole cost of $11,155,000. Somebody is going to want to know—I may want to know myself—what the New York and Port Chester cost, what was the development cost, what was paid for the stock, what was paid for the bonds, and what was paid for the different items. It seems to me that this report should read on such a date so many shares of stock were bought of such a party to be exchanged for so much and the whole should foot up $11,155,-

000 and should be a clear account showing how this money was disbursed.' It was in the midst of the panic of 1907 and Mr. Morgan was quite abrupt, very severe, and I felt very much humiliated and undeservedly so because I felt I was asking what the railroad was entitled to and I never got it."

Q. "What did he say?" A. "Mr. Morgan is dead and I have great regard for him. It was rather a humiliating scene and I prefer not to speak of it."

The witness explained that he stood in greater awe of Mr. Morgan than of any other man he had ever met and that the other directors probably shared this feeling. They did not want to contend with the financier although they had misgivings. After the meeting, however, they came around and discussed the matter with the witness privately.

Q. "What directors came around?" A. "Most of them were my Connecticut directors. I remember Mr. Skinner was there and Mr. Hemingway."

Q. "What did Mr. Hemingway say to you after the meeting with reference to this report?" A. "I cannot give the exact language, but it was along these lines: 'Well, you have been flying pretty high, haven't you, spending $11,000,000? What did you do it for?' I said, 'You can search me.' 'Well,' he said, 'don't you think you should have more information?' I said, 'I'll tell you what I'll do, Mr. Hemingway. I will appoint you a committee to go and get it from Mr. Morgan.' He said, 'No, you don't.' They were all willing that I should go and bark my shins, but they did not, any one of them, want to go and bark their shins. Mr. Skinner was present and I think Mr. Taft was there. My upcountry directors thought we ought to have more information and I did and said that they ought to get it, and I offered to put anyone on the committee to go to Mr. Morgan and get it, and they all ducked."

In 1916 a stockholders' suit charging mismanagement caused the directors to settle for $2,500,000, a sum which they paid into the treasury of the company.

Judge Hough pointed out that through this compromise "The individual defendants are buying their peace from the plaintiffs by paying money to the corporate defendant," and further that the only interest of the plaintiffs is to procure restitution for the company along with the recovery of counsel fees and expenses. The stockholders' counsel fees, approved by the Court, alone came to $833,333.33, which was deducted from the judgment.

The foregoing should give anyone a fairly good idea of the personal power possessed by the elder Morgan. I have even read a most respectful account by one of Morgan's financial brethren describing how the great man had a habit, toward the end of his life, of taking little naps at odd times—during directors' meetings, for example. On one such occasion during the discussion of some important problem, a director suddenly stopped in the middle of his sentence and, with much eyebrow wiggling, directed the attention of the assembled tycoons to Mr. Morgan, who had dozed off. Everyone immediately became quiet lest they disturb the master, and the man seated at Morgan's side, seeing him slump over a little in his chair, thoughtfully moved closer to Morgan and gently braced his shoulder against him.

After a while Morgan stirred, opened his eyes, and looked around the table. Immediately the interrupted speaker went on with his sentence, and the other gentlemen endeavored to act as though time had not stood still for five minutes.

CHAPTER XI

Peering wistfully down the vista of eighty-three years I find that some of the pleasanter memories of my life are those of the late 1890s and 1900s. Those years had a special charming quality. Partly the charm was that of the times—for it is now generally conceded that the Edwardian era did have charm—and partly it lay in the fact that the decade coincided with my thirties, when one has just the proper balance of youth and maturity to exact the last measure of zest out of people and experiences. Interspersed between my various business, law, and political activities was, as I have said, a quite active and pleasant social life, and a great deal of time spent riding, shooting, and fencing.

After our marriage, Mrs. Gerard and I spent frequent week ends at the hospitable homes of Mr. and Mrs. Oliver Belmont in Hempstead, Long Island, Mr. and Mrs. Stuyvesant Fish at Garrison-on-the-Hudson, and also at the house of Mr. and Mrs. George Gould, called "Georgian Court," at Lakewood, New Jersey. The Goulds entertained on a magnificent scale. They had not only a large and beautiful house, but, about a quarter mile away, they maintained what was called the "Casino." This held an indoor riding ring with tennis court in the center, and, in addition, a court tennis court, a racquets court, double and single squash courts, a gymnasium, and a beautiful swimming pool. After we had spent an active afternoon there, a bus would call at dinner-time to take us over to the main house. If anyone who had exercised too much decided to stay away from dinner in the house, he could have a simple dinner cooked for him in the Casino.

In 1904, in Paris, my wife and I and my sister-in-law, Harriot Daly, later Countess Sigray, were invited to dine with the pioneer Brazilian flier, Santos Dumont, at his apart-ment on the Champs Elysées. For some reason Mrs. Gerard and Harriot had gone to the dinner before me, and I was late in appearing. When I entered the dining room I heard their voices but couldn't see anyone until I looked up in the air. There they were, seated at a table the level of which was about eight feet above the floor. Dumont evidently liked to live up in the air as much as possible.

Bourke Cockran, the celebrated orator, was for years a great friend of ours. We often stopped with him at his place on Long Island, both before and after his marriage around 1905 to the beautiful daughter of Governor General Ide of the Philippines. No one could be a more amusing companion, and Cockran's friends never tired of his charmingly told anec-dotes of his political career and his early life in New York. He told me that once, on a Tammany excursion, he brushed up an acquaintance with a good-looking girl. Toward the end of the day she said to him, "You speak so beautifully that I thought at first you were an actor, but you dress so exqui-sitely that now I am certain you're a Broadway gambler"— surely a graceful compliment. Jay Gould, for whom Bourke Cockran had carried out some business, once gave him a tip on the market. Afterward Gould asked if he had used the tip. "No," said Cockran. "Why not?" inquired Gould. "Because," replied Cockran, "if you were perfectly sure about the tip you wouldn't have given it to me, and if you are not perfectly sure, I don't want it."

Bourke Cockran died suddenly in 1923 just after having described that day as the happiest of his life. He was a member of Congress and had just made an unusually successful speech. He named me as one of the executors of his will.

One of my closest friends was Louis Wiley, of the New York *Times*. He was not only business manager of that great publication but also contributed to its editorial councils. Wiley, who had lived at one time in Rochester in the beautiful Genesee Valley, founded the Genesee Society. Chiefly through his efforts its dinners in New York City were always a great success. My birth in Geneseo made me eligible, and on two occasions Wiley made me president of the society.

It was through Bourke Cockran, who was well acquainted with the Churchill family, that I first met Winston Churchill when, around 1900, he came to this country to give a series of lectures. His first was given in the old Waldorf, and I went to hear him and afterward met him. He was very young, very handsome, and spoke quite earnestly, but without the forcefulness that he possesses today, and he suffered at times from a slight stutter. I have recalled this occasion each time I've seen him during the past forty years, and particularly when I have listened to his masterpieces of oratory and phrase-making over the radio.

Since that remote day I have seen Churchill several times in various places. At one lunch—at Antibes in the South of France—my diary tells me, I had the Churchills and their daughter, almost as beautiful as her mother, Colonel and Mrs. Buzzard, Professor Lindeman, Sir Pomeroy and Lady

Burton, and Lord and Lady Wester Wemyss and their daughter. Lord Wester Wemyss, a high British admiral, represented the Allied navies at the surrender of Germany in the famous French railway car, and signed the Armistice as the representative of the Allied fleets.

My friendship with Arthur Brisbane began in our youth and continued until his death. During the early nineties he was courting Florence Pullman, the daughter of George M. Pullman, the "Palace Car King," at the same time that I was atttentive to her handsome younger sister, Harriet. One summer during the nineties, when Brisbane and I were both staying in town, we rode together every afternoon in the Park. As a rule one horse didn't give him enough exercise, and when one became tired he had a second horse brought out. After our rides we usually went to the New York Athletic Club for a swim before dining simply on a thick steak and a quart of burgundy.

Alfred McCosker, later the head of the Mutual Broadcasting System, was once Brisbane's office boy. When he had advanced to the rank of reporter, Brisbane asked him how he was getting on. "All right," said McCosker, "except that when I have to interview some great statesman, I am confused and embarrassed." "Never mind," replied Brisbane. "Just think of him as being in his nightshirt and your confidence will be restored."

My relatively carefree thirties, a period of zest tempered by dignity, was followed by a decade of the heavy responsibilities appropriate to the years when a man is thought to be in his prime. The transition from carefree man to man of cares came about promptly following my fortieth birth-

day. So promptly, indeed, that it might have been scheduled
from the famous lithograph that depicts the Seven Ages of
Man and in which the various stages shift precisely at ten-
year intervals.

In any event, I became forty on August 25, 1907. In September my mother died at Bar Harbor, and, in addition to
the sadness that must attend such a loss, there were the usual
changes in our family routine and the work of settling her
estate. Even while these affairs were under way new events
began to happen. In early October I was nominated as Democratic candidate for justice of the New York Supreme Court.
In the interval between the nomination and the November
election the Knickerbocker Trust Company crashed spec-
tacularly, and its collapse was the opening signal in the
disastrous Panic of 1907. I was a large depositor in the
Knickerbocker Trust as well as a member of its board of
directors, and the crash, coinciding with my candidacy for
the Supreme Court bench, placed me in a very hot and un-
enviable spot.

My nomination for the Supreme Court judgeship came
about quite unspectacularly. Although I had always been
active and, on occasion, quite helpful in New York Democratic politics, I had never asked for any reward nor shown
any desire for office. However, one day in the summer of
1907 Charles Murphy and I were discussing likely candidates
for various posts. One vacancy to be filled at the November
elections was that of justice of the New York Supreme Court.
When Murphy came to it on the list, I told him I'd like to
have the nomination myself. He was genuinely surprised by
my remark. When he saw that I was serious he replied, "Why,
I didn't know that you wanted any such position, but if you
want it—all right."

I was, thereafter, duly nominated as Democratic candidate and entered into what proved to be a very bitter campaign. Hearst, with his Independence League party, had nominated for the office of sheriff one of his employees named Max Ihmsen, to run against Tom Foley, Democratic leader of a downtown district. The power of the Hearst newspapers was used. not only against Foley but also against the entire Democratic ticket, including me. The fact that I was a director of the Knickerbocker Trust Company which, as I have said, closed its doors a short time after I was nominated, gave Hearst a fine opening for violent attacks upon me. I remember the cartoons about me in Hearst newspapers as quite amusing—which, I suppose, is the best way *to* remember political cartoons about oneself. One of them represented Thomas Fortune Ryan, who was then suspected of being a dominant influence in local Democratic politics, appearing at a window as a beautiful maiden and throwing me, as a rose, to Joseph Pulitzer, proprietor of the *World*—this presumably because I had been active in the legal affairs of the *World*. Another caricature represented me in bed with a character known as "Nigger Mike" who ran a saloon on the Bowery. The wherefore of this cartoon I could never gather. Still another pictured me as a ridiculous-looking little boy standing outside the Knickerbocker Trust Company inviting the public to make deposits.

As a matter of fact, the voters were probably much better informed about me by election day than they usually are about candidates for judicial office, for my connection with the Trust Company and my actions during the panic precipitated by its collapse were front-page news. In any event, my part in this unhappy affair apparently did not prejudice the voters against me.

CHAPTER XII

IN 1907 THE KNICKERBOCKER TRUST COMPANY WAS A MOST respectable institution. Charles T. Barney, its president, had the merit—but in some ways the disadvantage—of being slighty *persona non grata* with the elder Morgan. That is to say, he was not among those who came promptly to heel when Morgan cracked the whip.

The great, grim banker was not one to tolerate strongmindedness in anyone, as I believe I have indicated. At that time he exercised almost unbelievable power over the affairs of this country—a power which his firm continued to hold after his death, and which was only partially broken after the election of Franklin Roosevelt.

The House of Morgan, which has French and English branches, still controls—not through stock ownership in most cases, but through a sort of psychic influence exercised over the officers and directors—the great United States Steel Corporation, the First National Bank, Bankers Trust Company, the United Corporation (a great utility holding corporation), the General Electric Company, and the American Telephone and Telegraph Company, a large number of smaller corporations, and many railroads. They exercise this control by the force of gravity, as it were, and the habit stockholders have of mailing in their voting proxies to those in control of the company. Stockholders seem to give no thought to this matter, but in any case it is almost impossible for them to get together and put up an opposition ticket.

Because of the large amount of banking business that my family brought to the Knickerbocker Trust, Mr. Barney had made me one of the directors.

One day in October 1907 the Knickerbocker Trust Company directors were suddenly notified of a meeting to be held at three o'clock that afternoon. H. B. Hollins, a director who was known to be an intimate friend of J. P. Morgan, arose. He reported portentously that the street was full of rumors about the personal speculations of Mr. Barney in the Ice Company stock, and that, in consequence, Barney had resigned. Hollins then proposed that we elect as president a Mr. Higgins, an amiable old gentleman who was in the insurance business. Hollins further announced that the Bank of Commerce (a Morgan-controlled bank), through which the Knickerbocker Trust Company cleared its check balances in the Clearing House, had refused to clear in the future for Knickerbocker. This, of course, was notice to the world to commence a run on that institution.

The directors sent John Magee, a director, and me as a committee to try to persuade Mr. Snyder, president of the Bank of Commerce, to rescind his edict. Mr. Snyder had evidently received his orders, for he refused to reconsider. The Knickerbocker directors met that evening in the upstairs rooms of Sherry's on Fifth Avenue and Forty-fourth Street. Barney was asked to attend, but he was allowed to sit alone in the hall and took no part in the proceedings. John Magee and I presented our report.

Across the street from the Knickerbocker Trust at that

time was the predecessor of the Harriman Bank, then known as the Night and Day Bank. It kept open for deposits all night. All that night depositors who suspected the solvency of the Knickerbocker Trust were putting their checks in the Night and Day Bank to be presented at the Knickerbocker Trust for cash payment in the morning. We knew, too, that crowds of other depositors would be lined up when the bank opened, all anxious to withdraw their money.

The question before the directors was: Should the Knickerbocker Trust Company open in the morning? Two Morgan partners, Messrs. Steele and Perkins, were present and waiting in another room. The directors sent John Magee and me as a committee to interview them to see what assistance the Morgan firm would give if the Knickerbocker Trust opened.

To our inquiries Perkins and Steele said that they could make no definite promises but advised us to "go ahead and open and, about eleven o'clock, they would see what they could do for us." Of course this amounted to nothing.

When Magee and I returned with our report, I offered my opinion that the trust company should not open in the morning; that we had $11,000,000 in cash which we would lose in twenty minutes if we opened. Further, that if we *were* insolvent it would be a crime to allow money to be withdrawn; that it would be unfair to out-of-town depositors as well as to any who for other reasons did not join the run which would undoubtedly ensue. I added that if we did not open, every bank and trust company would close within twenty-four hours and then, after a short cooling-off period, all could open together. I stated that I was so sure of my position that I would insist that my vote in favor of not reopening the next day be recorded in the minutes of the meeting. But all the directors voted against me except John Magee, Alfred Hoyt,

Moses Taylor, and, I think, Charles Perin. I am sorry to record here that some of the directors had been preparing to withdraw money themselves through checks put in the Night and Day Bank across the street.

The result was as I predicted. The bank quickly paid out its $11,000,000 in cash. It then closed, and did not have the benefit of this cash to help in its reorganization.

After we closed, a dispute arose over the appointment of a receiver. Such appointments were political plums then, as they often are now, for receivers get large fees. An effort was made to have Herbert Satterlee, a lawyer and son-in-law of J. P. Morgan, appointed receiver. Fortunately, Bourke Cockran was a friend of Attorney General Jackson, an honest man, who was glad to look to Cockran for advice. The result was that the Attorney General brought about the appointment of Reginald Rives, a very distinguished and upright lawyer of New York; Mr. Thalman of Ladenburg, Thalman and Co., to satisfy Herbert Limburg, who was the attorney for Hearst; and Mr. Ide, who had been Governor General of the Philippine Islands and who was Bourke Cockran's father-in-law.

Of course those directors who had voted against my proposal to close the bank were not the ones active in the endeavor to rehabilitate the trust company. A fund was raised, to which I subscribed, to provide cash by the sale of stock, and in due time the company was rehabilitated, the depositors paid in full with interest, and the company was soon going again. I am very proud of the fact that the Attorney General, in his report for 1908, states:

"The resumption of business was due to the efforts of the directors led by Hon. James W. Gerard, D. Louis Boissevain, and William A. Tucker. . . ."

The Knickerbocker Trust afterward merged with the

Columbia Trust Company, which in turn merged with the Irving Trust Company.

Shortly before the closing of the Knickerbocker Trust, the State Banking Department had examined the affairs of the company and found it was in excellent condition. Why, therefore, was this panic brought about and why was it possible?

It was possible because at that time the Federal Reserve Act had not been enacted, and any bank or trust company, if suddenly asked for the full amount of its deposits, or even a large percentage of that amount, could not pay in cash. No bank or trust company keeps its deposits uninvested and in cash. It was often said of the 1907 panic, "Someone asked for a dollar and that started the crash."

As to whether there were deeply laid plans to bring on this calamity, I must leave the reader to judge from the following recital. A short time before this the United States Steel Corporation had been organized in New Jersey by the firm of J. P. Morgan and Company. Outside of the United States Steel organization was a large steel company called the Tennessee Coal, Iron and Railroad Company. On November 4, 1907, at the height of the country-wide panic that followed the closing of the Knickerbocker, Judge Elbert H. Gary and Mr. H. C. Frick, the head of United States Steel, called on President Theodore Roosevelt. They told him that a certain business firm—they did not give the name of the firm—would undoubtedly fail if help was not given. They informed him that among the assets of this firm was a majority of the securities of Tennessee Coal, Iron and Railroad Company; that application had been urgently made to the steel corporation to purchase this stock as the only means of avoiding a failure. President Roosevelt's callers then added that as a mere business transaction they did not care to purchase this stock, since it would bring little benefit to the United States Steel Corporation. They were aware, they continued, that the purchase would be used to attack them on the ground that they were striving to obtain a monopoly of the steel industry. They told the President that it had been the policy of the company, in order to prevent attacks of this kind, always to stop short of acquiring more than 60 per cent of the steel-producing capacity of the country. However, they felt that it was eminently to their interest—as it was to the interest of every responsible businessman—to try to prevent a panic and a general industrial smashup. They were, therefore, "willing" to make this purchase, which they would not otherwise do. They added that this course had been urged upon them by a combination of the most responsible bankers in New York. They declared that they did not wish to do this if the President decided that it ought not to be done.

The President replied that while he, of course, could not advise them to take the proposed action, he did not feel that it was his public duty to interpose any objections. The President embodied this in a note which he later sent to the Attorney General, Charles J. Bonaparte. Bonaparte replied to the President that the legal situation with respect to monopoly had been in no way changed, and that no sufficient ground existed for prosecution of the Steel Corporation. In his memoirs, however, President Roosevelt wrote that he acted purely on his own initiative and that the responsibility for the act was solely his. (See the *Memoirs* of Theodore Roosevelt.)

On November 5, 1907, the day following his talk with Roosevelt, Judge Gary gave an interview crowing over the acquisition of the stock, as follows:

The United States Steel Corporation has been negotiating for the purchase of a majority of the stock of the Tennessee Coal, Iron and Railway Company at par. The same price will be paid for all additional stock offered within fifteen days. The contract has been concluded by the finance committee of the Steel Corporation subject to formal ratification by the Board of Directors which will meet at four o'clock Wednesday, November 6.

By the acquisition of this property the Steel Corporation will increase its capacity by about 2½ per cent, making its capacity about 60 per cent of the total production in the United States. It is believed the purchase will eventually be of great benefit to the corporation and to the steel industry.

Mr. Frederick Lewis Allen in his book *The Lords of Creation*, page 140, has this to say about the interview of Frick and Gary with Theodore Roosevelt:

That Gary's explanation to Roosevelt was somewhat disingenuous is obvious. Roosevelt might not have been impressed had he been told that the immediate beneficiary of this transaction was a brokerage firm, that of George F. Baker's brother-in-law; that no single loan to the Schley firm was secured wholly by Tennessee stock; or that the development of the open-hearth process of steel-making was increasing the potential value to the Steel Corporation of the Tennessee's properties. It is also equally obvious that Roosevelt preferred not to question Gary and Frick too closely lest he discover something which it would be inconvenient to know. He could have pressed them for the name of the concern which was threatened with failure, but he chose not to. It is also clear that the transaction was not precisely an act of open-handed generosity on Morgan's part. It was a piece of business which he hoped would in time yield the Steel Corporation a good profit.

The President had not seen his way clear to balk the power of Wall Street, and the United States Steel had acquired its rival. But in every country in the world suicide, ruin, and panic followed the closing of the Knickerbocker Trust Company, which was the prelude to the Steel transaction. Remember that the United States Steel representatives told President Roosevelt that they didn't want the stock—that they only bought it to stop the panic. But after the panic was over observe that they did not try to sell the stock. They hold it to this day. As for stopping the panic—Steele and Perkins had the opportunity to prevent it the evening before the Knickerbocker Trust closed.

Charles T. Barney, the head of the Knickerbocker, committed suicide a few days after the crash. Frederick Eldredge, vice-president, jumped out of a second-story window and broke his legs. Naturally, I thought that the affairs of the bank were in catastrophic condition, and that I and the other directors were in a fearful scrape. But, as I have said, there was absolutely nothing the matter with the Trust Company. Those of us who participated in the reorganization were soon able to pay all obligations with interest. The stock we subscribed for to provide new capital became worth several times the amount we had paid for it. What we thought was a contribution became a good investment.

The House of Morgan was able in many cases to control many of its captive corporations without owning a majority of the stock, or even owning a sizable minority. Often these concerns were dominated merely by the use of nerve and possession of the list of stockholders—trusting folk, for the most part, who always signed over their proxies to the Morgan-controlled board of directors.

Perkins of the Morgan firm, to whom John Magee and I had appealed in vain to help the Knickerbocker Trust Company, was apparently not satisfied merely with the fall of that institution. In *The Lords of Creation*, page 26, Allen writes:

George W. Perkins, a partner in the House of Morgan, talked with the reporters who were waiting for news of the conference:

and the next morning there appeared in the New York *Times* and *Sun* an "official" statement which contained the scarcely diplomatic sentence, "The chief sore point is the Trust Company of America." Though the statement continued with reassurances that the conferences believed the company to be sound, that it had twelve million dollars in cash, and that as much more as might be needed had been pledged, the effect of that sentence was immediate. On Wednesday morning there was a terrific run upon the Trust Company of America.

During the 1904 campaign the president of the New York Life Insurance Company, one McCall, promised to give $50,-000 to the treasurer of the Republican party. Perkins, a trustee and vice-president of the Insurance Company, advanced $48,702.50 for which a check of the insurance company was given to Perkins. The check was drawn to the order of J. P. Morgan and Company of which firm, as I have said, Perkins was a member. In due course Perkins was indicted on a charge of grand larceny but was acquitted in the Court of Appeals. There was no law at that time, as there is today, forbidding a corporation to make political contributions.

In France, before the great Revolution and its reign of terror, there were brutal and arrogant nobles who oppressed the people and made harsh use of their feudal privileges, contributed no taxes, and kept in their own hands all political, military, even religious posts. But there were also decent nobles, quietly seeking to the best of their ability to do something for the poor people on their estates. But when the Revolution came and the tumbrils rolled toward the Place of the Revolution and the guillotine, no distinction was made between the good nobles and the bad. If the good nobles had been bold enough to stop the wicked ones in their oppression of the people, there might well have been no revolution.

In the United States of America we have had no nobles with titles and privileges. But we have had a band of predatory men in big business who have had little thought for the rights of even their own stockholders and still less for the rights of the public. If they had had coats of arms, William H. Vanderbilt's statement, "The public be damned!" might have been the device emblazoned on their shields.

And if, today, the mass of well-to-do people are being taxed to death, and their estates taken from their widows and children by the operation of enormous estate taxes, they have only themselves to blame. For too long they meekly sat back in awe of institutions—if you could call them such—such as the House of Morgan, and even joined with the retainers of the powerful corsairs in denouncing as a blackmailer, a Red, or a revolutionist anyone who dared to oppose this thinly disguised regime of self-interest. For the most part they have been afraid.

This haunting fear was well put by Woodrow Wilson in his book, *The New Freedom*, where he says:

Some of the biggest men in the United States, in the field of commerce and manufacture, are afraid of somebody, are afraid of something. They know that there is a power somewhere so organized, so subtle, so watchful, so interlocked, so complete, so pervasive, that they had better not speak above their breath when they speak in condemnation of it!

By the time the first excitement of the Knickerbocker Trust failure had died down and the 1907 panic was well established, Election Day rolled around. A great deal of the opposition campaign was devoted to pointing out what an evil fellow I must be, and many of the speeches dwelt scathingly on my connection with the Knickerbocker Trust. It was fortunate, then, that my friends were able to point out that I and my family had more than half a million dollars on deposit in the Knickerbocker on the day it closed, and that none of this money had been withdrawn. That was rather startling news in view of the cozy behavior of some of my fellow directors, and its revelation quite effectively disposed of the attacks.

Even with this point in my favor I was not too sanguine about the outcome of the election. My doubt was deepened on election night. I spent the early evening on the outskirts of the crowd in Times Square watching the returns being projected on a screen. When my picture appeared on the screen, a man in front of me turned to his wife and said, "He doesn't look to me like a judge—he looks more like a bunco steerer." This must have been a tribute to the fine, full mustache I wore at that time.

As soon as the returns began to come in, however, it became evident that I would win, so I went home to a peaceful dinner, and later in the evening I heard that I had been elected by a substantial majority.

As soon as things settled down, my wife and I sailed for Bermuda for a short rest. On the boat was Upton Sinclair, whose powerful book, *The Jungle*, exposing scandals of the great meat-packing industry of Chicago, had recently made a sensation. I gave Sinclair an account of the closing of the Knickerbocker and he put the story into a novel called *The Money Changers*. Unfortunately his knowledge of business was slight and he didn't get the details right. Moreover, he put in a woman conflict between Barney and Morgan—a literary device which, as the book turned out, was at best merely another distracting element in a tale which was below the Sinclair standard.

When the day came for me to ascend the bench to which I had been elected, I looked forward to a pleasant release from the hard toil and long hours that I had devoted to the law ever since I left school. Of course everyone understands that a judge has a pretty easy life.

Unfortunately, this happy dream does not materialize for those who occupy the bench of the Supreme Court of New York. I was not long in discovering that my previous labors at law were almost perfunctory in comparison to what I had to endure if I was to carry out my judicial duties satisfactorily. The actual hours spent in court were merely breathers between arduous hours of homework. A Supreme Court judge, if he is conscientious, must devote much of his time outside of court wading through a great mass of briefs, statutes, and notes. He must do this to keep his schedule up to date and—equally important—in order to appear omniscient before an endless procession of clever, well-prepared lawyers.

The only relief was in being assigned to jury cases, especially tort cases. These are so much of a routine nature as not to require the razor-sharp attention of the judge, and during these stretches it might be possible for him to compose sonnets or—under the guise of taking notes—catch up on personal correspondence. Many of these tort cases were against the street-railway companies, usually involving an injury sustained by a passenger. I can still recite verbatim the standard testimony of a typical plaintiff. Carefully schooled beforehand by his or her lawyer, he would render from memory, in a dull, mechanical manner, and with each syllable given identical stress, the following jewel:

"I boarded the car at Twenty-third Street and paid my fare. As the car approached Forty-fourth Street I signaled to the conductor in the appropriate manner that I desired to leave the car and for him to stop the car. And the car did stop. I then started to descend from the car to the street. With my right hand I firmly grasped the guard rail. Still firmly grasping the guard rail, and with one foot on the last step, I was endeavoring to place the other foot on the ground—but had not yet done so—when suddenly, without warning, the car started in motion. In consequence I was thrown violently to the ground and since then have not been the same woman."

Equity cases usually required homework, and as for the appellate term, I have sat with two other judges until all the arguments were heard and then gone home to find the entire side of my study piled high with briefs and other material on the cases, every bit of which had to be studied.

I had taken my place on the bench as a justice of the New York Supreme Court on January 1, 1908, and just before the elections in the autumn I was put on a hot spot. Judge Davis and I were detailed to hear the bitter election cases which were sure to come up in that autumn. Almost immediately Judge Davis was distressed to discover that one of his relatives was sick. He dodged out of town, leaving me to handle the election cases alone. Moreover, both Democratic and Republican parties stipulated that my decision was to be final and without appeal. Most of the cases involved district fights, but one of them was of especial importance. Hearst had formed what he called the Independence party. Although he was not a candidate himself in that year, his Independence party was supposed to control a number of votes, possibly enough to decide the mayoral election. However, the convention of the Independence party was foxily stolen by the Democrats of Tammany Hall, and the convention's endorsement was given to Judge Gaynor, the Democratic nominee. This act was challenged and the case was brought to court before me. Since I had just been elected by the Democrats, my position was difficult. I decided, nevertheless, that the convention of the Independence League had been improperly seized and struck the names of Judge Gaynor and the other nominees from the Independence League ticket.

This naturally enraged the Democratic leaders. Murphy himself was at first rather bitter about my decision. But when I told him that if I had decided otherwise I should have been pulled off the bench and that his leadership would be put in jeopardy, he finally became more amenable to reason. In the ensuing election, however, Gaynor won by a substantial majority, which somewhat blunted the wrath of the Democratic cohorts.

In many ways I had a great admiration for Charles Murphy. During the years that I knew him—that is from about 1900 or even before that, to the time of his death in 1924—our fast friendship was interrupted only for a brief time by this incident of the decision and later in 1919 when I had asked him to renominate Judge Newburger as a justice of the Supreme Court. I thought he would do this, but he finally nominated someone else. When this happened, Bainbridge Colby and I worked on the election committee of Judge Newburger, who ran as an independent candidate and was elected by an enormous vote.

Charles Murphy was thoroughly honest and despised methods by which previous Tammany leaders had enriched themselves. His word was absolutely dependable. Incidentally, I would have as soon thought of telling an off-color story to a lady as to Charlie Murphy.

He died in April 1924. I felt that we were especially close during the two or three years preceding his death. I was one of his pallbearers, and as I stood by his grave on a hill in the cemetery in Long Island City and looked at the towers of the city over which he had been the absolute political ruler for so many years, I felt that the public had suffered a great loss.

CHAPTER XIII

THE ARDUOUS DUTIES OF THE SUPREME COURT HAD ONE compensating advantage. The long summer recess gave me an opportunity to have protracted vacations with our friends abroad. Since it would have been injudicious not to utilize such an opportunity, Mrs. Gerard and I spent a short time in London each year from 1907 to 1912, followed by a stay on the Continent.

My diaries of this period record many illustrious names, and my memory evokes many brilliant gatherings. They lend poignancy to reflections on the melancholy change in the fortunes of many wealthy and aristocratic Britons and the contrast between the charm and opulence of this early era and the miseries of their ordeal in World War II and afterward. I recall visits with Burdett Coutts, an elderly American who had become a British citizen. His name originally was Ashmead Bartlett, but he had married a lady many years older, the Baroness Burdett Coutts. She was one of the richest women in England and principal stockholder of the celebrated Coutts Bank, and he had taken her name. He was a widower when we met him, and had a house on Piccadilly and a villa at Highgate-on-the-Hill, near London. We often lunched and dined with him. It was rumored at one time that both the Duke of Wellington and Napoleon III, when in exile in London, had been suitors for the hand of the rich baroness.

We were also invited frequently to the home of Lady Paget in.Belgrave Square, and to her place at Kingston-on-Thames, where she always had assembled a varied and interesting array of guests. It was at her house in London that I met Herbert Asquith, afterward one of the war Prime Ministers. I remember an instructive hour spent in her garden at Kingston with the beautiful opera singer, Lina Cavalieri and one or two other guests. Cavalieri demonstrated for our edification some of the exercises she used to keep her fine figure. Such exercises by women are habitual today, but in 1907 it seemed an exotic and faintly scandalous notion.

About this time I joined the Gun Club in London and competed with some success against many of the expert pigeon shots of England. It was at Ostend, I think, in 1911, that in a field of sixty-six I tied with a French baron for the Prix de Kursaal. In a field of sixty-six it was impossible to shoot a given number of pigeons, and the first miss eliminated the marksman. It was amusing to have the bettors approach a marksman and inquire: "You feel well?" "You digest your lunch well?" or "You sleep well?" If they were satisfied with this appraisal of your physical condition, they would place a bet on you. I have no doubt they cursed you bitterly for deceiving them if you lost.

For the summer vacation of 1909 Mrs. Gerard and I went to Scotland and took a shooting place called Stronelairg. Mrs. James H. Smith, the widow of the celebrated "Silent" Smith, lived not far away that summer at Tulloch Castle. Her daughter, Anita, was married there in September to Prince Miguel of Bragança, a son of the Pretender to the Portuguese throne. We attended the wedding at Tulloch Castle. It was most picturesque. Prince Miguel wore the red uniform of a Knight of Malta, his father that of an Austrian Hussar, and Count Sigray and Count Csekonics wore the national Hungarian dress. A full Highland band performed loudly on the lawn, and afterward pipers marched up and down in Highland dress and made a prodigious skirling.

A few days before the wedding Mrs. Smith asked me to come over to Tulloch Castle to draw up some legal papers. My firm for many years had been the lawyers for the Rhine-landers, and her daughter Anita was the daughter of William Rhinelander Stewart by Mrs. Smith's previous marriage. The papers which I prepared were signed by Prince Miguel and his father, and Señor Saldanha DeGama, representative of the Miguelista party of Portugal, and were to the effect that the marriage was not a morganatic marriage. In the event of Prince Miguel's becoming King of Portugal, the agreement gave Anita all the rights of a Portuguese queen, and provided that her children might inherit the throne. I tell of this contract with express permission of the family.

The eldest son of this marriage, John Bragança, like his brother Miguel, is a fine young man whom I have often unsuccessfully tried to get to learn Portuguese, on the chance that in the political changes of the future he might one day have a chance at the throne of Portugal.

That spring in London, when Mrs. Gerard was kept indoors by a cold, I accompanied the three beautiful daughters of the Duchess of Rutland to a fancy-dress party. The party was in the house of Lady Cunard whom I had known from early days in Bar Harbor. One of the sisters dressed in red, white, and blue as a French *tricoteuse*. Also present was Lady Diana Manners, in a dress of rough brown cloth with a leopard skin over one shoulder and with two horns, one branching from each side of her head. When I asked her who she was she answered, "Ildico, if you know who that was." I smiled blandly at this, but the thing worried me all evening. The next day I consulted the Britannica and learned the obscure fact that Ildico was the wife of Attila the Hun and said to have slain him on their wedding night.

Lady Diana Manners later married Alfred Duff Cooper, who became First Lord of the Admiralty, a post which he later resigned in protest against the weak policy of the Chamberlain government. Lady Diana, a celebrated beauty, appeared earlier in the movies, and made a great success in the part of the Madonna in Reinhardt's production of *The Miracle* in New York.

When Count Lâszló Széchenyi came to New York to marry Gladys Vanderbilt, Count Sigray ("Sigray" without the first name signifying that he was the head of the house), came with his friend, Count Lâszló, to attend the wedding and while here met my wife's sister, Harriot. He came to stay with us in Scotland in 1909. In 1910 he and Harriot were married and made their home in Hungary. Mrs. Gerard and I visited the Sigrays in the summer of 1910 at their country estate called Ivancz in the extreme southwest corner of Hungary.

While there I had a chance at the excellent Hungarian partridge shooting afforded by the estate. These partridges are raised by hand and then turned loose in great numbers. Wishing to make the best possible showing among the expert shots of Hungary, I had ordered in London a quantity of cartridges to be sent to Vienna. When I called for the cartridges, however, I found that they couldn't be released from the Customs without a permit from a certain American dentist who practiced in Vienna and who kept the teeth of Francis Joseph in order. It seems that Francis Joseph, prob-

ably after a successful tooth pulling, gave this dentist a monopoly on all sporting powders used in Austria and Hungary.
Legally, of course, he had no right to do this, but his decree
was respected as if it were law, so I had to go to the dentist's
office and pay ransom for my cartridges.

Except perhaps for Czarist Russia, no country was so feudal up to the time of World War I as Hungary, and in no
country was life more picturesque.

On one occasion I had supper with Sigray and a number of
his friends in the celebrated Restaurant Sacher in Vienna.
The proprietress, an eccentric old lady, smoked black cigars,
knew all the aristocracy of the central empires. I think the
Restaurant Sacher, perhaps under another name, appears
in the film *Meyerling*, which is about the death of the Crown
Prince of Austria, and also in the very successful play of those
great artists, the Lunts, called *Reunion in Vienna*.

Sigray was in the Hungarian Army during World War I.
After the war, when the Communists under Béla Kun for a
time had possession of Hungary, he joined Admiral Horthy,
afterward Regent of Hungary, who was organizing a White
Army to drive out the Communists. The Communists during
their months of power took possession of Sigray's country
place of Ivancz but did little damage. They had planned to
take the furniture to Budapest to put it in a museum in order
to show the populace how the rich lived. The only things they
stole were the wine, of course, linens, and some American
cookbooks. The Communists, with a sense of humor rare
among revolutionists, all signed the guest book.

When Admiral Horthy, with the aid of the Romanians,
overcame the Communists, Sigray was made governor of
western Hungary. He was in full power when the Emperor
Carl and Empress Zita, flying from Switzerland in a German

plane with the royal robes, crowns, and jewels in dress suit-
cases, landed in western Hungary. Sigray, being a Royalist,
went over to the Royalist side. With the aid of the Bishop of
Szombathely and Colonel Lehár (brother of the composer of
the *Merry Widow*), a little army was organized which then,
accompanied by Carl and Zita, marched on Budapest.

But, just as in the attempted escape of Louis XVI, there
were many delays. Large deputations were received, and
many banquets and masses were attended, so that by the time
the Royalists got to Budapest, the Regent Horthy, who probably liked his job, had organized a small army and armed the
university students. In the battle that took place outside of
Budapest about four hundred people were killed and the
Royalists were defeated. Later Counts Sigray and Andrassy
were put in jail. Since Hungary was supposed to be a monarchy with Horthy as regent, it was hard to prosecute them
for supporting the legitimate king, and they were soon released.

Carl and Zita were put on a British boat and sent down the
Danube. At Constantinople they boarded a British cruiser
which took them to Madeira. Here Carl died. His eldest son
is at this writing in America with his mother, sisters, and
brothers. He is a likable young man and has handled himself
so far with great skill and tact.

In World War II Hungary was forced into alliance with
Germany, but early in 1944 Count Sigray made a speech at a
session of the Hungarian upper House in favor of peace. The
Nazis considered this to be anti-German. Two or three days
afterward, the Germans occupied the country and seized
Sigray, Count Andrassy, and a number of other leaders of the
movement to restore the Hapsburgs.

Taken in charge by the Gestapo, Sigray, with a number of

other political prisoners, was imprisoned first in Hungary and then in the awful concentration camp of Mauthausen, on the Danube in Austria. He remained there for about a year, until he and his fellow prisoners were released by the advancing American armies. He made his way to the French zone, then to Switzerland, and finally to America. No care could overcome the ravages to his health, and on the day after Christmas, 1947, he died from the sufferings he had undergone.

Sigray could rarely bring himself to speak of the horrors of Mauthausen. But on one occasion, in describing some of the sights that had racked his soul, he related that a train bearing about five hundred prisoners, Jews of various nationalities, French, and others, arrived at the camp in the depth of winter. The captives were helpless with exhaustion, having been without food and even water for days. The Germans took them from the train, laid them in rows upon the ground, and poured icy water over them. Those who did not die promptly of shock and cold were machine-gunned. The Nazi guards explained that there was not room for them in the camp.

During his imprisonment and after Sigray's wife, Mrs. Gerard's sister, and their daughter remained on the Sigray estate in Hungary, even though the house was first occupied by the Germans and later by the Russians. Eventually they were able to make their way to Switzerland and thence to the United States.

The ten-thousand-acre Sigray estate has been confiscated by the Red government of Hungary. We here in America, still fat and complacent, remain indifferent to those who sow treason and who would have us become the slaves of a threatening dictator. We need a better conception of the hardships and horrors endured by the people of Europe, of which the sufferings of the Sigray family are an example.

In the summer of 1910 I stayed in Ostend for a time to compete in the pigeon shooting and enjoy the sea bathing. Staying at the same hotel in Ostend was an archduke of Austria—a man of tremendous dignity and aplomb. Whenever he entered the hotel's vast dining room, the orchestra leader would frantically stop whatever he was playing and launch the orchestra into a special Austrian air. After a few days of this I instructed the orchestra to play "Tammany" whenever I entered the room.

Hungary in those days was, as I have said, a feudal country. One day when we were shooting, Sigray posted me in a corner of a field to await a drive of partridges. While I waited I was made intensely nervous by two good-looking peasant girls who approached me and made extraordinary passes at me. I finally discovered that they were trying to kiss my hand, which they deemed their duty, since I was a guest of the lord of the manor. When we went out to shoot in the morning, the gamekeepers would come up and kiss the count's hand, and whenever we drove through the country, the small children used to line up by the roadside and chant a little religious song, the words of which recommended the count very favorably to the Almighty.

The Hungarian magnates had a most picturesque dress. Each family's traditional costume varies in color, although all are alike in their general cut. Sigray, for instance, when arrayed in full rig as a Hungarian magnate, wore light blue, snug breeches, a coat of white-and-gold brocade, Hussar boots with gold tassels and gold bands about the tops, swan-shaped gold spurs, and a scimitar. Over one shoulder he wore, with elaborate carelessness, a dolman, or extra coat, lined with fur and heavy with braid, and on his head a cap of sable with a diamond brooch in front and a white aigrette. It is a matter of great regret to me that in the early part of my life I never had the advantages of a Hungarian magnate's costume, but had to worry along on such glamour as is afforded by the uniform of my military school, the 7th and the 12th Regiments and the staff of the First Brigade.

While we were in London in 1910 I was invited, through the good offices of Bourke Cockran, to dine in the House of Commons with the leaders of the Irish party and many other dignitaries from Ireland. These were gathered in London to celebrate the change in form of the Coronation Oath, a change which removed the last insult in Great Britain to those of the Roman Catholic faith.

Afterward we all adjourned to the gallery of the House of Commons and listened to the debate which resulted in the vote that brought about this change. Few reference books supply the text of these changes and, for their historical interest, I include them here. It is astonishing that up to the accession of George V the kings and queens of England made the ancient declaration which follows:

The Declaration against Transubstantiation
(1 Will and Mary. Sess. 2. c.2.)

I A:B: doe solemnely and sincerely in the presence of God professe testifie and declare that I do believe that in the sacrament of the Lords Supper there is not any transubstantiation of the elements of bread and wine into the body and blood of Christ at or after the consecration thereof by any person whatsoever; and that the invocation or adoration of the Virgin Mary or any other saint, and the sacrifice of the masse as they are now used in the Church of Rome are superstitious and idolatrous, and I doe solemnely in the presence of God professe testifie and declare that I doe make this declaration and every part thereof in the plaine and ordinary sence of the words read unto me as they are commonly understood by English protestants without any levasion, equivocation or mentall reservation whatsoever and without any dispensation already granted me for this purpose by the Pope or any other authority or person whatsoever or without any hope of any such dispensation from any person or authority whatsoever or without thinking that I am or can be acquitted before God or man or absolved of this declaration or any part thereof although the Pope or any other person or persons or power whatsoever should dispence with or annuall the same, or declare that it was null and void from the beginning.

New Declaration under Accession Declaration, Act, 1910.
(10 Edw. 7. and 1 Geo. 4, c.29.)

I (here the name of the Sovereign) do solemnly and sincerely in the presence of God profess, testify, and declare that I am a faithful Protestant, and that I will, according to the true intent of the enactments which secure the Protestant succession to the Throne of my Realm, uphold and maintain the said enactments to the best of my powers according to law.

CHAPTER XIV

Under our political system, the successful aspirant for high office requires considerable of the dramatic actor in his make-up. It is an axiom of the stage that a good actor must live his role, and a truism that if a man plays a single role long enough, the assumed character is merged with his own. Thus, despite the testimony of some associates that Franklin Delano Roosevelt was a social snob, he radiated such a charming friendliness toward all kinds and conditions of men that the conviction of human brotherhood which he exuded, if not genuine, was at least indistinguishable from it. The character of the austere intellectual grew upon Woodrow Wilson until it became a fatal handicap to him as a leader. Theodore Roosevelt made a cult of physical vigor early in life, and so embellished the role with the passing years that T. R. became synonymous with hardihood and endurance.

In March of 1908 I had lunch at the White House together with my brother-in-law Marcus Daly II. When Teddy Roosevelt asked me if I were used to riding, I replied that I rode every day, sometimes riding two horses. Whereupon his daughter Alice, Mrs. Nicholas Longworth, spoke up and said, "Well, then, Father, you had better take them for a walk." So after lunch Roosevelt, his son-in-law, Nick Longworth, a gentleman named James Kidder, Daly, and I were driven out to Rock Creek Park in the President's car.

Roosevelt had mapped out, after much study, a sort of follow-the-leader steeplechase in the park, and he proceeded to run us over this course. He first crept out on a narrow ledge, only an inch or two wide, across the face of a rock overhanging Rock Creek. After that came various stunts, such as climbing a chimney of rock, until we finally reached a dam across Rock Creek where the water was deep enough for swimming. The President took off his hat and put his watch in it. I started to shed my coat, assuming that he meant to take off his clothes and go in swimming. Instead of that, he plunged into the stream fully clothed and swam to the other side. Of course we followed, with varying degrees of reluctance. Next he walked down to another deep place and swam back again. We then walked to Washington in our wet clothes. On the way the President dared Longworth and me to go into the Metropolitan Club in our bedraggled condition. I had lost my hat, all the buttons were gone from the front of my coat and waistcoat, and I was covered with mud and dripping with water. I would lie down occasionally on the sidewalk to let the water run out of my shoes. Without too much loss of dignity I managed to reach my room in the Willard Hotel by going up in the freight elevator. The President gave the newspapers a hilarious account of our follow-the-leader walk.

The President made quite a specialty of these excursions, and in the summertime sometimes led members of his cabinet and foreign diplomats to swim in the Potomac. He told me about one occasion when Jusserand, the French Ambassador, was one of the party. They were all stripped to the buff and ready to jump in the river when the President noticed that

Jusserand was still wearing gloves. "Why are you wearing gloves?" Teddy asked. "Ah," said Jusserand, "we might meet some ladies."

On February 22, 1909, after President Taft had been elected, we were in Washington, and I called on Roosevelt. Even then a break had occurred between him and Taft—I have never known why—and T. R. spoke of it, asking me what I thought the cause was. When Roosevelt was about to leave the White House in March 1909 I knew that no one would be paying much attention to him on his last day but would all be crowding about the new President. It seemed to be a good time to give him a going-away present, so I sent my secretary, Thomas McCarthy, to present to the President as a parting gift a handsome hunting knife which I had had prepared some months before by Dreicer, the New York jeweler. The handle was of gold, the top of the handle in the shape of an eagle, with ruby eyes, and on the side of the handle were engraved hunting scenes from Teddy's adventures. The President sent me back a penny in deference to the old superstition that a present of a sharp instrument will cut friendship unless it is paid for. I doubt that this fancy knife was of any use to Teddy on his African trip, and I believe it is now in a family museum at Oyster Bay.

When I was in Germany just before World War I broke out, Roosevelt sent me a letter to deliver personally to the Kaiser. It was a friendly letter. He spoke of his explorations in South America, his discovery of the River of Doubt, and similar matters. I never delivered it, for I felt that if war began, as seemed likely, the letter might be misinterpreted and widely misused by the Kaiser. I think Roosevelt appreciated my foresight, although he never spoke of the letter when I saw him afterward. But when the Society of the Genesee gave a dinner in my honor at the Harvard Club, he took the trouble to come all the way in from Oyster Bay to attend.

On one occasion when I arrived at the White House Teddy Roosevelt was discussing wrestling with another guest, a Briton. The talk became quite technical and finally Teddy summoned me to get down on the floor with him and show the visiting and surprised Britisher the particular holds under discussion.

After Theodore took office as vice-president, I think that he was very glad, for the publicity involved, to join the First Brigade New York National Guard in a field day at Van Cortlandt Park. He rode all day with the staff of which I was a member and at the end insisted on galloping all the way from Van Cortlandt Park to the stables at Fifty-ninth Street —a procedure which absolutely finished my lovely little horse. Those were the days of the strenuous life.

Theodore Roosevelt liked people and was at home with all sorts and conditions of men. On another occasion he invited me to spend the morning with him in his office while he received his visitors. An old army officer came in seeking a presidential appointment to West Point for his son. The President jumped up, took the applicant by both hands, and said, "Oh, my dear Colonel, why didn't you come in yesterday—I have just made my last appointment. If you had come in before, it would have been yours."

Maybe this was so, maybe not, but at any rate the disappointment of the colonel was softened.

Then, Hackenschmidt, the wrestler, appeared. Theodore felt the great wrestler's muscles, quite seriously expressed his admiration, and asked what food he ate to produce such strength. Next, a lovely actress, I think it was Billie Burke, received her meed of admiration. Finally a woman with two children came in. One of the youngsters handed the President a Teddy bear, saying, "This is for you." The President sent to the White House conservatory for flowers for the mother and searched his desk for old coins and souvenirs for the children.

These examples are typical of the welcome to all who came to see him. When they went away, they were Roosevelt partisans for life.

Woodrow Wilson, on the contrary, disliked people. He refused to see Elihu Root on his return from a mission to Russia; he refused to see Lord Grey when he came as British Ambassador, and he snubbed many of our own diplomats on their return from foreign posts.

As I relate later in these memoirs, I was with Wilson and his charming wife for four hours on my return from Germany in September 1916, and lunched with them at Shadowlawn, Long Branch. On my final return from Germany I was with him at his request for more than two hours, even though he was somewhat ill. When you had something vital to report, there was no question about seeing him, but he disliked unnecessary talk.

It is not generally known that at the time of his trip to Paris to the Peace Conference he had lost the sight of one eye perhaps because of ill health—but his resultant irritability was smoothed down by the charm and tact of his wife.

In these days a great deal of our so-called thinking consists of pasting a label, dictated by prejudice and gummed with ignorance, on every idea, political or economic. The label serves thereafter to identify it as "progressive," "reactionary," "good," or "bad," without the trouble of examining the contents.

One of these label conclusions which annoys me more than others is that Americans "exploited" Mexico, as if those who risked their money and expended their talents and energy in developing the country were comparable to pirates and plunderers.

The Cinco Minas property in Mexico, which I had a part in developing, provides a good example of what I mean. I, with my wife, her mother, and her brother, had formed a family syndicate to invest in mining ventures, and had sent out a young mining engineer named Henry E. Crawford to locate a suitable property. After examining several projects, he came upon Cinco Minas, in the mountains about eighty miles northwest of Guadalajara, in the State of Jalisco.

The Mexican proprietors were working only about two feet wide in a vein of comparatively rich gold and silver. To extract the metals they were using the century-old patio process. This involved first crushing the ore beneath stone rollers driven by horses or mules. A layer of the crushed ore was spread around a courtyard, or patio, then mercury was poured on the ore, and churned with it by the hoofs of horses and mules kept in motion around the patio by a small boy perched on the surrounding wall and armed with a long whip. The agitation of the ore with mercury formed an amalgam of gold and silver with the mercury. This amalgam was next heated in a retort; heat drove off the mercury, which was condensed for reuse and the gold and silver left in a fairly pure state. The whole primitive process was not only slow and wasteful of human and animal energy, but it failed to extract all the metal from the ore.

We paid the Mexicans an enormous price for the property, spent half a million dollars equipping it with modern machinery, and instead of working a vein two feet wide, worked a vein of lower grade ore sixty feet wide. Thus we gave employment at good wages to 1,300 men, instead of the 100 or so previously employed. We brought in a Belgian physician to care for the workmen and to instruct them in healthful living. We built a school, and initiated many other projects to improve the standard of living of the workers and others in the surrounding community.

This is not only a fair picture of the operation of our property but is typical of what happened almost every time American enterprise was devoted to the development of Latin-American resources. The local citizens have profited, learned new techniques of industry and agriculture, and prospered accordingly, as men always do when brains are applied to complement the gifts of nature. To speak of this as "exploitation" is to adopt the mental attitude of those who regard all capital as evil unless it is directed by the rulers of the state, preferably themselves.

I made my first trip to the Cinco Minas property in 1910, shortly after returning to New York from our visit to Hungary. Since we had made a large capital investment, I deemed it prudent to get to know the Mexican authorities, and, if possible, to avoid their ill will, particularly that of President Díaz, Mexico's strong-minded dictator.

As chance directed it, Díaz was planning at that time to celebrate the one hundredth anniversary of the commencement of Mexico's war of liberation against Spain, and he had invited all nations to send special representatives to Mexico for the event. This seemed a splendid opportunity to get acquainted with Díaz and his satraps under the most happy auspices. So I lost no time in getting some Democrat friends in Congress to introduce a resolution that the United States Government accept Mexico's kind invitation and send an ap-

propriate delegation to the ceremonies in Mexico City. The
bill proposed that the United States Commission include
three senators to be appointed by the Vice-President (which
I judged would insure the bill's passage in the Senate); three
representatives to be appointed by the speaker (I thought
that would get it safely through the House); and three citizens to be appointed by the President. This last, I thought,
would persuade the President to sign the bill. The legislation
went through with a whoop and I succeeded in getting President Taft to appoint me as one of the citizen representatives.
The other two were General Otis of Los Angeles, proprietor
of the Los Angeles *Times,* and Colonel Rook of Pittsburgh,
proprietor of the Pittsburgh *Dispatch,* both Republicans.
Each of us was given the rank of Envoy Extraordinary and
Minister Plenipotentiary.

With these titles, and with an appropriation from the State
Department, we started on the road to Mexico in two private
cars. Whenever the train stopped at stations in Mexico, it
was surrounded by curious crowds of Mexicans. I recall that
at Monterey, when we came out on the platform of our car
and saw the Mexicans who were standing about, no one
seemed to know what to do. The silent, mutual contemplation grew more awkward until someone in our delegation
commenced to sing. At the moment this seemed like a good
idea, and we treated the Mexicans to a selection of tunes
such as "There'll Be a Hot Time in the Old Town Tonight"
and the like. The natives appeared gravely surprised and
were restrained in their applause.

When we arrived at Mexico City, a delegation of ladies
and gentlemen who had been assigned to take care of us
escorted us to the Cobian Palace where we were to live. This
was a magnificent house which had been built by a well-to-do

cotton dealer named Cobian and had just been taken over by the Government to be used as the Ministry of the Interior. For our benefit the Ministry had fitted up the palace with beautiful furniture, had installed bathrooms, and provided a staff of forty-four servants for our party of fourteen. We were politely informed that we could spend no money. Whenever we gave dinners, we were furnished with food and wines. Each of us had at his disposal a chauffeur and an automobile, as well as a victoria with two men on the box wearing cockades in their hats. Since Díaz was quite anxious to show that he was on chummy terms with the United States Government, we were particularly requested by our hosts to appear at all the ceremonies. The rainy season was just setting in, so all the ceremonies took place in the early morning. I must record that we were a queer-looking lot at nine in the morning in full-dress suits, the time-honored uniform of American diplomats.

For our hosts an emotional high point of the centennial occurred on the evening of September 15, when, as is the yearly custom, the President of Mexico, in the full view of the populace, rang the ancient bell whose clamor marked the opening of the Mexican war for independence. In 1810 it hung in the parish church of the priest Hidalgo, who rang it as a prearranged signal to summon his parishioners to arms. In time the bell was moved to the National Palace in Mexico City. To ring it, the President had to climb through a window onto a small projecting platform. By custom, as the President rings the bell, he shouts "Viva Mexico." It was once customary for him to add "and death to the Spaniards," but this sentiment was dropped some years before the centennial.

On this special occasion the patriotic feeling of the populace was naturally at a high pitch. The ceremony took on a powerful additional flavor from the fact that many in the crowds that filled the great palace square harbored much the same feelings toward Díaz that their forebears had had for the Spanish governors a century before.

When, therefore, Díaz asked me to step out on the platform with him while he rang the bell, I judged that the invitation was not merely a polite gesture of inter-American friendship. My presence was calculated to be a fortuitous form of life insurance. With this prospect in mind, then, I partook of just enough of the President's champagne at dinner to give me the courage to intercept casually any bullets that might be attracted to the President while he was doing his bell chore. All things considered, it was a perfect setting for a Mexican political assassination. The citizens were at the height of their tequila-nurtured fiesta spirit; the occasion symbolized the revolt of the masses against oppression; and now—climbing out on to the small, unprotected, second-floor platform in the full glare of hundreds of festive electric lights—was an iron-fisted dictator that many of the well-armed spectators below considered distinctly ill fitted for the task of ringing a liberty bell. Pondering these things, I climbed out on the platform in the wake of the President. Díaz wasted no time in posturing, but smote the bell with one hand, waved once to the populace with the other, intoned a hoarse "Viva Mexico," and was pushing past me to get back through the window before I had had a chance to brace myself for the Winchester slugs. No bullets were fired, however, and I felt that my own dignified retreat from the platform was the anti-climax of a thwarted martyr.

Mexican newspapers at that time were under strict censorship—as is always the case in dictatorships. As a natural consequence, Mexico City was filled with gossip and rumor.

This state of affairs affected us in an amusing way. Senator Guggenheim, a vice-presidential appointee, hadn't come down with the delegation because of a coming election and Representative Fairchild, for the same reason, left soon after his arrival. Inevitably a strong rumor spread about Mexico to the effect that we had had a terrific fight among ourselves, that Congressman Fairchild had killed Senator Guggenheim. The gossip continued that we had buried Senator Guggenheim at midnight in the patio of the Cobian Palace and hurried Congressman Fairchild out of the city. To those who believed these tales we must have seemed like very picaresque characters indeed.

The night before we left, there was a great ball in the National Palace. I bade good-by to Díaz and said to him, "Mr. President, when I come to Mexico again, I hope to speak better Spanish." Solemnly he answered, "When you come again, I am afraid I shall not be here. I have made two great mistakes. I have not introduced universal education soon enough, and I have not forced a division of land so that the people could become small proprietors. I have commenced this in the neighborhood of Lake Chapala, but I am afraid it is not soon enough."

At the banquet that evening Mrs. Gerard and I were seated at Díaz's table with about thirty others. Along the center of the table miniature electric bulbs were set in a bank of tropical flowers. I was told afterward that shortly before we went in to supper an electrician checked these lights and discovered a bomb under the table with two wires leading to the street outside.

President Díaz had predicted correctly, for shortly after our departure a revolution that had been smoldering during the centennial broke out. He was driven from Mexico, his train fired upon as he fled. He died an exile in Europe.

At the conclusion of the centennial I left Mexico City for Guadalajara, from where I would set out for our Cinco Minas mine. I had to wait several days in Guadalajara, and during that time was pleasantly entertained by the governor of the State of Jalisco, Señor Cuesta-Gallardo. Following Mexican custom, he did not invite me into his home, but entertained me at a restaurant, and afterward drove me around the streets and pointed out the sun-baked glories of the city.

I asked Cuesta-Gallardo how he had happened to become governor, and he told me the story with evident zest and satisfaction. The señor, it seems, had been a self-respecting haciendero with a good following. One day President Díaz arrived in the state with his entourage, and Cuesta-Gallardo, as an act of simple loyalty and devotion, rode out to meet him. As an additional mark of courtesy he took with him two thousand well-mounted men, armed to the teeth. Díaz was apparently a quick judge of character, for at the end of Cuesta's charming little welcoming compliments he immediately said, "Señor, I think you are just the person to be governor of Jalisco."

I went by train on the new Southern Pacific line from Guadalajara as far as it then had been built along the west coast of Mexico. There I got out and drove for some distance, and then mounted a mule for the rest of the journey to the Cinco Minas property. Crawford was installing the new mining equipment, beginning the development which enabled us to work the mine for sixteen or seventeen years. We took from it more than 33,333,369 ounces of silver and about 233,-495 ounces of gold. This, of course, was far from being all profit. The ore was low grade and from the value of the gold and silver produced was deducted the expense of production.

When I was in Germany in 1914 the United States Marines occupied Vera Cruz. This caused great resentment in Mexico and there was a riot at the camp. Of our staff of about twenty-eight Englishmen and Americans one was killed and the others had to leave. After three or four months, when things had quieted down, the American and English staff went back to the mine, expecting to find that the costly machinery had been destroyed. On the contrary, the miners had kept everything in apple-pie order and met the returning staff with a brass band.

When this news was cabled to me, I immediately cabled back, "For heaven's sake, buy the band a new set of instruments." It was done.

During the succeeding years of the revolution we had repeated trouble in Mexico, but managed never to lose an ounce of silver, although bandits sometimes laid siege to the mine. On one occasion a bandit chief put a pistol to the stomach of our engineer and demanded ten thousand pesos. He finally compromised for a pair of old shoes. The war cry of the bandits was, "Viva Christo Rey [Long Live Christ, the King]," for they mixed a little politics with their vocation and claimed to represent the Church party.

After the fall of Díaz I met the family of the new President, Francisco Madero, in New York, and often lined up the President's father and brother in the front row of the Ziegfeld *Follies,* which seemed to be the entertainment they enjoyed most. Don Francisco Padre, as the father of the President was called, was a Mexican of the finest type, who spoke French and had been educated at the University of Antwerp.

On our return from Mexico in 1910 I organized the Mexican Society, and we gave several banquets to visiting Mexican statesmen. But as the tempo of the successive revolutions increased, the turnover in statesmen became so great that the Society was swamped and soon fell into innocuous desuetude. My friendships with many of the leaders of Mexico kept on, however, despite the ebb and flow of their political fortunes.

CHAPTER XV

LATE IN 1911 IT BECAME APPARENT TO THOSE MORE OR LESS skilled in politics that the old Republican Guard would turn down the bid of Theodore Roosevelt and nominate someone else as the party's presidential candidate. Norman Hapgood was then the editor of *Collier's Weekly*, and I often met him as he rode his sorrel pony in Central Park. In the course of our conversations we agreed that it would be a bold and worthy stroke if Theodore Roosevelt were to be nominated on the Democratic ticket.

When I offered this suggestion to Charles F. Murphy, he immediately hailed it as a splendid idea. Such unorthodox tactics were no novelty to him. In a previous mayoral election he had taken the candidates for Comptroller and for president of the Board of Aldermen off the Republican ticket, and on their pledge to accept no other nomination, named them on the Democratic ticket and carried them to victory.

As our plan evolved, it was arranged that I was to write a brief article urging the Democrats to nominate Theodore Roosevelt. Hapgood agreed to print this on the cover of *Collier's* so that even those who did not buy the magazine, but merely saw it as it lay on the newsstands, could glance over this short article and be converted to its proposition.

It has been the custom for a long time, of course, for the Democrats to hold a dinner in Washington on January 13, the birthday of Andrew Jackson. In a presidential year this gathering affords an especially valuable opportunity for the exchange of views and for many intrigues. When the New York delegation arrived in Washington for the 1912 Jackson Day Dinner, Mr. Murphy and I were deep in conspiracy. "You sit with me in my room at the Shoreham Hotel on the day of the dinner," he said, "and when people come in and talk to me, I will say that you have a candidate. Then you can spring your Roosevelt proposal, and we'll see how they take it."

I think the first visitor was popular Mayor Fitzgerald of Boston, widely known as "Honey Fitz."

"Mr. Murphy," Honey began, "we have a splendid candidate in our governor, Governor Foss. You ought to consider him."

To this Murphy countered, "Well, Jim here has got a candidate. Go on, Jim, tell him about your candidate."

I then enlarged on the advantages of nominating Roosevelt on the Democratic ticket, but Fitzgerald was so nonplused by what he had heard that he seemed hardly to have strength to back gasping out of the room. We tried the idea on several others with about the same results, and finally Murphy concluded it was no use. "They have no imagination," he said. "Get your article back from *Collier's Weekly*. We'll have to call it off."

The result is history. Theodore Roosevelt was refused the nomination by the Old Guard. William Howard Taft was nominated, and the ensuing split in the Republican party when Roosevelt ran on the Bull Moose ticket resulted in the election of Woodrow Wilson. To this day I cannot tell just how strongly my idea appealed to Roosevelt. I had gone to

Washington several times to lunch with him, each time enthusiastically reporting on the plan to him. He didn't disapprove, but, as a then loyal Republican, he never gave it his formal approval.

Part of the summer of 1912—I was still a judge and had a two-month vacation—I spent in Ostend, while my wife visited her sister in Hungary. I went to Scotland for the "Glorious Twelfth" of August 1912 (Scots for "opening of the grouse season") with Lord Cowdray at his great stone castle, Dunecht, near Aberdeen. When I told Cowdray that one of my great-grandfathers had come from Aberdeen, he grinned and said: "I am going to make trouble for you. I am going to put that in the newspaper."

Soon afterward a paragraph to that effect did appear in an Aberdeen newspaper. In due time, just as my host had predicted, I received a letter from a man who said that he was a tobacconist. He demanded to be informed why I should be stopping with lords when he, descended from the same family, was forced to keep a small shop in Aberdeen. After some thought I wrote him that my great-grandfather had had the nerve to leave Aberdeen and seek his fortune in America. I suggested that he do the same.

I am indebted to Lord Cowdray for still another insight into the mental attitudes that prevailed in Great Britain. In the summer of 1911 I was one of a house party at his place south of London. One morning, as I lounged on the window seat of my room, I observed for the first time the strict caste system that exists—or did then—among the servants at large English country houses. As I gazed idly out the window, I was startled to hear a loud, authoritative voice calling imperiously for Judge Gerard.

"Judge Gerard!" shouted the voice. "Come here immediately."

By craning my neck I saw my valet trotting toward the voice, and it dawned on me that valets and maids were called by the names of their masters and mistresses, and took on the social ratings of those whom they served. Even in the servants' hall their seating at tables corresponded to that of their employers in the dining room. From the imperiousness of the voice it could not possibly have been less than the aide to a royal duke—perhaps even the major domo himself.

One hunting day I was sitting on a rock, waiting for a bird drive to commence and chatting with Lord Cowdray, when a confidential mood came upon him. He was at that time one of the richest men in England. After a lengthy account of his various properties and interests he added, "Do you know that there has never been a day in my life when I have not been kowtowing to somebody?" The climax of his talk was an offer to take me in as a partner in his contracting business. I was greatly tempted; it was a great compliment from so skillful a businessman.

He had in mind the construction of a great road which would traverse Cuba from end to end. Such a road later came into being, but I think that we would have done much better with the project than the contractors who afterward built it. The eventual cost to the Cuban Government was enormous. My consideration of this Cuban project went so far as a discussion with Cowdray and the Cuban Ambassador to this country one night in the St. Regis Hotel. But I had other irons in the fire, and I was forced to forego the idea of partnership, even though, as I say, I was vastly complimented. Cowdray's son, Clive Pearson, who carries on the business so successfully, did not inherit the title, being the younger son. Lady Cowdray, a most interesting and intelligent woman, was an example of how much a wife can help a man in his career. I know that Cowdray depended on her judgment of people and on her advice in all things.

After I left Scotland, some premonition, perhaps, induced me to visit Berlin, which I had never seen, and after a few days there I joined Mrs. Gerard in Paris, and returned to the United States.

I have related how I tried to make Theodore Roosevelt the Democratic nominee in 1912. The Democratic convention that year was held in Baltimore, and I took a house there, having brought with me some of my fellow judges, Judge Seabury and Judge McCall, as guests. Since a judge of the Supreme Court cannot hold any other office, and as in New York State delegates are officially elected, we couldn't be delegates to the convention. But there was nothing to keep us from being interested onlookers.

I was for Champ Clark, who was a splendid American. Clark was beaten in the convention by Woodrow Wilson. Possibly his defeat came about through his own bad judgment and that of his supporters. When he was leading in the vote, an adjournment was taken, even though Ollie James, the chairman, had warned the Clark supporters of the possible consequences. During this breathing spell provided by the recess, the Wilson partisans gathered such strength that Wilson became the nominee.

When an ambassador is appointed, the White House announcements are unctuously flattering and give no hint of the pulling and hauling, the promises and maneuvering, and the blasted hopes that have preceded the appointment. It is frequently more difficult to become a diplomat than it is to be one.

It had always been my ambition to be an ambassador, and after the election of President Wilson, in 1912, my desire was realized. President Wilson's decision to appoint me Ambassador to Germany was brought about, I think, by the friendly intervention of a combination of Tammany, Senator James A. O'Gorman of New York, William G. McAdoo, William F. McCombs, and William Jennings Bryan. Bryan, in particular, helped me because my father-in-law had so lavishly supported him in his '96 campaign. For a while Colonel E. M. House, the Harry Hopkins of the Wilson administration, very cleverly succeeded in persuading me that he had been the principal factor in my appointment, but this conviction wore off. The first offer to me was the post of minister to Spain, but I demurred. Senator O'Gorman telephoned me the advice to take Spain or I might get nothing. But I replied, "No, I want to be an ambassador or nothing." Then he told me that the Spanish post would be made an embassy, and on that basis I consented to accept it. Shortly after this talk I sailed for Europe without waiting for anything definite to be settled.

I have heard that a number of gentlemen whom Wilson had proposed to send to Germany were in each instance turned down by the Kaiser. It is the custom, of course, to appoint a man who is *persona grata* to the country to which he is to be sent. Finally someone close to the President said, "Well, let Gerard go to Germany and try his luck with that hoodoo job!"

The post had an unhappy reputation. At least two of the ambassadors who preceded me in Germany had gotten into some sort of a mess, although the fault was not their own. Ambassador Leishman, who immediately preceded me, was in disfavor in Berlin because his very attractive daughter had become engaged to one of the greatest catches of Germany, the Duke of Croy. Leishman had been employed by a large steel corporation presided over by H. A. Frick in Pittsburgh. When the anarchist Berkman attempted to assassinate Frick, it was Leishman who saved him by grabbing the knife which Berkman held. Leishman's own hand was severely cut in the process.

Ambassador Hill fared poorly because the Kaiser had once met Lloyd Griscom and his wife, and was most anxious to have them sent to Berlin. Poor Hill arrived disconsolate at his post, knowing that he was not the man the Kaiser wanted as American Ambassador.

I imagine the Kaiser found me acceptable because he thought I was a mere socialite who would do a lot of entertaining and not bother about Germany's ambitions. I understand that when Bernstorff returned to Germany in 1917, after America entered the war, the Kaiser reproached him for having passed favorably on my appointment and for not knowing that I could, when necessary, be rather hard-boiled. Of this, Bernstorff writes in his memoirs:

A further reason for his displeasure at the time was told me subsequently at Constantinople by the Kaiser himself. He said that I had "let him down most dreadfully" when I had recommended Mr. Gerard as American ambassador to Berlin.

I sailed for Europe to join Mrs. Gerard in Paris on the first eastern voyage of the great German liner *Imperator* (which, after the war, became the Cunard liner *Berengaria*). The ship was in mid-Atlantic when I received a wireless that I had been appointed Ambassador to Germany. I was asked to preside at the ship's concert, during which I made a short speech. It seemed most appropriate to speak in German. As

I was quite unfamiliar with the language, I composed my speech in English and then had it translated into German by Henry Morgenthau, Sr., who was soon to be our Ambassador to Turkey, who was also on board. Coached by Morgenthau, I managed to read the German version well enough to impart to most of my listeners the gist of my remarks.

Henry Morgenthau performed a great work in Turkey. After World War I and at the close of the war between the Turks and the Greeks, he was appointed to superintend the very difficult task of transferring Turks in Greece to Turkey and the Greeks in Turkey to Greece. This he did with great skill and tact, for which he has never been accorded adequate credit.

Mindful of my grandfather Angel's unprofitable experience with the United States Senate, I stayed in Paris and London until I had word that the Senate had confirmed my appointment. There was the inevitable delay while a southern senator, whose strict policy it was to fight the nomination of any person who had ever criticized the South, spent some time looking up my record in that particular. Happily, my past was spotless.

On the Fourth of July 1913, at an American banquet in Paris, I sat next to Edward Herriot, afterward Premier of France, mayor of Lyons, senator, et cetera, and one of the most prominent statesmen of France. In the course of our conversation he told me that he thought the French nation was over-civilized and over-refined. "What we need is a war," he proclaimed.

A year later his wish came true. During the bloodletting that France underwent during the ensuing four years, I occasionally recalled Herriot's remark, and wondered if the carnage was sufficient to satisfy his patriotic sentiments. Certainly, in retrospect, World War I did not appear to create a more virile and healthier France.

When Herriot visited this country during the early 1930s, New York's Mayor John P. O'Brien appointed me as a committee to receive him, so I boarded his ship and interpreted for him when the reporters fired questions at him. Before he left he gave a luncheon aboard a French liner and had me sit next to him. I had an engagement and had to leave early, so I asked him whom he wanted put in my place when I left. With true French grace he said, *"Votre souvenir."* Certainly the French can still most charmingly turn a compliment.

When, finally, my diplomatic appointment was confirmed, Mrs. Gerard and I went to Berlin and had a brief visit with Ambassador Leishman, who gave me wise counsel about the German court and officials. When he had gone over the ground, he added, with mock concern, "I have now some bad news for you. There is not a good-looking woman in all Germany. If you see one, she will undoubtedly be a foreigner."

I subsequently found that his gloomy prediction was not entirely correct, for there were quite a number of statuesque and handsome German women in Berlin. But in general he spoke truly, for the usual type looked as if it had been scrubbed with a stiff brush, starched and ironed, and an expression of contentment stenciled on.

We returned to America in July, and I resigned as a Supreme Court justice. I went immediately to Washington to take my oath as Ambassador, to receive my instructions from the State Department, and to thank President Wilson for my appointment. I had some difficulty finding out what my ambassadorial duties were. When I sought to question my new colleagues in the State Department, the usual reply was, "Oh, just go over and be an ambassador!" I *was* told, however, that

I would be expected to make a short speech when I presented my credentials to the Kaiser. Indeed, making short speeches, as I found out, is the most popular number in an ambassador's repertoire. Thus instructed, I prepared to leave for Germany in September.

After my preparations were complete, I went to Newport in August for a short stay. On the train going up was the Grand Duke Alexander of Russia, whose acquaintance I had made before. We spent the time in conversation, during which he said, "I am very sorry for you, Gerard. You are going to have a pretty hard time with those Germans; they are a hard people to get on with." At least he was more definite than the State Department.

CHAPTER XVI

Wﾟ

W HILE WAITING IN PARIS I HAD TEA ONE AFTERNOON WITH
Mrs. Charles Marshall of New York in her apartment, and
there met the ex-Queen Maria of the Two Sicilies, a person-
age who I had supposed had died long ago. Her husband, the
last King of the Two Sicilies, who had reigned in Naples over
southern Italy and Sicily, was driven from his throne by the
combined forces of Garibaldi and Victor Emmanuel. But the
last fight of this Bourbon king was ennobled by the magnificent defense of the Fortress of Gaeta by Queen Maria. As a
small boy I had seen, in a gallery in Munich, a large picture
of Queen Maria touching off a cannon in the course of her
brave battle. Meeting this tall and distinguished old lady in
real life was an experience comparable to being transported
back to the Court of King Arthur.

Much has been written about the drab, rundown little
structures that the rich United States provided, in the past,
for its diplomatic representatives in foreign capitals. In 1913
American ambassadors reporting for work did not find the
beautiful embassies that exist today, but were compelled to
lease houses at their own expense. When I arrived in Berlin
on October 6, 1913, I found that the United States Government had rented as an embassy for one of my predecessors,

Mr. Hill, a two-family apartment house ridiculously unsuitable as an embassy. By good luck I found that the old Hatzfeld Palace was vacant and I rented it for $16,000 a year —almost as much as my salary of $17,500. In addition to the building's imposing appearance, it had the advantage of being excellently located on the Wilhelm-Platz. Across the square was the Chancellor's palace and next to that was the Foreign Office. This proximity proved extremely useful after the war broke out, for it soon became necessary for me to consult with the Foreign Office at all hours.

Not for more than a month after my arrival in Berlin was I able to present my letters of credence to the Kaiser. On the appointed day, however, he sent, to convey me and my staff, several carriages with glass sides and white-wigged coachmen, just the kind which Cinderella's fairy godmother provided to take her to the ball. The Kaiser received me and my staff in the Royal Palace in Berlin. The better to impress us, he was dressed in the striking black uniform of the Death's Head Hussars. With the grim skull and crossbones insignia on the front of his busby and his up-pointed mustache, he looked very fierce indeed. There is a story that one of the kings of Prussia, coming back to the palace from his father's funeral, found the rooms hung with quantities of black cloth and decorated with skulls and crossbones—apparently in tribute to the departed. His thrifty soul revolted at the waste, and he declared, so the story goes, "There is cloth enough here to uniform a regiment." This thought grew on him, and, after a decent mourning interval, he had the cloth made into uniforms and thus called into being the celebrated Death's Head Hussars.

The Kaiser had refused to receive my predecessor because of his dissatisfaction with the marriage of the latter's daugh-

ter to the Duke of Croy. So I presented not only my letters
of credence, but my predecessor's letters of recall. Then, as
directed by the State Department, I made a little speech
stressing the "great work for peace" accomplished by the
Kaiser.

During the winter a friend of mine had informed me that
the Kaiser had designed the chapel in the recently completed
castle at Posen. He suggested that if I wished to please the
Kaiser, I should visit that chapel. The scheme was simple:
"The next time you see him, the Kaiser will ask what you have
been doing lately. You will say that you have been visiting a
most beautiful chapel, and he will say, 'Where?' and then you
will say, 'In the castle at Posen,' and then you will be in good
with him—ja!" The plan seemed so unlikely that I decided to
try it. So—tongue in cheek—and accompanied by Allison
Armour of Chicago, a great friend of all those connected with
the German Court as well as the royal family; Mrs. Ernest
Wiltsee, an American who afterward became Princess Bittetto; Mr. and Mrs. Robert K. Cassatt and Mrs. Gerard, I
descended on Posen. Some German acquaintances tried to
play a joke on us by recommending that we stop at a certain
hotel. Had we done so we would have found ourselves
marked as Polish sympathizers, for I soon found that the town
of Posen was divided into two camps. There were Polish and
German hotels, shops, cafés, newspapers, and so on. If a Pole
went into a German shop, the Polish newspapers next day
would say, "Who is this traitor to Polish tradition who
bought a pair of sneakers yesterday in a German shop?" Conversely, a German would be accused of treachery to the
Fatherland if he bought so much as a pencil in a Polish shop.

The Kaiser had built this castle in Posen thinking to please
the Polish population, but I was told that on the night the

castle was opened with a great ball, the Polish people standing in the streets threw ink through the windows of the carriages going to the ball.

My Posen expedition, however, was a great success and turned out as my German friend had predicted. Shortly after my return I met the Kaiser at some ceremony, and he asked politely about my recent activities. I replied, "I have been seeing a most beautiful chapel." He asked where, and I said in the castle at Posen, whereupon he twirled his mustachios with great satisfaction and exclaimed "Ha!" several times. I will give him credit, however, for having designed what I thought was a really beautiful chapel.

Certain statements of the Kaiser, made before my arrival, led me to believe that he was a fierce, Attila-like ruler. Actually, Kaiser Wilhelm at heart was rather a good-natured man with a fierce front. He was very vain and inclined to swagger, and his statements sometimes shocked the statesmen of Europe. One of his remarks, for instance, went like this: "I have been influenced by five men: Alexander the Great, Julius Caesar, Theodoric II, Frederick the Great, and Napoleon. Each of these men dreamed a dream of world empire. They failed. I have dreamed a dream of German world empire and my mailed fist shall succeed."

I found Wilhelm less fierce than these words would indicate—he had dreams of world conquest perhaps, but those dreams were vague and unformed. For all his saber-rattling, I think he felt—as Marshal Foch later told me the French felt—that "war was a dangerous adventure."

On the Kaiser's birthday, January 27, 1914, I arranged to have our embassy building on the Wilhelm-Platz illuminated with lines of electric lights. No other embassy did this, and I heard afterward that the Kaiser was quite pleased by the compliment. After a religious service in the palace on the morning of that day, all of the ambassadors stood in a circle, and the Kaiser made the rounds, speaking a few words to each. He talked to me for quite a long time, and in the course of the conversation warned me that we in America ought to look out, that Mexico was full of Japanese colonels, all working against us. He also said that he had done everything possible to make friends with France, but since the French didn't seem to want his friendship, they would have to beware, as something might happen in the future. Of course his overtures to the French, whatever they were, did not include the sorest point of all between the two nations, the return of Alsace-Lorraine.

It is a commentary on our scant knowledge of things European that I had been, as set forth in my commission, appointed Ambassador to a place which did not exist. The President, under his hand and seal, had named me as Ambassador to Germany. Technically, there was no such place as Germany. There was the German Empire, which was made up of twenty-two separate kingdoms, grand duchies, duchies, and principalities, and the three free cities of Hamburg, Lubeck, and Bremen. There was also the former French territory of Alsace-Lorraine, which, at the end of the Franco-Prussian War, had been awarded to Prussia. Each one, except Alsace-Lorraine, had its own ruler, some had constitutions, and each of them sent a full diplomatic representation to the Kaiser's court in Berlin. One at least, the Grand Duchy of Mecklenburg-Strelitz, had no constitution at all. The Grand Duke was an absolute ruler. By his mere order he could cause the execution or imprisonment of any one of his subjects.

The German Emperor ruled all of these units through the Chancellor, who was appointed by him, and through the chiefs of the General Staff, the Marine Cabinet, and the Civil Cabinet. Each of these appointed the personnel of their respective departments. The country was civilly governed by functionaries appointed from above.

There was a little similarity between our American political structure and the German, for these kingdoms vaguely corresponded to our forty-eight states. But over all was the Kaiser, who was not Emperor of Germany, but German Emperor.

Two typical examples will show what a Cloud-Cuckoo-Land Germany was under its emperor. At the head of the alphabetical list of German states was *Anhalt*. This was a duchy, a constitutional and hereditary monarchy. This little duchy of about eight hundred and eighty-eight square miles had at the head:

> The Duke with a Minister of State
> President of the Chamber of the Court
> Grand Master of the Court
> Grand Master of the Horse
> Grand Master of the Court of the Duchess
> Marshal of the Court
> Two Court Huntsmen
> Grand Mistress of the Robes
> Ladies of the Court of the Duchess
> A Seneschal
> An Intendant of the Theater and Chapel of the Court
> An Aide-de-Camp
> Grand Marshal of the Court of the late Dowager Duchess
> Ladies of the Court of the Princess

And at the end of the alphabetical list was *Wurttemberg,* a kingdom—a constitutional monarchy hereditary in male posterity, which, in addition to supporting a king, maintained such hereditary dignitaries of the Crown as:

> Hereditary Marshal of the Kingdom
> Hereditary Grand Master of the Court
> Hereditary Banneret of the Court
> Chancellor of the Orders
> Head of the Cabinet of the King
> Councillor of the Court
> Superior and Second Preacher of the Court
> First Doctor of the Court
> Royal Directors and corresponding Marshal of the Buildings and Gardens of the Court Library and Court Theater
> An Aide-de-Camp
> Ladies of the Court for the Princess and Princesses
> Minister of State
> Privy Council
> Upper and Lower Chamber, constituting the local legislature and with ministries of war, foreign affairs, finance, interior, justice, education, and so forth, its army forming the Thirteenth Army Corps of the Army of the German Emperor.

Each of the little kingdoms, duchies, and principalities had a similar organization, although in some of them, as I have said, there was no legislature whatever.

Many foreign countries accredited ministers to these local courts. The English Ambassador in Berlin was accredited to a large number. The local rulers were very jealous of this and resented the fact that the Ambassador of Turkey and I were not accredited to any of the German states. The King of

Saxony, thus frustrated, made it a point to ask that the newly arrived ambassadors of Turkey and of the United States of America be presented to him. This gave him the opportunity to enjoy his privilege of refusing to shake hands with them on the ground that they had not been accredited to Saxony. I remember when it happened to me. It was on the Emperor's birthday in 1914, during the interval between the acts at the gala celebration at the opera. The King of Saxony asked that I be presented to him, a command that I could not have refused even if I had wanted to. When I put out my hand, he put his behind his back and fairly bristled with self-satisfaction and righteousness. A German friend asked me later how I had gotten on with the King. "All right," I said, "except that I can't understand him." My friend said, "Don't mind that; neither can we." The King spoke a Saxon dialect that was almost incomprehensible to the Germans of the North, who spoke pure German, the language of Hanover.

All of these states named delegates who formed the Bundesrat, or Imperial Council, in which they had a varying number of votes, Prussia having the largest. In a general way this body corresponded to our Senate. The Emperor could not, for example, declare an offensive war without the consent of this Council. Then there was the Reichstag, or Parliament, the members of which were elected by male suffrage.

In the Kingdom of Prussia there was a House of Lords and a Chamber of Deputies, the members of the latter being elected by a peculiar system of circle voting. The population was divided into circles according to wealth, a system which made it possible for a very rich man, voting all by himself in circle number one, to have as many votes as ten thousand people voting in circle number three.

It is important to remember that the population of the

great part of Germany had been absolute serfs until a recent period. For instance, in Mecklenburg-Strelitz the people were not freed from serfdom until about 1817, at the time my grandfather had been practicing law in New York for five years. Therefore the transition to the autocratic rule of Hitler, after a short Republic experiment, was a comparatively easy change from the Germany of before the last war with its circle voting, its recently freed serfs, its states with no constitution whatever.

Augustus Caesar, who inherited, as it were, the dictatorship of his Uncle Julius, never would accept the title of "king." The word "emperor" is derived from the Latin word "imperator" or "commander of the troops," the title by which the Caesars were known, and the family name of Caesar is the basis of the words "Czar" and "Kaiser" in the central empires. Always, from the time of Augustus and for many centuries afterward, the fiction of the Roman Republic was that consuls, tribunes, and senate governed at Rome. Actually, as in the Kaiser's Germany, absolute power of the Praetorian Guard, which later made and unmade the rulers of the Roman Empire, was paralleled in Germany by the rule of the General Staff. This group never went so far as to assassinate or elect an emperor but nevertheless exercised at times, especially in war, the balance of power.

No dictators, as a rule, burst suddenly into being, but acquire power gradually. There are countless examples of this in history; one of the more recent, perhaps, being Napoleon III. He was first elected a deputy after the Revolution of 1848 had driven out Louis Philippe. Then he became President, later Prince President, and finally, by his *coup d'état* with the aid of the Army, made himself Emperor and secured the suffrage of the people of France by promising that the

Empire meant peace. I am convinced that if dictatorship ever comes to America it will be in the guise of preserving us from some catastrophe, internal or external, real or pretended.

The nobility of the Central Empires was quite numerous because by custom every son of a prince or duke or count usually held the same title, as did his children also, and so forth ad infinitum. Moreover, some counts in Germany ranked ahead of princes—a circumstance which will illustrate the difficulties of arranging place cards for a formal dinner.

This confusion of titles and precedence was rooted in the history of middle Europe. After the Napoleonic Wars, and the destruction of the ancient Holy Roman Empire, many of the nobles who had ruled over little states were "mediatized" when their states disappeared as political entities. This meant that those nobles, in their quality of head of a state within the Holy Roman Empire, were given the right of equality of birth with the royal houses. Thus a mediatized noble could marry royalty or a commoner, and in either case the marriage would be legal not only in law but also for transmission of a title. It is well known that many titles in Germany and Austria had their origin in the love affairs of various monarchs and princes. These origins, while possibly a little irregular, are not, of course, exclusive with the German nobility. Four of England's proudest dukes are descendants of various mistresses of Charles II: the Duke of Buccleugh is descended from Charles and Lucy Walters; the Duke of Richmond from Charles's French mistress, Louise de Keroualle, who was sent to England by Louis XIV for the express purpose of fascinating the Merry Monarch; the Duke of St. Albans is descended from the little orange seller, Nell Gwyn; and the Duke of Grafton owes his title to Barbara Villiers, who was still another of Charles's playmates.

The Count Neipperg, who belonged to a mediatized house, ranked ahead of the Duke of Courland, as did also Counts Platen and Fugger. The Dukes of Courland were descended from one Biron, who was only a cook but who had succeeded nevertheless in winning the affections of an empress of Russia. After the fall of Napoleon, his wife Marie Louise lived with a Count Neipperg in a duchy which had been given to her in Italy. When she sought from the Emperor of Austria the right of her children by Neipperg to bear their father's name, the Emperor refused, but he said they might call themselves Princes of Montenuovo, that being the Italian translation of the old German word Neipperg, which means New Mount, or Neu Berg.

The Counts Fugger were the descendants of the great bankers of Augsburg. The Velzers, another banking house, once owned the whole country of Venezuela as the result of a loan transaction with the Emperor Charles V. The Fuggers were among the most powerful bankers of the Middle Ages and had their own representatives in all the countries of Europe. The regular confidential reports that these representatives were required to send to the main office always included the local gossip and scandals, as well as business reports, and are fascinating reading.

During my first winter in Berlin I found that Germany was so well organized for war that even the social life was regimented. At a pre-1914 court ball the magnates of the Empire were ranged according to rank on one side of the ballroom and the diplomats on the other side, the wives of the ambassadors being seated. When everyone was in his proper niche, the Emperor and Empress, accompanied by the princes and princesses, made their entry. Prominent in their train was a six-foot-six guardsman in high boots, silver breastplate, and a silver helmet surmounted by a silver eagle. Next came the royal huntsman wearing a long, green-brocaded coat, a white wig, and a three-cornered hat and carrying a spear with a silver head. Finally, an array of princes and officers in uniforms of all colors closed the procession. This impressive array then "made the circle" of the room, the Emperor taking one side and the Empress the other. They talked for a few moments to the ambassadors on one side and the dukes, duchesses, chief of staff, and so forth, on the other. After this was over, the imperial couple sat on the dais to watch the dancing. The dances were formally stylized and had been carefully rehearsed by the young ladies and officers who took part in them.

Late hours were unknown, for nothing was allowed to interfere with the efficiency of the young officers who had to rise at an early hour for drill. At any court ball, for instance, we were required to be in the ballroom at a quarter after eight, and the affair was over about a quarter of eleven. At a beautiful ball given by the Crown Prince and Princess, and at which we were the only diplomats invited, Mrs. Gerard and I arrived at nine o'clock, sat down to a three-course cold dinner, then went up to the ballroom. At eleven o'clock a supper was served and the ball was over.

Even the Presentation Court commenced at about eight o'clock. This court was popularly known as the *Schleppen Cour* (from the word which means a tow, as of boats) because the ladies, on their stately passage around the throne room, literally towed long trains, many of them easily ten or twelve feet in length. Pages dressed in white stood at the corners of the room with long sticks in their hands with which to straighten out the trains of the ladies as they made the turns. Mrs. Gerard's dress was of gold cloth and her train was of green velvet with gold bowknots scattered on it and trimmed with silver fox.

The Emperor and Empress were seated on thrones, on a large raised dais with steps on which were grouped the royal family and the highest dignitaries of the Court. Mrs. Gerard had to stand in front of the dais and announce in a loud voice the names of the ladies she was presenting. These ladies made their stately progress across the room about twenty-five feet from the dais and made low curtsies to the throne as their names were called.

I then presented the men, calling out their names like a butler as each made a bow. Each person presented, after his bow or curtsy, backed out of the room and Mrs. Gerard followed the ladies and I the men. When I had left, another embassy went through a similar process. We presented Mrs. Luce and Miss Luce (no relation to the celebrated writer and ex-congresswoman), Mrs. Robert K. Cassatt of Philadelphia, Mrs. Ernest Wiltsee, who is now the Princess Bittetto, and Mrs. Norman Whitehouse. All these ladies were handsome and beautifully gowned, and I was afterward told that the Emperor was quite pleased. The Kaiser tried very hard to make the German Court as smart and impressive as the British Court, but could never quite bring it off with the inimitable British flavor. In the same way, his Kiel Regatta was never more than an awkward imitation of Cowes. He asked me once why more foreigners did not come to Berlin in the short season, but I imagine he knew the reason.

These 1914 court ceremonies were the last to be held in Germany. Not being accredited to the lesser German courts, I never visited them. Most of the provincial kings and princes suffered from an acute inferiority complex and were uncomfortable in their jealously guarded royal prerogative. I was told that in Saxony the King and Queen sat at a table playing cards while the court and people to be presented filed past them making low curtsies and bows, the royal pair apparently paying no attention to the proceedings. When we were in Germany there was no Queen of Saxony, the royal consort—who was born an Austrian archduchess—having eloped with her children's tutor. The members of the Austrian imperial family have always been notorious for their wild love affairs.

CHAPTER XVII

Delicate diplomatic duties confronted me during my first winter in Berlin. I sought to persuade the Germans to sign the so-called Bryan peace treaties, which provided that the nations pledge themselves to negotiate for one year before resorting to war. Foreign Minister von Jagow declined, telling me frankly that Germany's greatest asset was her readiness for sudden assault. Germany had no objection to signing such a treaty with the United States, he assured me, but if they did so other powers would ask similar agreements. If they signed with other powers, privately willing to disregard the treaties and commence a lightning war, they would be convicted of bad faith. If they refused to sign, the refusal would be almost equivalent to an admission that they contemplated war. It was a complex problem.

About this time the Germans made an attempt to create a government monopoly of oil. Their plan was to take over the properties of the American Standard Oil Company, condemning them just as we would exercise the right of eminent domain over land needed for a park. Standard Oil's president hastened to Germany for a conference with me, but I was obliged to tell him that nothing could be done to halt the seizure, provided compensation was paid. I softened the blow by confiding to him a helpful idea. My proposal was that the German Government must not only compensate the company for its plants, but also for its good will, the value of which would be determined from the company's earnings.

When I advanced this claim, the Chancellor said in astonishment, "You don't mean to say that President Wilson and Secretary Bryan would do anything for the Standard Oil Company!" My answer was that my instructions, as well as my principles, required that I give all American citizens the same protection, regardless of whether they were friendly to the Wilson administration. The result was that the projected seizure of the Standard Oil Company plants was dropped. The oil company had to agree, however, to keep a specified large amount of lubricating oil and gasoline always in storage in Germany. This was an obvious preparation for the approaching war.

Under the domination of the Prussian military caste the government was acutely war conscious, despite the dissatisfaction of the mass of the German people with the militarism of their rulers. An occurrence significant of this popular resentment was the Zabern Affair. Troops garrisoned in the Alsatian town of Zabern became embroiled with the townspeople and a lieutenant cut down a lame shoemaker. In the anti-military riots that followed, the Military inadvertently arrested the President, the judges, and the state attorney of the local Supreme Court, all of whom had been caught in the crowd. The lieutenant who had slashed the shoemaker with his sword, a young and typically zealous officer-caste product, was sentenced by a court-martial to a year's imprisonment. But a higher military court then acquitted him on the ground that he had acted in "self-defense." The Social Democrat members of the Reichstag who represented the mass of the people immediately attacked the Chancellor, Von Bethmann-Hollweg, and for the first time a vote of censure against the Chancellor was passed in the Reichstag.

Other countries never grasped the significance of this affair, but it caused great excitement in Germany and showed the government that the people were in a mood to turn away from extreme militarism. This rapidly growing pacifist sentiment was, I believe, one of the reasons that led the rulers of Germany to force the nation into war in 1914, before pacifism became too powerful to resist.

During this period the upper classes were kept in line by a system of orders and distinctions. One honorary title was that of counselor. A man attaining some eminence in law, architecture, finance, or commerce was given the title of counselor, and later—if he had been a good boy—he became a Privy Counselor, still later a Court Counselor, and eventually he might be given the title of Excellency. If a businessman or lawyer did not obtain one of these titles after a certain period in life, the suspicion grew that something subversive was hidden in his past, for of course no one who opposed the government received one of these official distinctions. Such a stigma would distress his family and hurt his business. Beside the title of counselor and its variations there were a number of decorations and orders in Prussia. The Order of the Black Eagle was chief of the list and then came the Order of Merit, the Order of the Red Eagle, the Order of the Crown, and the Order of the House of Hohenzollern. In addition, each of the little kingdoms, dukedoms, and principalities also had its decorations and medals. All of these tinsel distinctions served to placate and discipline the people and keep them subservient.

But if there were many rewards for the loyal and faithful,

there was also severe punishment for those who set themselves in opposition to the Hohenzollern rule. There was a crime called *lèse-majesté,* which might be translated as "contempt of majesty." Under its provisions, critics in the Empire were prosecuted. For instance, a writer who had criticized the conduct of an ancestor of the Kaiser in connection with the election of the Emperor Charles V in 1519 was convicted of lèse-majesté for this reflection on the Emperor's forebear.

One of my first concerns, naturally, was to become as familiar as possible with the German language, the people, and the customs. The appallingly complex political organization of the Empire was no small bite to digest, and the language, with its wide, sectional variations of idiom and pronunciation, also took a lot of work. Inevitably I had to look to Germany's past to help me understand many puzzling aspects of its present. In the years since 1913 I have constantly been struck with the importance of the effect of Germany's bitter history on her actions and her national mental attitudes.

As a unified nation Germany was not very old, and her population is not homogeneous. Many important elements of the population are not of Germanic stock. In Prussia, for example, the mass of the population are descendants of Slavs who were conquered by the Teutonic Knights. Thirty miles up the River Spree from Berlin is a country where, protected by forests, canals, and marshes, there was a colony of the original inhabitants of Germany before the coming of the warlike Knights. There are the Wends, still speaking their ancient Wendish language, in addition, of course, to German.

There is no doubt that the numerous wars which have swept over Germany through the centuries had a psychological effect upon the German people, producing fear and with it a sense of inferiority, only partly compensated by an air of braggadocio and a will to conquer.

The old Holy Roman Empire, which disintegrated in the wars of Napoleon in 1806, was at that time headed by the House of Austria. After this dissolution the old Empire assumed the title of Emperor of Austria for its head. From 1806 until the King of Prussia was proclaimed German Emperor in 1870 there was neither Emperor of Germany nor German Emperor. The old Empire in 1806 consisted of more than three hundred separate dukedoms and principalities and was aptly said by Voltaire to be "neither Holy, nor Roman, nor Empire."

For a long time the emperors of the Holy Roman Empire fought to rule Italy, and were constantly at war in Germany and in Italy with the party that took the side of the Pope. The Pope's partisans took their name from the Castle of Welf, while the members of the opposing or Germanic Imperial party were known as the Ghibellines. About the year 1268 the combined forces of the Pope and the French had it out with the last of the Hohenstaufens, defeated him in southern Italy, and beheaded him. After this, the Hapsburg emperors who succeeded the Hohenstaufens withdrew behind the mountains and ceased to take such an active interest in the affairs of Italy. There is a memorable little sidelight on history in the story of the siege of the Castle of the Welfs by the Emperor Conrad, to whom the garrison surrendered. The Emperor, however, promised that each woman might carry out what valuables she could. When the gates were opened and the women of the besieged stronghold appeared, each one had her husband on her back. The Emperor Conrad, urged by his generals to seize the husbands, replied, "An emperor must keep his word," and so the women of Welf saved their husbands.

Again, at the time when Charles V was Emperor and Luther opposed him, religious wars swept over Germany, but it was in the Thirty Years' War that the German lands suffered the greatest damage. This war lasted from 1618 to 1648. The conquering Swedes invaded from the north and the Catholic armies of Tilly and Wallenstein swept over Germany from the south. In this holocaust the population of Germany was reduced from twenty-four millions to four millions. Only the ruthless survived, and this had an effect, I am convinced, on the German character. It was after this war that polygamy was legalized, even priests being permitted several wives in the endeavor to restore the population. Human flesh was on sale in the butcher shops of Heidelberg.

Then, in the eighteenth century, came the wars of Frederick the Great, and following them the wars of Napoleon. In 1866 Prussia and the small northern German states allied with Italy, defeated Austria, assisted by Saxony, Bavaria, Wurttemberg, Hanover, Nassau, Hesse-Cassel, and Hesse-Darmstadt. Just before the war of 1866 Prussia waged a successful war against Denmark for possession of the duchies of Schleswig and Holstein. This was followed by the blitz war of 1870 that resulted in the defeat of France and the capture of the French Emperor, Napoleon III, in a few months.

War is inbred in the German people, and thereby it came about that the war-minded German General Staff held the greatest power. This was true until the rise of Adolf Hitler, but it is significant that he attained supreme power by being more frenzied and maniacal in his belligerence than the General Staff. His internal conquest would have been impossible otherwise.

After World War I the army of Germany, by the Treaty of Versailles, was reduced to 100,000 men. The German generals made this small army the training corps for the army of experts which took only six weeks to conquer France in the spring of 1940. It was history over again. After the Battle of Jena in 1806 and the fall of Prussia before Napoleon, the Prussian Army was reduced to 40,000 men. A great part of the population was successively passed through this army for training, and contributed mightily to the fall of Napoleon in 1813 and at the Battle of Waterloo after Napoleon returned from Elba.

In 1913 everything in Germany was subordinated to preparation for war. The high consideration given to the officers and even to the men of the Army showed the set of the national mind. Control of the Army was kept in the old Prussian military families. Even in the last war the high officers of the Army usually had the "Von," the name-symbol of the Prussian *Junker* class, before their names, although the Nazi regime made it possible for qualified men in the ranks to be graduated into the commissioned groups.

In the spring of 1914 Colonel House came to Berlin to see the Kaiser and stayed with us in the embassy. I had the greatest difficulty in explaining to the Germans, who are precise about matters of status, exactly what his position was. Although he had no political office whatever, he represented President Wilson just as if he were the Grand Vizier of the Caliph of Baghdad. And although his title of colonel was honorary, deriving from an appointment to the staff of a state governor, the Germans, to whom a military title is a sacred thing, were convinced that he was some sort of military man.

Thus, when I insisted that House be given an audience with the Kaiser, they arranged the meeting at a military ceremony held in Potsdam in May. In a way this was fortunate, for as a military man House was bound to merit more respect in the Teutonic mind than he would have received had they suspected he was a mere politician.

Colonel House and I were invited to Potsdam on the day of the *Schrippen Fest*. Ever since the time of Frederick the Great, a body of picked troops stationed at Potsdam was honored with a lunch each year at which the soldiers ate *Schrippen*, which are white rolls, instead of the usual black bread, and were visited by their Emperor and his staff. Afterward Colonel House and I were feasted in the company of the Kaiser and about sixty of the military dignitaries of the Empire in the distractingly awful Shell Hall, as it was called, in the then new Potsdam palace. The chamber was called the Shell Hall because in its plaster walls were embedded stones and shells collected from all over the world. The Emperor was in excellent spirits during the luncheon. At one point he looked across the table at the colonel and me, who were arrayed in dress suits amid all the brilliant regalia of the sixty officers, and commented that we looked like a couple of undertakers—"indeed, a couple of crows"—and that we spoiled the picture.

After luncheon the Kaiser talked for a while with Colonel House. On this occasion the Kaiser proposed an alliance of Germany, England, and the United States for the purpose of keeping the peace. Of course nothing came of this; the stage was already set for the opening of the Great War.

I also arranged for a meeting of the colonel with the Chancellor, the Minister of Foreign Affairs, and many others, and the renowned Admiral von Tirpitz came to our house to dinner. The Emperor had instituted at Kiel his imitation of the Cowes yachting week, and in the summer of 1914 Mrs. Gerard and I were invited by Allison Armour to spend this week at Kiel with him on board his yacht the *Utowana*. Naturally, the arrival of the Kaiser aboard his yacht *Hohenzollern* required an appropriate setting. To this end all the warships and yachts in the long, narrow harbor were arranged in line, with the sailors lined up manning the rails. When all was ready, the Kaiser's large yacht made its entrance. On the top bridge stood the Kaiser. He presented a most surprising spectacle. He was dressed in tight white breeches, white coat, high black boots that came halfway up his thighs, a shining silver breastplate, and a silver helmet surmounted by an eagle. He carried an enormous sword, and, as the ultimate oddity, wore spurs! Nothing could be more indicative of the Kaiser's character than this attire adopted to inaugurate a peaceful yachting week.

That evening, after dinner on the *Hohenzollern*, the Kaiser drew me over to the rail and muttered, "Did you see what those fellows did to me the other day in the Reichstag?" He was referring to an episode at the recent adjournment of the parliament. The custom was to call for cheers for the Emperor. Usually the Social Democrats politely left the chamber before cheers were proposed. This time they had remained in their seats, refusing to rise. "Pretty soon," the Kaiser continued, "something will start that will fix those fellows." Of course he meant the war, but I thought that he merely had in mind more repressive measures against the Social Democrats.

On Sunday afternoon launches darted like dragonflies over the waters at Kiel, heralding the fact that the heir to the Austrian throne had been assassinated at Sarajevo.

The Kaiser left early Monday, but insisted that the festivities continue, presided over by his brother, Prince Henry.

The next evening Mrs. Gerard and I dined with the Prince of Monaco on his yacht. Everyone among the brilliant gathering appeared to believe that the assassination would not bring war. Upon my return to Berlin, I found all the diplomats unanimous in believing that, in spite of the strong action taken by Austria against Serbia, everything would be negotiated and war avoided.

On July 31 Mrs. Gerard and I lunched at the Hotel Bristol, a gathering place for the diplomats in Berlin. The Turkish ambassador, Mouktar Pascha, who was celebrated among the diplomats in Berlin for always being wrong in his predictions, was also lunching there. I went over to his table and asked him what the outcome was to be. He assured me that everything would be settled and that there would be no war. Therefore, "coppering," as it were, his prediction, I went immediately to our embassy and cabled to Washington as follows:

"Germany's efforts for peace having failed a general European war is absolutely inevitable."

The phrase about "Germany's efforts for peace" was added on the likely assumption that the Germans were familiar with our cipher.

CHAPTER XVIII

THE BRIEF TIME THAT SEPARATED MY ARRIVAL IN BERLIN in October 1913 and the outbreak of war the following August gave me only a fleeting opportunity to learn my new job and to become familiar with the people and customs of Germany. It was particularly necessary, of course, for me to know the leading figures in the government and in Berlin society, and I devoted the peaceful winter of 1913–14 largely to that duty. With spring came the tension of the impending war, and with summer, the war itself. After that there was little social life and little or no free time in which to enjoy it.

The first time I went to the Royal Palace I was tremendously impressed, as I climbed the great staircase, by the guard of honor drawn up at the top with kettledrums and trumpets. Each member of the guard was dressed in the uniform of the era of Frederick the Great, with long white gaiters, cocked hat, and white wig. Just as I was about to approach this guard, I heard a friendly voice behind me say, *"Ah, guten Abend, Excellenz,"* and discovered an extra waiter who had officiated at *Tafeldecker* in our house, standing at the head of the stairs in the Kaiser's livery. The fact that the divinely appointed Kaiser hired extra waiters like anybody else gave me renewed confidence to face the formal guard of honor, who were drawn up in formidable array, rumbling their kettledrums at the approach of an ambassador.

An enormous American Negro named Bronson called on me one day with some small request, and noting his fine appearance and great height I thought I would impress the Germans by hiring him as a second porter to stand at the door. However, after a week or two I was obliged to dismiss him. I found he had initiated my German servants into a game known as "craps," and was proceeding to extract their life savings from them—a serious thing to do to a German. Shortly afterward, a handsome German girl called at my office. When I asked her mission, she inquired for the whereabouts of Mr. Bronson, and when I asked her why she was interested she said, "He is my best young man." The ordinary Germans had not yet been converted to delusions about the purity of the master race.

Every ambassador in Berlin had a porter who, on state occasions, wore a long coat with a baldrick across his chest and an enormous cocked hat. He carried a baton like a drum major's, with which he rapped on the floor a certain number of times on the arrival of each distinguished guest. Also, every prince and ambassador had what was called his *Leib-jäger*, or body huntsman, who was dressed in green broadcloth, carried a beautiful gold dagger in his belt, and wore a cocked hat—in our case with red, white, and blue plumes. His undress uniform was made of green cloth with the traditional Tyrolean hat with a chamois tail at the back.

There were, of course, a number of extra-wealthy Germans in Berlin, but their fortunes in general were not so large as those of the very rich Americans and English. Frau Krupp-Bohlen, apparently the richest person in Germany, possessed a capital of about $70,000,000. For second place it was a race between Prince Henkel-Donnersmarck and the Kaiser, who were each worth about $60,000,000.

When we first arrived in Berlin, we were required by custom to give two receptions. One was for the enormous diplomatic body in Berlin, which included, as I have related, not only representatives from all the countries of the world, but from the twenty-two German states and three free cities as well. The second reception was for all those people who were called *hoffaehig*, or "fit for Court." The hoffaehig group consisted of the Prussian military caste, the old landowning families, and the numerous provincial nobility, and were, almost without exception, an egregiously dull and uninspiring lot. Rigidly excluded from this group were the commercial magnates, the manufacturers, artists of all sorts, writers, publishers—in short, the really worth-while and interesting individuals in Germany. To meet these people I had to seek them myself outside of diplomatic or court circles.

At the second reception the officers of the Army were introduced to me by a special officer sent by the Military, while the others were introduced by an official known as the "Introducer of Ambassadors." Possibly knowing what was in store for me, the army officer whose duty it was to introduce the army officers at our reception was a gentleman bearing the extraordinary name of *Der Pfoertner von der Hoelle,* "the porter of hell."

As I say, I made a point in Berlin of meeting not only the members of the Government, the Court, and Berlin society, but the prominent people in the business and even theatrical world. I dined one night during the war with Herr Fuerstenberg, who was head of a large bank, and I had the pleasure of sitting next to a young actress whose name I have forgotten, but who had visited America before the war in a pantomime of Reinhardt's *Sumurun*. She had played the part of the Beautiful Slave of Fatal Enchantment. Evidently she thought that her training in fatal enchantment would extract secrets from me, and she did her best during dinner, posing some extraordinary questions.

This reminds me of an occasion when I was going to inspect a prison camp a hundred miles from Berlin. I was in a private compartment on the train, and the conductor came to me just as we left Berlin and asked if I had any objection to his putting a lady in my compartment, since the train was crowded. I naturally agreed, but later, when I had occasion to pass along the corridor, I noticed that there were empty compartments. When the lady arrived—she proved to be an attractive blonde—she dropped her handkerchief (the traditional little square of cambric), her purse, and many other movables in her possession in order to attract my attention, but I remained hidden behind a newspaper. A few days afterward I told an officer friend who was in the General Staff that if they wanted to catch me they had better send a better-looking agent.

The three German officials with whom I conducted the bulk of my official business were Von Bethmann-Hollweg, who was Chancellor during all the time I was in Germany; Von Jagow, who was Secretary of Foreign Affairs until 1916; and Zimmermann, who was Von Jagow's Under-Secretary of Foreign Affairs and who became minister in 1916 when Von Jagow was ousted.

Theobald von Bethmann-Hollweg was a pleasant, likable man of good appearance and enormous physical stature. Unlike most of the previous chancellors, he was not of noble birth, but came from a well-to-do banking family in Frankfort. Undoubtedly it was this background that made his manner so agreeable and his mind so flexible, for he had none of the military class's single-mindedness and inflexibility. In both his manners and in his pliant personality he stood out among the usual run of German political bigwigs. I liked to talk with him. His point of view was reasonable—even when he disagreed with me—and he had nothing of the German habit of trying to overwhelm one with his personality so as to make his auditor feel like a small white worm—a trait I had to endure in many of his countrymen. He correctly predicted that the adoption of ruthless submarine warfare as a definite policy would bring the United States into the war. In this belief he was opposed by Admiral von Tirpitz, who had been primarily responsible for building up the efficiency of the German Navy, and who wanted to exploit it to the utmost. Von Bethmann-Hollweg finally drove Von Tirpitz out of office, but from his retirement Von Tirpitz conducted a campaign in favor of ruthless war which in the end obtained the support of the Army and finally of the Kaiser.

Von Jagow was a skillful diplomat, adroit rather than forceful, and quite pleasant to deal with. He was of the old Prussian nobility, but long years as ambassador to Italy and in other foreign posts had taken much of the Prussian starch from his manner and thinking. When I called on him, he always kept me for a long time, apparently to practice his English—a language he insisted on using with me, who would have much preferred to practice my German on him. He often lunched with us, and devoted more time to learning English idioms than he did to his plate.

When the British first captured a German submarine crew, Winston Churchill, then First Lord of the Admiralty, said that because of their inhuman acts the crew shouldn't be treated as ordinary prisoners of war, but should be thrown into a common jail like the felons they were, and this was done. In reprisal for this the enraged Germans picked a number of English prisoners of war—twice the number of the German undersea crew—and clapped them into ordinary jails in Burg and Magdeburg. They went to great trouble to pick young officers of the best-known English families, and selected as one choice the son of the last British Ambassador to Germany, Sir Edward Goschen. Young Goschen was recovering from wounds, and when I heard this, I attacked Von Jagow not only for putting a wounded man on the reprisal list, but also for violating ambassadorial courtesy. Von Jagow, who had become quite nervous with the war and whose nerves grew steadily worse as the war progressed, burst out crying and said to me, in a plaintive voice, "You are a terrible ambassador." Nevertheless, I obtained the release of young Goschen and sent him back to England accompanied by one of the doctors of my staff.

What finally caused Von Jagow's political downfall was the poor showing he made whenever he had to appear before the Reichstag to answer questions. Von Jagow was not adept at the catch-as-catch-can of parliamentary debate, and he cut a poor figure as government spokesman on these occasions. In any event, while I was on a short visit to America in 1916 he was dismissed from his post, and Zimmermann, the Under-Secretary, was appointed Foreign Minister in his place.

Zimmermann lacked the advantage of being of a noble family like Von Jagow, but he was of tougher fiber. I always got on very well with him, however, although on one occasion, when we were discussing the sinking of the *Lusitania*, he said to me, "Your government doesn't dare to do anything against my government because we have five hundred thousand trained German reservists in the United States who will rise in arms if your government attempts anything against mine."

As he knew America didn't have much of an army at that time, I said to him, "That may be, but we have in America five hundred thousand and one lampposts, and that is where the reservists will find themselves hanging the morning after they try to rise!" He blinked at me a couple of times, but made no reply.

Zimmermann went over completely to the side of the army and navy officers who advocated unrestricted submarine warfare, and, with his consent and the forced consent of the Kaiser, the orders for those merciless attacks were issued in January 1917.

CHAPTER XIX

THE OPENING GUNS OF THE GREAT WAR CAME WITH THE startling abruptness of a thunderclap to most of the foreign diplomats in Berlin. They had been practically unanimous in predicting a peaceful solution, partly because they didn't realize that the German military ruling class, having prepared for a war, intended to have one regardless of any nonsense about obligations.

With well-kept secrecy, considering the size of the task, the country had been thoroughly prepared for the war, and on the very day it was declared—August 4, 1914—millions of reservists donned field-gray uniforms and began to draw the enormous stores of military equipment that had been made ready. In an incredibly short time an enormous, well-trained, and well-equipped army was mobilized and on the march.

As more and more nations became involved in the war with Germany and her allies, the American embassy became an ever busier place, for the United States had been asked to take over the Berlin affairs of several of the belligerents. In a short time after the outbreak of hostilities I found myself representing the interests of Great Britain, Japan, Serbia, Romania, and, later on, the minuscule Republic of San Marino, which had thrown its weight against the Germans too. Berlin diplomatic circles were beset with grave problems of all sorts, some of them practically without precedent, for it had been a long time since a grand-scale war had occurred in Europe. In the beginning there were many procedures and niceties of protocol observed that later, as the war grew longer and more bitter, were forgotten or ignored.

When I first arrived in Berlin, our embassy consisted of the First Secretary, Joseph C. Grew, who has since represented our country so ably in Japan and elsewhere; Willing Spencer, the Second Secretary; Albert R. Ruddock, Third Secretary; Lanier Winslow, my private secretary, and two clerks. Shortly before the war Roland Harvey, a career diplomat, came to take the place of Willing Spencer, who was promoted to a post in South America. As war came and our duties multiplied, our embassy staff was augmented by the arrival of John R. Jackson, former Minister to Cuba, to Greece, and to Romania, and by a number of volunteers—Boylston Beal of Boston, and Ellis Dressel of Boston, whose knowledge of German was especially useful.

We soon acquired many other hard and earnest workers. Lanier Winslow became the Third Secretary, and Barclay Rives, formerly in our diplomatic service in Austria, and Oliver Harriman, a career man, came to help me. A most welcome addition was Alexander Kirk, recently our Minister to Egypt and Saudi Arabia, and later to Italy, a most skilled diplomat.

Lithgow Osborn, later conservation commissioner of the state of New York, and later Minister to Norway, and Captain Walter Gheradi, who later became an admiral, was our naval attaché, aided by Captain Herbster. Admiral Gheradi proved himself most efficient in getting news about the Germans, submarines, and so on, and Captain Herbster, going about Berlin, picked up a great deal of useful gossip in the course of his routine duties. An American navy surgeon, Dr. Karl Ohnesorg, not only took good care of us all in the embassy but also did splendid work investigating conditions in German prison camps.

Robert M. Scotten, later Ambassador to Ecuador and New Zealand, and Hugh Wilson, later our last Ambassador to Germany, were sent by the State Department to assist me and performed most useful services, as did Rivington Pyne, Grafton Minot, and Charles Russell, the latter now helping to represent our country at the United Nations. Christian Herter, now making a great record in Congress, was another helper.

As conditions in the prison camps and the plight of the prisoners became more acute, a number of doctors were sent to help in the inspections of camps, among them the eminent Dr. Daniel J. McCarthy, who has written a most interesting book of his experiences; Dr. Alonzo Taylor of Leland Stanford University, and Dr. Jerome Webster, who has accomplished such wonders at the Presbyterian Hospital in New York in the reconstruction of battle-torn faces. When I returned to Germany in December 1916 I brought Lieutenant Angel as an additional naval aide and Herman Oelrichs as an additional secretary, but despite this added help, the work of the embassy was an enormous task, and I cannot too highly praise the organizing ability of Grew, who kept the embassy's business in order and everything running smoothly.

I regard Joseph Clark Grew as our top diplomat today. His long experience in the State Department, his official residence in Germany and other parts of Europe, his outstanding career as Ambassador to Turkey, and, above all, the splendid record he made in his stay as Ambassador to Japan, all qualify him for high place in our diplomatic service. What a great Secretary of State he would be! In fact, our embassy seemed to be a school for ambassadors. Not only Grew, but Wilson in Germany, Alexander Kirk in Italy and Egypt, Scotten in Ecuador, Osborne in Norway were all outstanding representatives of our country.

With every German completely preoccupied with the war effort, the customary social life was quite abbreviated, so that for the most part our conviviality eddied around our own embassy and among a few resident Americans.

The late Seymour Conger, Berlin correspondent of the Associated Press, was always pro-American in his outlook and was a most helpful friend during this period, as was also Carl W. Ackerman, who represented the United Press. Ackerman has carved out a noteworthy career and is now the dean of the School of Journalism at Columbia University. His then chief, Roy W. Howard, whose force, courage, and vision have put him at the head of the powerful Scripps-Howard newspaper chain, was another welcome wartime visitor.

I had leased a large shooting preserve about eighteen miles from Berlin for what became practically my only exercise and relaxation. Occasionally I would motor there in the afternoon to shoot Hungarian partridges, pheasants, roebucks, ducks, and geese. Thanks to strict enforcement of the laws against poaching, game was plentiful, it was a welcome addition to our larder, and, while I was shooting, my chauffeur usually managed to buy a few eggs from nearby farmers.

My first and most pressing concern was my responsibility toward those prisoners of war, both civilian and military, who were citizens of the nations I represented in Germany. I deemed it my duty to see that the prisoners were well treated, and with the grudging permission of the German authorities, made inspection trips to some of the prison camps. It was not long before our State Department cabled to me that my inspections of the prison camps were irritating the Germans, and I was therefore ordered to desist. I cabled to Washington that in that case they had better give up protecting the interests of the British and the other countries whose affairs I was handling, and that it was plainly my duty to make these inspections. The State Department withdrew the order.

In my efforts to obtain proper care for the prisoners, I sent many notes to Von Jagow which remained unanswered. I then notified Chancellor von Bethmann-Hollweg that if my notes were not answered in a satisfactory manner, I would take a chair, put it in the street in front of his palace, and sit there until I received a reply. The Chancellor, thus prodded, finally authorized me to deal directly with the German military authorities. This was a radical change in diplomatic procedure; a diplomat is supposed to deal only with the head of the government or the Minister of Foreign Affairs. In any event, I was permitted to arrange a meeting of a representative from the Foreign Office, one from the Ministry of War, one from the General Staff, and Count Schwerin, who was in charge of the civilian prisoners quartered near Berlin. It was agreed that I and ten of my staff could visit the prison camps and talk to the prisoners out of earshot of the camp officers.

But despite these assurances of co-operation by the Government and the Military, I encountered a great deal of opposition.

The first British prisoners had been captured during August and September, and had only lightweight uniforms and no overcoats. When I proceeded to buy heavy underwear and other articles for them in Berlin, I was stopped by the Germans; they said it was their obligation to furnish these articles for prisoners. Notwithstanding this assurance, the warm clothing was not furnished for some time.

At the outbreak of the war there were fifty thousand or more German civilians of military age in England and about eight thousand British civilians in Germany. The Germans offered the exchange of all for all, but the British would exchange only one German for one Englishman, since, obviously, an all-for-all exchange would have added a full army corps of men to the German forces. The upshot was that no exchange was made, and the eight thousand British travelers were shut up near Berlin on a race track called Ruhleben, six to a box stall, or in the hayloft with their cots jammed together.

The prisoners' food, because of the British blockade on Germany, was insufficient, but we arranged that packages of food could be sent to the British prisoners from London. After World War I, about 1929, an international convention held in Switzerland laid down rules for the treatment of prisoners of war, and these were agreed to by many of the nations. To some extent the rules were drawn to avoid repetition of the war-prisoner experiences in Germany during World War I. Japan, it might be noted parenthetically, was not a signatory to the Geneva convention. She did not want the idea of surrender suggested to her troops.

In Ruhleben many of the prisoners became mentally unbalanced as a result of the privation and monotony of their lives. D. John R. Mott of the Y.M.C.A. arranged through his able assistants, Rev. Archibald Hart and Dr. Conrad Hoffmann, to build a library in this camp. When I met some of the prisoners in London after the war, they told me that this library had saved their reason, by giving them a place to read, write, and escape from the deadly routine of camp life and dreary contemplation of their melancholy predicament.

The opening of the war found thousands of Americans stranded in Germany, many without money and without passports. I gave them passports, but the question of money was difficult and caused hardship and delay. The Germans would not honor letters of credit and traveler's checks, but I finally arranged to have the Dresdner Bank pay out a reasonable sum on all letters of credit presented, providing that I had stamped these letters with the seal of the embassy. Later, and after the first strain of mobilization was over, I was able to arrange for special trains which took Americans to Holland, whence they could take a ship to the United States. My secretary, Lanier Winslow, sat in the lower hall issuing railway tickets, and Mrs. Gerard and Mrs. Ruddock sat in the ballroom assigning steerage passage on the ships of the Holland-America Lines.

I had the advantage of representing a powerful nation, and so was heard respectfully in my pleas concerning treatment of the prisoners. In the last war our interests were represented by Sweden or by Switzerland, countries that had been somewhat in awe of the conquering Nazis. Those who accepted the responsibility of protecting the interests of the nations at war with Germany in World War II failed most lamentably, albeit with some excuse. The horrors of the German prison camps shocked the world—a world which will never quite forgive the German people.

In 1915 a number of Americans were still marooned at Carlsbad, in Austria, and I arranged with the German Government for a special train to take them out. Among them was Frank Munsey, who gave a great dinner in my honor for about eighty guests at the Ritz when I visited America in the autumn of 1916. He showed his appreciation in many ways up to the date of his death.

As 1915 wore on the prisoner question became more and more difficult. The problem, in brief, was that while the number of prisoners constantly increased, the quantity and quality of the food given them (excepting the parcels from home) decreased, a condition partly caused by the efficient British blockade. Had it not been for the package system which we arranged, the British prisoners would have suffered more severely, as the Russians, in fact, did, for the camp rations given by the Germans were hardly sufficient to keep them alive. I saw Russians surround British prisoners who were opening packages, in pitiful hope that a few crumbs might fall upon the ground to be retrieved. The French seemed to be as badly neglected as the Russians, but since the Germans were then only a few miles from Paris and occupied a large part of France, the inability of the French populace to help was understandable.

The Germans devoted a great deal of thought and cunning to getting their money's worth out of the prisoners. For example, in a burst of applied psychology they segregated in one camp the Irishmen from the batches of British prisoners they had captured. Then they sent the renegade Irishman, Sir Roger Casement, to seduce them from their allegiance to the King and induce them to join the German Army. Out of a camp of thousands of Irish prisoners, only about thirty-five joined the Germans. I visited this camp of loyal Irishmen at Limburg.

Before the war Casement had been in the British service. He did very good work in exposing conditions in the Congo and consequently was knighted by the British Government. However, he became violently anti-British and pro-Irish, and was living in Germany at the beginning of the war. Later, when he went with an expedition of Germans that landed on the coast of Ireland, he was immediately arrested, sent to London, tried for treason, and hanged.

Some years after the war I talked with an American who had been in Berlin during the rioting that followed the Armistice. He had stayed at the Hotel Adlon. One day when there was fighting outside his window he was fascinated by the actions of a German soldier who had climbed to the top of the Brandenburg Gate. From that vantage point he seemed to be indiscriminately potting the unfortunate citizens of Berlin. After the fighting had died down my friend tactfully questioned this sniper and found that he was one of those Irishmen who had joined the German Army through the efforts of Casement. His explanation, delivered with a strong Irish brogue, was quite reasonable: "OI'm wan of Casement's victims," he said, "and OI'm having a hell of a good time killing Germans."

At the outbreak of war all the Japanese in Germany were imprisoned. However, I procured their release as soon as possible and got permission for them to leave the country. Popular hate against the Japanese was intense because the Germans had been disappointed in their hope that Japan would enter the war on the German side. In fact, when a crowd was serenading the Japanese embassy with this hope in their hearts, the Japanese were packing their trunks preparatory to leaving Berlin. We gave shelter to a number of these Japanese in our embassy until I could arrange for their departure, and I sent Lanier Winslow with them as far as Munich where they had to change cars on their way to Switzerland. I must say that I found them grateful. When

Mrs. Gerard and I arrived in Zurich on our departure from Germany in 1917, we found a little group of Japanese waiting in the railroad station to greet us. The next day in Berne a delegation of them called and with elaborate ceremony gave me a clock. Later I was given the Grand Cordon of the Paulownia flower by the Emperor of Japan.

Although the Japanese did not agree to the Prisoners of War Convention of 1929, in February 1942 they did pledge to abide by the rules of the 1929 Convention. Early in 1942 a ship loaded with supplies for war prisoners was waiting in San Francisco to sail to Japan, but the departure was canceled because of the inability of the Japanese and the American governments to agree on a system of distribution. Since that time eyewitness accounts and confessions during the Japanese war-crimes trials have left no doubt of the sadistic barbarism with which the Japanese frequently treated Americans and prisoners of other nationalities.

Early in 1944 my brother Sumner, whose own two sons were serving with the Pacific forces, was aroused by reports of brutalities to prisoners. He wrote to Secretary of War Henry L. Stimson, recalling that my help to the Japanese prisoners in Germany in 1914 had brought me a decoration and a personal letter of thanks from the Emperor, and suggesting that a reminder of this to the Emperor might bring some relief to our prisoners. Sumner's letter to Secretary Stimson concluded:

The entire country is horrified and aroused at what these same Japanese are now doing to those of our men in their power. . . .

According to some opinion nothing can be done. We can only inflict punishment after complete victory. But till then, perhaps two or three years, how about the prisoners, the number of whom is bound to increase?

I spoke to my brother yesterday about this situation and the possibility, however remote, of capitalizing on his past services. He is eager to help. It would seem to come down to whether or not any feeling of gratitude can carry over when an enemy is desperate and throws to the winds all decent instincts and, secondly, what may be the method of approach. A direct appeal from a civilian to the head of a belligerent government is perhaps impossible and one should avoid the risk of misinterpretation. But there remains the press and the radio.

You, Sir, know the ropes better than either of us and you may think of something that may be worth trying.

Yours sincerely,
Sumner Gerard

The offer was politely declined by Secretary Stimson, on the ground that a "gesture" toward the Japanese "might be susceptible of misinterpretation by them." I shall always believe this to have been an error in judgment. There may have been, to be sure, some reason to avoid such an appeal to the Emperor by a private citizen, but a momentary appointment to the State Department would have circumvented this objection. It seems to me that any approach which offered the slightest hope of mitigating the horrors to which our men were subjected was worthy of the fullest exploration. Secretary Stimson's reasoning on the matter is explained in his letter declining my offer:

February 15 1944.

Dear Mr. Gerard:

I very much appreciate your letter of January 31, 1944, communicating the generous offer of your brother, the Honorable James W. Gerard, to lend his assistance in the matter of attempting to obtain better treatment of American prisoners of war and civilian internees held by the Japanese.

In view of the action already taken, I do not believe it would be advisable at this time to make any gesture toward the Japanese which might be susceptible of misinterpretation by them. This would apply, I think, in especial degree to the use of the good offices of a private individual, even one so distinguished and so favorably situated as is your brother vis-à-vis highly placed Japanese.

I regret that circumstances make it impossible for the War Department to accept your brother's kind tender, for I can well understand his eagerness to be of help. Please convey to him my warm personal regards as well as my grateful appreciation of his thoughtfulness.

> Sincerely yours,
> (*Sgd*) Henry L. Stimson
> Secretary of War

At least I could have stirred up those neutral diplomats who were representing us and who were supposed to look after our prisoners and who might have helped in many ways those of our men in enemy prison camps.

Politics are somewhat like an iceberg, in that a large part of what goes on is generally invisible. I was more than usually handicapped in this respect in a political involvement that took place shortly before the outbreak of war and while I was at my post in Berlin.

The governor of New York, William Sulzer, was removed from office after impeachment, and was succeeded by Lieutenant Governor Martin H. Glynn. Thus in the fall elections of 1914 there was a governor to be elected as well as one of the two United States senators from New York.

In the Democratic primary Secretary McAdoo, probably with the approval of President Wilson, backed John A. Hennesey for governor and Franklin D. Roosevelt for senator. The Democrats nominated me—although I was out of the country—to run against Roosevelt in the primary. Glynn and I won. My majority over Roosevelt was about 73,000. In the election, however, I was beaten by the Republican candidate, James W. Wadsworth, by what was at that time the usual Republican majority of about 60,000.

Many observers thought that I might have won except for two developments. In a meeting of the Republican Union League Club I was subjected to particularly violent attacks, and Wadsworth supporters flooded the western part of New York State, always strongly Protestant, with circulars stating that I was a Roman Catholic. Since I was in Germany I had no opportunity either to meet the attacks or to affirm my Protestantism and denounce the introduction of falsehood and religious issues into the campaign.

I believe that the Union League regretted the unfair attack, because when I returned to the United States I was invited to speak at a special meeting of the club—the first time, I think, that a Democrat was so honored.

In addition to the defeat of Franklin Roosevelt in an election, the episode was historic in that it was the first time that a candidate for United States senator was absent from the country during the entire campaign. I never regretted the outcome, believing that the consequence of my remaining in Berlin gave me a larger and more exciting role in the momentous history of the succeeding years.

CHAPTER XX

Early in august 1914 president wilson sent me a message through the State Department stating that the United States stood ready at any time to mediate between the warring powers. He directed me to present this proposal to the Emperor in person. An audience with the Emperor was arranged for me for the morning of August 10. The Emperor was seated at an iron table in the little garden of the palace in Berlin, on the banks of the River Spree. In formal language I made my offer. It was declined. Then the Emperor asked me to sit down and talk to him. It was, of course, my business to be as agreeable as possible to those in authority, and so I said to the Emperor that it appeared that his troops would soon capture Paris, whereupon he would be able to dictate peace.

The Emperor, on one of the few occasions that I saw him in a thoughtful mood, hesitated for a moment and then said slowly, "No, the coming in of the English has changed the whole situation. They are an obstinate race. They will never stop fighting."

After some further discussion the Emperor said he would send a personal message to President Wilson in answer to his offer. He then wrote in pencil, on some large telegraph blanks lying on the table, a personal message to the President. Mainly it consisted of various excuses about the declaration of war. Of the most historical interest is that part of the message referring to Sir Edward Grey, the British Minister of Foreign Affairs, and the violation of Belgian neutrality.

The message was as follows:

For the President of the
    United States personally:

10/VIII 14.

1. H.R.H. Prince Henry was received by his Majesty King George V in London, who empowered him to transmit to me verbally, that England would remain neutral if war broke out on the Continent involving Germany and France, Austria and Russia. This message was telegraphed to me by my brother from London after his conversation with H.M. the King, and repeated verbally on the twenty-ninth of July.

2. My Ambassador in London transmitted a message from Sir. E. Grey to Berlin saying that only in case France was likely to be crushed England would interfere.

3. On the thirtieth my Ambassador in London reported that Sir Edward Grey in course of a "private" conversation told him that if the conflict remained localized between *Russia*—not Serbia— and *Austria,* England would not move, but if we "mixed" in the fray she would take quick decisions and grave measures; i.e., if I left my ally Austria in the lurch to fight alone England would not touch me.

4. This communication being directly counter to the King's message to me, I telegraphed to H.M. on the twenty-ninth or thirtieth, thanking him for kind messages through my brother and begging him to use all his power to keep France and Russia— his Allies—from making any war-like preparations calculated to disturb my work of mediation, stating that I was in constant

communication with H.M. the Czar. In the evening the King kindly answered that he had ordered his Government to use every possible influence with his Allies to refrain from taking any provocative military measures. At the same time H.M. asked me if I would transmit to Vienna the British proposal that Austria was to make Belgrade and a few other Serbian towns and a strip of country as a "main-mise" to make sure that the Serbian promises on paper should be fulfilled in reality. This proposal was in the same moment telegraphed to me from Vienna for London, quite in conjunction with the British proposal; besides, I had telegraphed to H.M. the Czar the same as an idea of mine, before I received the two communications from Vienna and London, as both were of the same opinion.

5. I immediately transmitted the telegrams *vice versa* to Vienna and London. I felt that I was able to tide the question over and was happy at the peaceful outlook.

6. While I was preparing a note to H.M. the Czar the next morning, to inform him that Vienna, London and Berlin were agreed about the treatment of affairs, I received the telephones from H.E. the Chancellor that in the night before the Czar had given the order to mobilize the whole of the Russian Army, which was, of course, also meant against Germany; whereas up till then the southern armies had been mobilized against Austria.

7. In a telegram from London my Ambassador informed me he understood the British government would guarantee neutrality of France and wished to know whether Germany would refrain from attack. I telegraphed to H.M. the King personally that mobilization being already carried out could not be stopped, but if H.M. could guarantee with his armed forces the neutrality of France I would refrain from *attacking her, leave her alone* and employ my troops elsewhere. H.M. answered that he thought my offer was based on a misunderstanding; and, as far as I can make out, Sir E. Grey never took my offer into serious consid-

eration. He never answered it. Instead, he declared England had
to defend Belgian neutrality, which had to be violated by Germany on strategical grounds, news having been received that
France was already preparing to enter Belgium, and the King of
Belgians having refused my petition for a free passage under
guarantee of his country's freedom. I am most grateful for the
President's message.

William, H.R.

That afternoon I talked with Von Jagow in the Foreign
Office, and he asked me bluntly, "You had an interview today
with the Emperor; what happened?"

I told him of the message, and he said, "I think you ought
to show that message to me; the Emperor, you know, is a
constitutional emperor, and there was once a great row about
such a message."

I showed him the cable, and when he had read it he declared earnestly, "I think it would be inadvisable for us to
have this message published. In the interest of good feeling
between Germany and America, if you cable it, ask that publication be withheld." I complied with his request, and President Wilson never published the message.

When I returned to America, after the breaking of diplomatic relations, I wrote my first book, called *My Four Years
in Germany*. In it I published a facsimile of the message.
Whereupon the official *North German Gazette*, not knowing
that the original message, in the Kaiser's own hand, was in
my possession, stated: "We are, in these circumstances, in
the position to give the assurance that a telegram of the
Kaiser of this nature does not exist."

The Berlin *Tageblatt*, a publication having a large circulation, printed a lame and silly explanation on August 13, 1917,
and Reventlow, writing in the *Tages Zeitung*, said, "Kaiser

William had possibly for his answer written down notes and given them to Gerard, and it was not a question of a direct communication of the German Kaiser to the President. Mr. Gerard has therefore, again in this respect, lied, which is not surprising."

The German newspapers and Reventlow had not seen my book with its facsimile of the Kaiser's telegram headed in his own writing: "To The President Personally." Later, when they saw the facsimile, the newspapers complained bitterly of the Foreign Office for making a denial of a fact which could not be controverted. One of them lamented that, anyway, before I had been permitted to see the Kaiser, he should have been warned of my "insidious personality." I had the Kaiser's message beautifully bound by Tiffany and sent it to President Wilson.

The blockade of Germany was so effective that not only did the civil population suffer for the want of food but, as I have said, it was only because of the food-package system that we had instituted that British prisoners were able to keep in fair health. A tragic result of the blockade was that the people of Belgium, cut off from food supplies, were in danger of starvation. However, an arrangement was eventually made by which a commission for the relief of Belgium was created. At its head was Herbert Hoover.

Under the aegis of the Hoover relief committee, the Allies subscribed a large sum. Farmers and others in the United States contributed a substantial sum in money or grain. The British allowed the relief ships to pass through the blockade, and the Germans permitted them to land.

I was one of the honorary chairmen of this commission and was able to be of considerable help to Hoover in his negotiations with the German Government. On December 31,

1914, I had obtained the assurance of the German Government in writing that from that date on it would prohibit the requisitioning of food or forage of any kind whatsoever which would require replacement by importations by the American Committee for Belgian Relief. Foreign Minister von Jagow later sent me a letter which follows:

My dear Excellency:

Many thanks for your kind letter of the 1st instant enclosing a copy of the telegram of Mr. Hoover. Herr von Bethman-Hollweg and I retain the most pleasing remembrance of Mr. Hoover and both he and your Excellency may rest assured that the Imperial Government maintains its former attitude to afford the humanitarian work of the Relief Commission on the part of Germany every possible support.

On April 18, 1915, Von Jagow again wrote to me assuring me that the German submarines had been directed to allow the ships of the relief commission to proceed unmolested if they were recognized by their marks of identification.

Hoover's commission had undertaken not only to furnish food to the Belgians, but also to that part of France occupied by the Germans. While Grew and I were at the Kaiser's headquarters at Charleville-Mézières, we were taken to various small places in the vicinity to witness the workings of this system. While driving about the country I had observed at work in the fields a number of women and girls who looked as artificially rustic as the chorus in *Cavalleria Rusticana*. When some of Hoover's workers met me I learned the explanation for these strange-looking peasant women. In their desperate need for field hands the Germans had seized many young women and men in towns such as Lille and Roubaix and set them to work on the farms. I approached the Chancellor about this practice, and the matter was later taken up by President Wilson. It required the assistance of the King of Spain, the Pope, and other neutrals to procure some modification of this procedure.

It is indicative of the extent to which civilized standards were abandoned in World War II that Germany, in addition to using prisoners of war to supplement her labor supply, made slaves of noncombatants in the occupied countries. Postwar disclosures of the hideous brutality of the concentration and slave-labor camps sickened the entire world. I wish I could believe that all civilized peoples, revolted by that evidence of retrogression toward barbarism, had reacted with a determination that it should not happen again. But our fragmentary knowledge of what transpires behind the Iron Curtain of Soviet dictatorship indicates that behavior more fitting to brutes than men continues to be the policy of despotism.

Dr. Mott of the Y.M.C.A. undertook work to alleviate the condition of the prisoners of war in Germany, having regard rather to the mental, spiritual, and intellectual side of their lives. The work was financially backed by the McCormick family of Chicago, Cleveland H. Dodge, John D. Rockefeller, Jr., and others. A building was erected in the prison camp at Ruhleben and much was done to help the prisoners in other camps throughout Germany.

It was the habit of the Germans to put some prisoners of each Allied nation in every prison camp. At the camp of Wittenberg, some imperfectly deloused Russians were placed in the camp with French, British, and Belgians, and infected the others with typhus. Captured Allied medical officers, who had been kept with their own troops in the camp, protested to the camp commander at the inclusion of the typhus-laden

Russians in the same camp. The camp commander replied, "You will have to get to know your allies," and thus automatically condemned a number of French and British prisoners of war to death. While the typhus was epidemic, the Germans themselves deserted the camp.

In this particular camp were kept a number of fierce dogs which were trained to attack persons wearing British and French uniforms. Many of the prisoners were bitten by them. When I called on Von Jagow to protest about this savage business, I said, "I am a good shot with a revolver. Suppose I go back to Wittenberg and shoot some of those dogs! What can you do about it? As an ambassador, I am above the law." Soon after this conversation the dogs disappeared from the camp.

The immunity from arrest enjoyed by an ambassador had its usefulness. Some Americans in Berlin, headed by a bookshop keeper and an expatriate dentist, organized what they called "The League of Truth" and attacked President Wilson. At the statue of Frederick the Great they placed a large wreath with a streamer bearing the inscription, "Wilson and his press do not represent America." When I told Von Jagow that I was going to climb over the railing and remove the wreath and its offensive streamer, he quickly had it removed. The League of Truth then announced that they were going to publish a book attacking me. I called on the head of the League, in his bookshop, and told him that if he printed anything about me that I didn't like, I would burn his shop down. He tried to have me indicted for threatened arson but got nowhere because of my diplomatic immunity.

For my aid to British subjects at the opening of the war I received the thanks of the British Government. On August 29, 1914, the British Ambassador, Cecil Spring-Rice, delivered a communication to Secretary Bryan by direction of Sir Edward Grey, asking that the "warm thanks" of the British Government be conveyed to me. The communication to Mr. Bryan was as follows:

A report by Sir Edward Goschen, lately His Majesty's Ambassador at Berlin, on the events at Berlin which took place both before and after the outbreak of war between Great Britain and Germany, has been laid before Parliament and, as you have doubtless noticed, has appeared recently in the American Press. It contains cordial recognition of the great assistance of a personal nature rendered to the British Embassy by the United States Ambassador and his staff. Mr. Gerard repeatedly visited the Embassy of his own accord, undeterred by the very hostile attitude of the crowd and, often at considerable risk to himself, extricated many British subjects from difficult situations.

It is a pleasure to me to inform you that I have received Sir Edward Grey's instructions to request that a warm thanks of his Majesty's Government may be conveyed to Mr. Gerard.

CHAPTER XXI

In the early months of 1915 it became apparent that the German blitzkrieg had lost its initial force. The push for Paris and the German sweep to a quick victory had failed. After seven months of war the Allies and the Germans had dug in face to face in the trenches which extended from Switzerland to the Channel, while on the high seas there seemed little chance that the submarines of the Empire would starve England into surrender. A gigantic naval blockade and a long war faced Germany. In February 1915 the victory promised the German people seemed far away, if not impossible. The Kaiser, from the balcony of his palace, had said that before the leaves fell from the trees the soldiers would be back in their homes. Berliners said later he must have meant pine trees. The government now fearfully realized that revolution might well be the answer of a starved people to the militarists who had led them into a fatal war.

After the war began I was requested to send all my communications to President Wilson in a highly peculiar manner. I would write a letter to Colonel House and put it in an unsealed envelope addressed to him. This letter was then enclosed in a sealed envelope, which was addressed to the President. I have never been able to understand this elaborate device, unless it was to enable President Wilson to say that he had never received a letter from me on some particular subject which might have become the basis for dispute. These letters, of course, were put in our diplomatic pouch and sent to the State Department at Washington, being carried by couriers from Berlin to London. On quite a number of occasions these couriers were detained, sometimes for days. Their bags were taken from them but returned later with their contents apparently untouched.

The Germans did not decipher our codes till after the war. Nevertheless, they knew that the quickest way to the ear of Washington was through me, and in due course it was intimated to me that Germany was ready to make peace. This came first from our military attaché, Major Langhorne, who was later falsely accused of pro-Germanism. Langhorne arranged for me to be conducted by devious passages to the private quarters of Admiral von Tirpitz in the Admiralty Building. Nothing substantial came from this interview. But soon other Germans high in authority were more specific—so specific, indeed, that I felt justified, on February 11, 1915, in sending President Wilson the following cable in code

It is my conviction that if a reasonable peace proposition were offered Germany very many men of influence would be inclined to use their efforts to induce Germany to accept the proposition. If peace does not come immediately a new and protracted phase of the war will commence. It will be fatal to hesitate or wait a moment; success is dependent on immediate action. It is my belief that if you seize the present opportunity you will be the instrument of bringing about the greatest peace which has ever been signed, but it will be fatal to hesitate or wait a moment.

The response to this cable was an instruction from President Wilson to refer everything to Colonel House, who, the communication specified, had been "fully instructed and commissioned to act in all these matters." Colonel House was then in London. I had anticipated the cable from Washington and had written him the following:

"Germany will make no peace proposals, but I am sure if a reasonable peace is proposed now (a matter of days, even hours) it would be accepted."

And to Washington I cabled:

"Yours about Colonel House received. Favorable moment is passing."

Having heard nothing by February 13, I cabled that I "had not sent my long cipher without having good reason."

At that time the United States theoretically stood in the position of being able to force the Allies to listen to reasonable peace proposals by threatening to embargo exports of munitions to them. But, as letters from Colonel House to me show, the British did not want to make a peace that, in substance, would have sent the warring powers back to their corners. They wanted the utter defeat of Germany.

The following letter from Colonel House to me is illuminating:

Feb. 16
The President has just repeated to me your cablegram to him, and says he has asked you to communicate directly with me in the future. Until we can get together and form a code of our own, I would suggest using the green code. There are many difficulties in starting negotiations quickly as you have proposed because the three allies must all be reached. As I wrote you before, I can see no insuperable difficulty here, and if no raid either by air or sea is made upon noncombatants in the near future, I shall feel hopeful that something may be soon started. If such a raid or raids be made, it would be impossible for this Government to

move. If they did, there would be a storm of disapproval that might sweep them from office.

Sincerely yours,

(*signed*) E. M. House

Please keep me informed in every way possible.

Colonel House apparently was avid to monitor the Berlin-Washington diplomatic correspondence. In addition to the cable which I had already received informing me that Colonel House was "fully commissioned to act" he himself reminded me of my duty in his February 16 postscript. In his own handwriting were those words from House: "The President has just repeated to me your cablegram to him, and says he has asked you to communicate directly with me in the future. . . ." All authority, therefore, had been vested in Colonel House, and as I was directed to report to Colonel House direct, the President ceased to be even a conduit of communications.

On February 19 Colonel House wrote me as follows:

Feb. 19, 1915.

AMERICAN EMBASSY
LONDON

His Excellency,
    The American Ambassador,
        Berlin, Germany.

My dear Judge:

Your letter of the 15th came to me yesterday. I immediately saw Sir Edward Grey. He said it was utterly impossible to make any such hasty proposal as you thought the situation required.

If things had gone on quietly for a few weeks longer, I feel sure we could have gotten these belligerents together, but the blockade has, for the moment, brought everything to a standstill.

As far as I can see, there is no prospect now of my getting to

Berlin soon, so I take it, we will have to let the matter drift until another period of deadlock ensues.

I sincerely hope that the good relations between Germany and the United States will not be interrupted. I know how earnestly the President desires to be on good terms with all, and I am sure that your every effort is bent in that direction.

It is a great disappointment to me that I cannot be with you at an early date, but this unexpected phase has upset all plans.

With warm regards and good wishes, I am.

Faithfully yours,
(*signed*) E. M. House

In *Grey of Fallodon*, by George Macaulay Trevelyan, the author writes, "It was at the request of Colonel House himself that arrangements were made for intimate and secret communication between Grey and the 'President's friend' on account of 'the hopeless leakage of the State Department' as House called it."

Certainly Colonel E. Mandell House occupied a unique position in the annals of American diplomacy. He, who had never been appointed to any position and who had never been passed upon by the Senate, was "fully instructed and commissioned" to act in the most grave situation. I have never ceased to wonder how he had managed to attain such power and influence.

In 1911 Colonel House wrote a thoughtful book, published anonymously, called *Philip Dru, Administrator*. In this book the hero becomes dictator of the United States following a civil war. In fact, Dru becomes a sort of Messiah, ordering the world about at his own sweet will. He is utterly without patience for the democracy of the United States. The Supreme Court is deprived of its right to pass on the constitutionality of laws, and in the field of foreign affairs "Germany was to have the freest commercial access to South America and she was invited to develop those countries both with German colonists and German capital." Germany was to have "a free hand in the countries to the southeast of her and Asia Minor." Moreover, Canada was to be "surrendered" by Britain to the United States.

My favorite passage in the book deals with naval ship design. Philip Dru's battleships were to have newfangled turrets. "Around these turrets ran rims of polished steel, two feet in width and six inches thick. These rims began four feet from the water line and ran four feet above the level of the turret decks, and were so nicely adjusted with ball bearings that the smallest blow would send them spinning around, therefore a shell could not penetrate because it would glance off." Surely this is one of the noblest passages in the whole body of writings on naval design.

The colonel admitted the authorship of this book. I once told him that every anonymous author left in his work something by which he could establish his authorship. On page seventy-three, for example, one character says to another, "If you will dine with me in my rooms in the Mandell House tonight, I shall be delighted. . . ." Thus we have the author —E. Mandell House. He admitted this to me but would never tell what "Dru" meant.

The break between Wilson and House came at the Paris Peace Conference. House asked me once if I knew why it happened. I think that I know the reason for the break, but its disclosure would injure people still alive.

As the conflict wore on into the first spring, the issue of unrestricted submarine warfare precipitated recurring crises. At times I expected hourly to have to pack our bags and leave

Germany. I particularly expected such a break after the sinking of the *Lusitania* in May 1915. One day shortly after that tragic event Zimmermann came to lunch with us. While I was talking to someone else, I overheard snatches of his conversation with another guest, a young American girl who had married a German. When Zimmermann left, I asked her what he had said about the *Lusitania*. She told me she had expressed the fear that, because of this incident, war would ensue between Germany and America, but that Zimmermann had replied, "Don't worry. We have had a cable from Dr. Dumba (the Austrian Ambassador to the United States) saying that Bryan had told him that the stern note sent by America was only meant for public consumption."

I grabbed my hat and rushed across the square to the Foreign Office and saw Zimmermann. He was still in an amiable mood, having consumed his usual two quarts of Moselle at lunch, and he readily asserted, "Certainly it is so: I will show you the cable." He handed me a cable signed by Dr. Dumba which read, "Have had a conversation with Secretary Bryan and he states, 'Pay no attention to the *Lusitania* note which is only intended as a sop to public opinion.'"

This cable placed me in a difficult position. Bryan was not only a friend of long standing, but was my chief as head of the State Department. I finally decided to cable Colonel House what Zimmermann had told me, using a special cipher known only to him and to me. The result, of course, was that he informed President Wilson, who immediately intervened in the matter, and Bryan publicly denied the alleged conversation related by Dumba.

Early in 1915 I informed the Foreign Office and the Chancellor that I would like an audience with the Emperor in order to discuss the question of prisoners of war and other

disputed matters. It was the rule in Berlin that an ambassador
could see the Kaiser at any time. But in this instance my requested audience was put off from day to day and week to
week. I finally asked Major Langhorne to tell the Kaiser that
it had been so long since I had seen him that I had forgotten
what he looked like. Langhorne did this and reported to me
that the Kaiser had replied, "I have nothing against Mr. Gerard personally, but I will not see the ambassador of a country that sells arms and ammunition to the enemies of Germany."

This answer was especially interesting since Germany
herself had been the agent by which such arms shipments
were made legal under international law, with the undoubted motive of preserving Germany's profitable munitions business. With this in mind, I wrote a note to the Chancellor saying that although I had several times requested an
audience with the Kaiser, I had now changed my mind and
therefore begged him to take no further trouble about the
matter. The reaction to my note was salutary: I was invited
to go to Potsdam almost the next day.

When I arrived at the Postdam Palace, I was straightway
taken to the Emperor. I found him dressed in a field-gray uniform and standing over a map-littered table. He strode
toward me across the room and, shaking his finger under my
nose, began to storm. "You are to understand," he cried,
"that I will stand no nonsense from America and America
had better look out after the war!"

As this thoughtful statement did not merit any answer that
I could think of, I remained silent and outwardly calm. He
next said accusingly that he had seen a picture of American
warships escorting ships built in America for the British
Navy. I assured him that this was not so. Then he charged

that a large loan had been floated in America for Great Britain and France. I replied that the first American loan to a belligerent was a loan to Germany, and that if he would send one of his aides to telephone the Foreign Office the fact could be quickly verified. Incredulous, he dispatched an aide on this errand, and the aide returned to report that my story was correct.

The Emperor, now deflated and certainly calmer, then went into what might be called his religious phase. He said to me, "Don't you believe that God is fighting on my side? Look where my armies are, and see what the Germans have accomplished." I could think of no apt reply to this one and said nothing, solacing myself with the happy thought that an ambassador should not involve himself in a religious controversy. When I continued to answer him with polite "hmm's" he dropped the *Gott mit uns* inquiry and talked in a natural manner of other matters. The gist of his conversation was that President Wilson had disqualified himself as a mediator, and that when the proper time came, he and his cousins George and Nicky would make peace.

The German Government was divided on the subject of unrestricted submarine warfare, the indiscriminate torpedoing of Allied ships. The more thoughtful officials realized that if it were carried too far America might be forced to enter the war. On the other side were the Prussian military element, the Navy, and their adherents, who believed that such tactics could starve Britain and France out of the war before America could be very effective. The opponents, who included the Kaiser in his weak, undecided way, were for the most part people such as Von Jagow and Von Bethmann-Hollweg who had been out of Germany often enough in their careers to have gained a better understanding of Anglo-American viewpoints, and who did not underrate the potential strength of America. The result was exactly what they had predicted.

Early in 1916 Colonel House arrived in Germany and took up the submarine question directly with the Chancellor. But he was unable to work out any definite agreement, and the situation seemed hopeless.

After the colonel's departure, the critical issue of the S.S. *Sussex* arose. The sinking of the *Sussex*, a Channel boat, caused forty deaths and injury to several American passengers. In this controversy the United States took the position that while the Germans had the right to torpedo merchant ships, they must first call on the passengers and crew to surrender and put them in safety before sinking a ship. I must add that to a certain extent I sympathized with the German point of view. I had sent the following letter to Colonel House embodying my views:

A submarine is a recognized weapon of war as far as the English go, because they use it themselves, and it seems to me to be an absurd proposition that a submarine must come to the surface, give warning, offer to put passengers and crew in safety, and constitute itself a target for merchant ships, which not only make a practice of firing at submarines at sight, but have undoubtedly received orders to do so.

I believe that if the Germans had stuck obstinately to their defense that merchant ships should not be armed, their view would have prevailed. It did not seem reasonable to require a submarine to surface and demand the surrender of an armed merchantman. For inevitably, as soon as the passengers and crew were safely in the lifeboats, the ship's gun crew would have a vulnerable target in the surfaced submarine. The Germans made a great deal of this point, but they weakened its force with other arguments of less validity.

In any event, after the *Sussex* incident it seemed that Germany and America had come to the point of an open break. However, some German friends suggested that I should go to northern France, where the Kaiser then was, and try to settle the grave issue with him in person. I consented to make this attempt only if I were requested to do so by the Foreign Office. A day or two later Von Jagow broke the rule requiring that I and not he should initiate a call. He called at the embassy and proposed that I go to the headquarters of the Emperor. I agreed, and taking Joseph Grew with me, traveled to the town of Charleville-Mézières in the Department of the Ardennes.

Days later I was told that I was to lunch with the Emperor. Accompanied by the Chancellor and Grew, I was escorted to a little château outside of the town. Grew and I wore silk hats and that garment least admired by the Kaiser—and now passé for diplomats—the frock coat. I was taken alone by the Chancellor into a garden on a gently sloping hillside below the château. Here I found the Emperor strolling—splendid in uniform. It was one of those moments the Kaiser loved, and he had apparently rehearsed his lines for it. As soon as I had drawn near he came to the point, so to say, and let me have it. "Do you come like a great proconsul bearing peace or war in the folds of your frock coat?" he intoned.

This surprising question at first caused me to glance down at my coat to see what folds he could mean, and then I realized he was indulging his flair for historical allusion. Dimly I recalled the episode in Roman history in which Quintus Fabius Maximus, Roman envoy to Carthage before the

Second Punic War, made two folds of his toga and grasping a fold in each hand, held them up and said, "In these folds I carry peace and war; choose which you will have." "Give us which you prefer," was the reply. "Then take war," answered the Roman, letting his toga fall. "We accept the gift," cried the Carthaginian senators, "and welcome."

To this twentieth-century Carthaginian I replied, "No, Your Majesty, I come only hoping that the difference between two friendly nations may be adjusted." It was the best I could do at the moment.

The Emperor first discussed the notes which had been sent by the United States Government. He remarked on what he termed their "discourteous tone," laying particular stress on the fact that we had charged the Germans with carrying on warfare in a barbaric manner. On the contrary, he said, as Emperor and head of the Church, he had carried on war in a knightly manner.

Touching on the British naval blockade, which he spoke of as an effort to starve Germany and keep milk for children from coming in, he said that before he would allow his own family and his grandchildren to starve, he would "send a Zeppelin over Windsor Castle and blow up the whole royal family of England." Some years later I quoted this remark to King George V and I'm afraid it quite upset him.

In the discussion of the submarine question which followed, the Emperor compared a passenger on an enemy ship to one traveling in a cart behind the battle lines—he had no just cause to complain if he was injured. With some asperity he asked me why America had done nothing to stop violations of international law by Great Britain and why we had not broken the British blockade. In answer I said that I could not recall any note sent by my government which had made any general charge of barbarism against Germany; that we had complained only of the manner in which the submarine was used. I also said that we could never agree to take any action against Great Britain, or any other country, in return for a promise made by Germany, or any other country, to keep the rules of international law and respect the rights and lives of our citizens; that all we demanded was our rights under the recognized rules of international law and it was for us to decide which rights we would enforce first. I then repeated a conversation with the Chancellor in which I had said that if two men entered my premises and one stepped on my flower beds and the other killed my sister, I should undoubtedly first pursue the murderer of my sister. Persons traveling in enemy merchant ships, I continued, were in a different position from those traveling in a cart behind the enemy's battle lines, because the land travelers were on enemy territory, while the sea, beyond the three-mile limit, was free.

Continuing to discuss the blockade, I reminded him that it was not our business to break this embargo, that there were plenty of German agents in the United States who could send food ships and test the question. I pointed out that one ship, the *Wilhelmina*, laden with food from the United States, had been seized by the British, who then compromised with the owners, paying them, I believed, a large sum for the cargo. I referred to the fact that during the Civil War we had taken exactly the same stand against Great Britain, with reference to shipments destined for the Confederacy, as Great Britain now took.

Both the Emperor and the Chancellor spoke of the warning that had been given before the sailing of the *Lusitania*. To which I answered, "If the Chancellor warns me not to go out on the *Wilhelmplatz*, where I have a perfect right to go, the fact that he gave the warning does not justify his killing me if I disregard his warning."

After more talk on generalities, we finally went into the château where the Emperor's aides and guests were impatiently waiting for lunch. I sat between the Emperor and the Prince of Pless. Conversation was general for most of the time, and subjects such as the suffragettes and the peace-ship expedition of Henry Ford were discussed with every appearance of light-heartedness. After lunch I again had a long talk with the Emperor. The result of this exchange of views was a note sent to America by Germany conceding the American position and agreeing not to sink ships without first putting the passengers and crew in safety. It was the breaking of this pledge at the end of January 1917 which eventually brought us into the war.

Its observance in the intervening months, however, was of incalculable influence on the course of history. It permitted the United States to sustain the Allies to considerable degree, and it allowed this country time to reach a degree of preparedness which materially shortened the period before victory. I consider it one of the two particularly outstanding services that I performed as ambassador. The other, of course, was the extent to which I was able to alleviate the suffering of Allied prisoners of war.

The Germans themselves credited me with preventing for two years their full use of their most powerful weapon, the submarine. Writing in the *Tages Zeitung* for August 14, 1917, Count Reventlow, influential newspaperman, asserted:

In the U-boat crisis Mr. Gerard has been able to play a decisive part. He was, like Mr. Von Bethmann-Hollweg, entirely of the view that the German Empire must give in to the demands of the United States and constantly showed himself wonderfully informed about what steps each inner circle would for the moment take.

The influence of Mr. Gerard is all the more a shameful and heavy reproach for the official leadership of Mr. Von Bethmann-Hollweg since this American Ambassador, while an intriguer, was not a personality.

But when Gerard said anything, or wished anything, or threatened anything, that imported always a fear-exciting event, and he was finally sly enough to seize and use this halo to the limit. That a man like Gerard has been able all these years to win and keep such a position and such an influence over German affairs is without example.

Germany's wartime ambassador to the United States, Count von Bernstorff, wrote a book called *My Three Years in America,* published in 1920 (the title and plan of which he copied from my first book). In it he says of me that:

On account of his anti-German tendency, Gerard was not popular in Berlin. He regarded it as a personal slight that the most important submarine warfare and peace negotiations should have been carried on partly in Washington and partly by Colonel House in Berlin. The Ambassador wanted therefore to use the opportunity of the *Sussex* incident to assert himself, and expressed a desire to visit G.H.Q. and explain the American point of view in person to the Emperor.

The fact is, as I have related, that affairs were at an absolute stalemate both in Washington and Berlin, and the first suggestion that I should attempt to settle the question with the Emperor personally was made by Dr. Ludwig Stein, who published a diplomatic magazine called *Nord and Sud* and whose articles bore the pen name of "Diplomaticus." Then Herr Hecksher, a member of the Reichstag, came to see me and put the same question, and after that Von Jagow called in person. After I had returned from seeing the Kaiser at General Headquarters in France, I gave a gold cigarette case to Dr. Stein inscribing it to a *"Wirklicher Geheimner Galvanizator."* I meant to commemorate the fact that it was he who had galvanized a deadlocked situation into a lively negotiation.

After the war Dr. Stein came to this country, and at his suggestion a fund was organized for the assistance of German intellectuals, physicians, artists, writers, and so on. I was chairman, and Mr. Stettinius, father of Edward R. Stettinius, Jr., afterward Secretary of State, was treasurer. We were in the process of raising a considerable sum when the German embassy refused to half-mast its flag upon the death of President Wilson. After that we never got a dollar.

In the autumn of 1916 the issue of submarine warfare strained relations between the United States and Germany to the breaking point. The German Army, Navy, and the great mass of the population had been promised a quick peace if the Navy were allowed to resort to "ruthless submarine warfare." They demanded a resumption of that campaign. Thinking men, such as the Chancellor and Von Jagow, appreciated what it would mean to provoke the United States into war and held out as long as possible, and it was at their request that I decided to visit America and discuss these subjects with the President.

In September 1916 Mrs. Gerard and I sailed from Copenhagen on the *Frederick VIII,* a Danish boat which, with great flags and letters illuminated on its sides, hoped to escape sinking by the submarines. On board were Herbert Bayard Swope and his wife, and William Bullitt and his wife, and their stimulating conversation enlivened the long hours of the voyage. As we approached the shores of America, Swope knocked at my cabin door about one o'clock one morning and told me that the captain thought I should be told that U-boats were operating ahead of us and had just sunk several ships in the neighborhood of Nantucket Island. All the next day the air bore the smell of oil from one of the destroyed tankers. Swope wrote a thoughtful book on his observations and experiences called *Inside the German Empire*, which he dedicated to me. It had a substantial and deserved success.

When we landed in New York I was given a great reception at the New York City Hall. Afterward I visited President Wilson at his large house called Shadowlawn, at Long Branch, which he then occupied. For four hours the President listened intently to my report of conditions in Germany and my belief that if he could not force an early peace, he would have to face a war. At lunch a cake was served which the President said had been sent to him by a "German-American." A strain of caution prompted me to refuse my share, but the President and Mrs. Wilson partook largely of this gift. I doubt if they would have done so later.

On December 4, 1916, Count von Bernstorff cabled the Chancellor the following report:

House told me in strict confidence question of Mr. Gerard's return has been thoroughly discussed by him with Mr. Wilson and Mr. Lansing. Mr. Gerard's unpopularity in Berlin and his unfriendly manner were well known here. However, no satisfactory successor was available, and Mr. Gerard is at least straightforward and does exactly what he is told. He has received very detailed instructions here and is even quite enthusiastic over the idea of assisting in bringing about peace. . . . He was certainly right in his prediction of the unrestricted submarine campaign.

In all my writings and speeches since the war I had never once referred to Count Bernstorff, as I was uncertain as to his real attitude during the war. But I am now certain that he was genuinely in favor of keeping the peace between Germany and the United States and bitterly opposed the ruthless submarine war. He and Von Jagow to the end, and Bethmann-Hollweg for a time, held out against the generals who presumed to direct the political as well as the military policies of the Empire.

Bernstorff was the protégé of Prince von Bülow, sometime Chancellor, a tricky politician whose memoirs are a mass of adroit, deliberate, and monumental lies.

Personally, I found Count Bernstorff an engaging companion, a man with an agile, non-Prussian, and international mind. But an index of his character is found on page 175 of his second book. He writes that, during his mission to Constantinople after the war, he learned to like and "respect" Talaat Bey, the man, he admits, who had a hand in the massacre of 800,000 helpless Armenians.

CHAPTER XXII

A T THE END OF DECEMBER, ON ORDERS FROM THE PRESI-
dent, I returned to Germany. Mrs. Gerard accompanied me,
and again we took the long, cold, wartime route across the
stormy North Atlantic around the top of Scotland. In Copenhagen we delayed a few days to arrange for the transportation of about two tons of food that I had brought from the
United States. While we were there, President Wilson's celebrated note seeking a basis for peace was transmitted through
our legation in Copenhagen. It arrived in Berlin a few hours
before I did, and Grew had immediately presented it to the
Foreign Office. However, by that time it was obvious to me
that the President's note would have no effect.

I was informed through various channels (which even now
I cannot disclose) of the imminence of a return to merciless
submarine warfare. I knew of this on the night of a great banquet given to me in Berlin at which I said in a speech that the
relations between Germany and the United States had never
been better. Both the President and Colonel House had urged
me to show myself exceptionally friendly to the Germans.
Knowing that the break would soon come, I was delighted to
follow these orders. I knew that if I showed myself exces-
sively friendly, criticism of the Wilson administration by the

great mass of German-Americans would be blunted when relations were finally broken.

During my absence Zimmermann had replaced Von Jagow as head of the Ministry of Foreign Affairs. Zimmermann had completely fallen in with the desires of the military to risk a break with the United States. On the last day of January a brief note from him asked me to call at the Foreign Office at six o'clock. At that meeting he informed me that Germany had marked off large parts of the seas for unrestricted warfare. Any ship, enemy or neutral, that ventured into these areas was to be sunk without notice. I had, a few days before, transmitted a warning to Washington that this would probably occur.

On the third of February 1917 I received a cable directing me to break diplomatic relations with Germany. In compliance I called on Zimmermann and demanded my passports, following this with a note to the Foreign Office making the same request formally. I heard nothing from the Foreign Office until a day later, when, returning to my office from a walk, I found Count Montgelas. Montgelas had the rank of Minister, and headed the Foreign Office department which handled American affairs. I asked him why I hadn't received my passports. He told me that I was being delayed because the Imperial Government didn't know what had happened to Count Bernstorff. There had been rumors, he added, that German ships in American ports had been confiscated by our government. I replied that I was quite sure that Bernstorff was being treated with every courtesy and that the German ships had not been confiscated. I said, moreover, "I do not see why I have to disprove your idea that Bernstorff is being maltreated and the German ships confiscated. It is for you to prove this; and, at any event, why don't you have the Swiss

Government, which now represents you, cable to its Minister in Washington and get the exact facts?"

"Well," he said, "you know, the Swiss are not used to cabling."

Then with a flourish he produced a document which turned out to be a reaffirmation of the Treaty of 1799 between Prussia and the United States with some very extraordinary clauses added to it. He asked me to read this, and either to sign it or to get authority to sign it. If it was not signed, he said, it would be very difficult for Americans to leave the country, particularly the American correspondents. I read the treaty over. It provided, among other things, that German ships in our ports should be given a pass, recognized as binding by all the enemy sea powers, to a home port or to another port of its master's choice.

"Of course I cannot sign this on my own responsibility," I said. "I will not cable to my government unless I can cable in cipher and give it my opinion of this document."

"That," he replied, "is impossible."

"Then I shall not cable at all. Why do you come to me with a proposed treaty after we have broken diplomatic relations and ask an ambassador who is held as a prisoner to sign it? Prisoners do not sign treaties and treaties signed by them would not be worth anything." And I added, "After your threat to keep Americans here, and after reading this document, even if I had authority to sign it I would stay here until hell freezes over before I would put my name to such a paper."

When I told the American correspondents then in Berlin of Montgelas's threat, all of them, even the pro-German ones, urged me not to consider them or their liberty where the interests of America were involved. Montgelas was a gentleman, and I learned later that in this conference he had acted on orders that were distasteful to him personally.

During the following week I was not allowed to telegraph instructions to the American consuls throughout Germany, nor was I, my staff, or my servants permitted to use the telephone. Every time I left the house I was followed by three or four heavy-footed German detectives. I managed to shake them off by traveling on the subway. I would get off at a station and then, when they had gotten off, suddenly jump on again as the train was starting. In this way I managed to secure the delivery of some letters which Samuel Gompers, our great labor leader, had entrusted to me for leaders of labor in Germany.

I sold two prize-winning American saddle horses to the proprietor of a circus, and he asked if there was anything else that I wished to sell. I sold him some guns and other articles which I didn't want to carry out, and then he said, "Anything else?" My American associate, Frank Hall, who was standing behind me, said, "Why don't you sell him that uniform?" He referred to the fancy diplomatic uniform I had acquired but never used when I first came to Berlin. When my predecessor had given me information about Berlin Court life, he mentioned that I would have to wear a uniform.

"But," I said, "we have no uniform."

"Then you can copy mine," he replied.

So I ordered a complete outfit from his London tailor. When I arrived in Berlin and found this uniform and its gaudy accessories laid out on my bed, I shivered at the thought of what the American newspapers would say if they learned of it. There was a coat covered with gold lace, trousers with a broad gold stripe, a piratical cloak, a cocked hat

with white feathers, and a sword. I called on Count Eulenburg and asked him if I had to wear a uniform.

"I will give you the same answer that I gave one of your
predecessors," he said. "The answer is 'No.' Your predecessor,"
Eulenburg continued, "then asked, 'Would you rather have
me wear a uniform?' and I again answered, 'No.' Then he said,
'Well, I am going to wear one anyway,' and proceeded to
wear something that he had designed himself."

At any rate, I sold the never-used uniform to the Lord of
the Circus. I have no doubt that in later years as the ringmaster cracked his whip and engaged in repartee with the
clown, some reference must have been made to the American Ambassador's uniform worn by the ringmaster.

The diplomats representing Soviet Russia appeared at the
coronation of George VI in plain dress suits, but at the end
of 1943 they suddenly adopted a uniform as splendid as that
of any country. As the French say, *"Plus ça change, plus c'est
la même chose."*

When the French and Russian ambassadors to Germany
left for their homelands in August 1914, they were not allowed to proceed directly but were disdainfully sent to Denmark. German guards stood over the French Ambassador
with drawn pistols when his train crossed the Kiel Canal,
doubtless to frustrate any effort he might make to block the
canal by tossing a piece of German *patisserie* through the
window. The French, at the same time, sent the German Ambassador to France directly back to the German border in a
special train, amid the usual courtesies, and the Germans—
their ambassador safely returned—thoughtfully stole the
train.

Naturally these incidents were fresh in the minds of the

members of the diplomatic corps who remained in Berlin, and undoubtedly each of us wondered just what sort of exodus he would have if the fortunes of war required him to leave for home.

For two and a half years I had often said jokingly to Von Jagow and Zimmermann, and even to the Chancellor, "When I leave Germany, you can't treat me as you treated the other ambassadors." When the break in diplomatic relations finally came, I told Zimmermann that I would insist on my choice of routes. Since it was not then possible to get to Russia and home from there, I chose Switzerland. Finally the word came that I would be permitted to leave. The Germans gave me a special train with a car for Mrs. Gerard and myself. I took with me all the embassy staff and all of the correspondents and other Americans who wanted to leave, in all about a hundred and twenty people. Our train left at 8 P.M. from the Potsdamer railway station, in the heart of Berlin. There was no demonstration; the German onlookers seemed dazed rather than excited by our exit. I had the impression that they realized that our departure symbolized their eventual defeat. Count von Moltke, the Danish Minister, sent his car to take us to the station.

When I had at last been informed that we were to be allowed to leave Germany, I decided, despite the delay and the discourtesies, to bid a personal farewell to the Chancellor, of whom I was very fond. I sent word across the square to the Foreign Office that I was coming over to see him for a purely personal visit. Nothing either of us said, my message continued, would be put in any blue book, or red book, or white book. I had a pleasant talk with the Chancellor for about half an hour or more. As I stood up to leave, he remarked, "I must say that we Germans do not understand the psychology of other nations." This phrase, I believe, summed up the whole situation of the German ruling classes.

Several of the higher-ups from the German Foreign Office —and all of the neutral diplomats—appeared at the railroad station to see us off, as did a number of Americans who had decided to stay in Berlin. These sent up a vigorous cheer as our train pulled out of the station. The Germans had sent a General Staff officer and an officer from the Foreign Office to accompany me to the frontier. I had filled the train with all our remaining wines, cigarettes, and other comforting things, and entertained these officers en route. When they said farewell to us at the Swiss frontier, I presented each one with a gold cigarette case with the date engraved, which I had obtained before leaving Berlin.

The train stopped at Zurich, and we had supper in the station restaurant with Harold McCormick and his wife, who was a daughter of John D. Rockefeller, Sr. They entrusted me with the care of their son, Fowler McCormick, a fine young man—now chairman of the International Harvester Company—who thereafter remained with us until I turned him over to his grandfather's representative as our train from Key West stopped at the railroad station of Daytona, Florida.

After resting a day or so in Berne, the Swiss capital, we went to Paris. There, at the request of British Lord Esher, I had an interview with General Lyautey, the celebrated conqueror of Morocco, who was then France's Minister of War. When Lyautey said that he "supposed the Germans had exhausted their reserves," I had to reply: "No, General, I am sorry to tell you that I have seen many new regiments drilling."

Lyautey asked many searching questions about what was going on inside Germany and I gave him, of course, my best knowledge. I also had interviews with Briand, Poincaré, and others. I was invited to visit the French war front but regretfully declined, for I felt it my pressing duty to hurry back to the United States and make my report.

From Paris we took the train to Spain and while waiting for the train to start from the Paris station, I struck up conversation with a little French soldier who stood on the platform. I asked him about his ideas of the war. He answered, "My father and grandfather were both killed in wars with the Germans. I feel that we have got to end this danger forever and go on with the war." (He would have been discouraged, I am sure, if he could have foreseen that his own son might be voicing the same thought in May 1940, and—who knows? —his grandson in 1965?!) His conviction was quite different from that of a number of the French higher-ups in 1917. They seemed ready to quit the war, and in truth it was only the entrance of the United States shortly afterward that prevented a movement in France for a negotiated peace.

We spent a few days in Madrid, looking about for a method of getting home, and while there were entertained by the Spaniards as well as by our excellent Ambassador, Joseph E. Willard. King Alfonso asked that I be presented to him, and Mr. Willard took me to the palace one morning about eleven o'clock. I was immediately shown into a small room alone with the King.

Alfonso first pressed me to accept an enormous cocktail, saying that he understood that American gentlemen always drank in the morning. I managed to dodge this without renouncing my gentility, and in answer to his questions told him what I could about the war situation in Germany. He brought up the subject of conditions in his own country and said he wanted American capital to come to Spain. I replied,

"But you have a great deal of capital here in your own country."

"Yes," he said, "but the capitalists put their money in government bonds and sit in front of the cafés nibbling olives and drinking wine. They won't venture their money in any speculation which has a spice of danger." Then he added, "I suppose you want to know where I stand in this war. My sympathy is with France, but remember that I am an Austrian grand duke and the son of an Austrian grand duchess."

After the war, when the Spanish novelist Blasco Ibáñez wrote attacking the King, charging that he had been against the Allies during the war, I published an account of this part of my interview with Alfonso, and through our then Ambassador Moore received the thanks of the King.

From Madrid we went to LaCoruna, a seaport in the extreme northwestern corner of Spain and sailed from there on the *Infanta Isabella,* a fairly large ship, for Havana. This seemed to be the safest way to cross the Atlantic.

The Duke of Saragossa, a noted amateur locomotive engineer, drove our train for some hours after it left Madrid, crossing the Guadarrama Mountains over steep grades. When he had finished his turn of duty, he came into the dining car and ate with us in his overalls, wiping his hands on cotton waste—just like a real engineer. He said it was the ambition of his life to come to America and see the pretty girls and the big locomotives.

After a pleasant voyage we landed in Havana and straightway crossed to Key West where we boarded a train for Washington. As the trains stopped frequently at the stations in Florida, crowds had gathered to greet us, and at St. Augustine my old friends Frank Munsey and Chauncey Depew joined the crowd with a hired band. Chauncey Depew pulled me to one side and said, "Young fellow, don't let this get into your blood. If it does, you will never have a peaceful moment thereafter, because this sort of thing never lasts—in America, at least."

When we got to Washington, Senator McAdoo and Frank Polk were at the station to meet me and expressed President Wilson's regrets that he was ill with a cold and couldn't see me that day. He wished me to stay over in Washington in order to see him the next day. The next afternoon I gave the President a two-hour report. During this interview the President suggested that if war were declared, I should go around the country making speeches and explaining the situation. This I promised to do.

It is quite a pleasant feeling to be received into the arms of New York City—a great many people have been, and they all seemed to enjoy it. Back in 1917 the art of welcoming a returning hero was not so highly developed as it later became under the regime of Mayor Jimmy Walker, but it was probably less stereotyped and more emotional. My reception was not, as I say, so elaborate as those of the late twenties but it had a considerable thrilling quality. Naturally the drama came from the fact that to the onlookers my arrival was a reminder that America might soon be at war.

John B. Stanchfield was chairman of the reception committee, which included my old friend Clarence H. Mackay, and the entire committee escorted me in automobiles to City Hall where I was officially received. Speeches were made by Mr. Stanchfield and Mayor Mitchel, and in due course I made a short speech on the steps of City Hall. I said:

We are standing today very near the brink of war, but I want to assure you that if we should be drawn into the conflict, it will be only after our President has exhausted every means consistent with upholding the honor and dignity of the United States to keep us from war. I left Berlin with a clear conscience because I felt that during all my stay there I had omitted nothing to make for friendly relations and peace between the two nations.

The precarious peace persisted until an overt act came in the sinking of another ship. Then a declaration of war against Germany was demanded from Congress by President Wilson on April 6, 1917. On that night we were with Mr. and Mrs. Lewis Iselin in their box in the Metropolitan Opera House. Suddenly, during an intermission, newsboys were heard crying extras—"all about the declaration of war." I found one of the directors of the Metropolitan in the lobby and said to him, "Aren't you going to do something—aren't you going to have the orchestra play 'The Star-Spangled Banner'?"

"The Opera House," he replied, "is neutral."

I immediately went to the front of our box and in a loud voice called for three cheers for President Wilson. The audience responded with a will. The opera was De Koven's *Canterbury Pilgrims,* and my act so shocked one of the German songstresses that, as the audience rose and cheered, she keeled over in a faint.

CHAPTER XXIII

IT WAS GERMANY WHO DECLARED WAR, AND THE RESPONSI-
bility for that declaration must rest upon the German General Staff. The German lower classes, who well understood
that they were cannon fodder, had no wish for war. In 1911,
when war threatened because of the incidents at Agadir, a
great gathering of the plain people in the Tempelhofer Feld
raised their hands and voices in protest against war. In 1914
they had no time to protest. They were hurried into war before they knew what was happening.

In this question of the outbreak of war it must be noted
that Sir Edward Grey missed a great opportunity. If, in the
beginning, he had told the German Ambassador that England
would go to war against Germany (it may be that he had no
authority to make such a statement, but there are times when
bluffs are justified) and his bluff had succeeded, the world
might have been spared a great war—a war which sowed the
seeds of another and greater one twenty-five years after. Had
such a bluff failed, England would have been in no worse
position than if it had never been made. As I wrote for the
supplement of the Encyclopaedia Britannica: "It is a pity that
when Sir Edward Grey was at Oxford the American game of
poker was not part of that university's curriculum."

An interesting guide to Sir Edward Grey's actual attitude toward Germany—and toward the war which had just begun—is contained in a letter written to me by Prince Lichnowsky, German Ambassador at the Court of St. James's. When Lichnowsky returned to Germany I made his acquaintance, and on August 27, 1915, he wrote me the following letter giving what he claimed to be the attitude of Sir Edward Grey at the time of the breaking of diplomatic relations between Germany and Great Britain. This letter I publish for the first time.

Telephon	Kuchelna
Bolatit z 2	Oberschlesien
Aug. 27.	15.

Dear Mr. Gerard,

I should like you to know exactly what happened the last time I saw Sir Edward Grey. Owing to a communication that Sir Edward wished to see me before I left London, I took leave from him at his private lodging. What Sir Edward said was this:

"It has been the most terrible decision I ever had to take in my life. I want you to know that I shall always be ready to mediate, provided I am still in office."

On my remark that although I had always expected that Great Britain would protect France, I nevertheless thought that the British position would have been stronger if he had remained neutral as an umpire, Sir Edward answered:

"No—I can also withdraw if things don't go as your military people think they shall go. We don't wish to crush Germany."

I immediately made a note of it when I came to Berlin and delivered it at the Foreign Office because I thought it essential for my government to understand that, as I always had reported before the war and have said since, there was no wish on the British side to destroy Germany, and that Sir Edward had shown even in the last moment his good will for future mediation. I regret to have to acknowledge that the way the Chancellor interpreted my report amounts to a misrepresentation and that I have drawn the attention to this fact by a letter I recently addressed to the Foreign Office. Pray make the use you think proper of this statement, but of course avoid publication as I am bound to remain silent as long as the war lasts although I have, as you will be aware of all this time, endeavored to explain why Great Britain joined and to oppose as much as possible the anti-British feeling.

Hoping to find you in Berlin when I come to town again, I am, dear Sir.

Very sincerely yours,
Lichnowsky

If there had been any delay, any discussion of war, as in 1911, I am satisfied that war could have been averted. The General Staff knew this and desired an immediate declaration of war by the Emperor. However, according to the Constitution of the German Empire, an offensive war could not be declared solely by the Emperor, while the Emperor alone *could* declare a defensive war. Hence, it was first proclaimed that French fliers had flown over Nuremberg and that French troops had crossed the Belgian frontier. This story justified a declaration of war by the Emperor alone and the German violation of Belgium's neutrality. No shred of proof has ever been advanced to justify the Nuremberg story. On August 10, 1914, in the personal letter which he penciled in my presence to President Wilson, the Kaiser wrote that the neutrality of Belgium was violated for strategical reasons.

I was told by Von Gwinner, the head of the Deutsche Bank, that when, at the last moment, the Emperor still hesitated to declare war, the officers of the Staff threatened to break their swords over their knees if he did not sign the declaration. In an article I wrote after the war I mentioned this, whereupon

Von Gwinner denied that he had ever made such a statement to me.

I have always wanted to get to the bottom of this, so in 1938 I commissioned a friend of ours who was going to Holland to visit the former Kaiser in exile at Doorn to ask the Kaiser two questions. In due course I received from our friend the Kaiser's answer in the following letter to Mrs. Gerard, written on the notepaper of Hasn Doorn:

Hasn Doorn

August 26, 1938.

Dear Mrs. Gerard,

True to my promise to Mr. Gerard, I asked the Emperor yesterday about the two points which I noted down at the time, namely:

(1) Did the generals and officers of the General Staff threaten to break their swords across their knees if His Majesty refused to sign the declaration of war in 1914?

To this the Emperor said, "Nonsense. There was no such conference and such a thing never took place. In fact," he added, "almost every head of the Staff and, indeed, of the important departments both Army and Navy, were on leave at the time." He considers this fact as one of the most conclusive proofs that he was not expecting or preparing for war.

In a previous chapter I have spoken of the breakfast with the Kaiser at Potsdam to which I took Colonel House before the war in 1914. After breakfast the Kaiser and Colonel House had a private conversation about a proposed alliance. My second question for the Kaiser was about that conversation, as follows:

(2) Was France to be included in an alliance proposed by Germany in May 1914 between Germany, England, and America?

To this the Emperor said that the proposal had been made but France was not mentioned as it was a foregone conclusion that had such an alliance matured, France would obviously have been forced to join in.

When a murder has been committed and there are several suspects, the law examines what motives each suspect might have had. For Russia and France, 1914 was too early for possible military success. In France a law making the period of military service three years instead of two, bringing a great increase in the standing army, was soon to be effective. In Russia a reorganization of the army had been decreed, but not begun, and the strategic railways planned for the Polish frontier had not been constructed, although the money for their construction had already been furnished by France. Belgium had voted universal military service, but the universal service had not started. England seemed occupied by affairs at home and her small standing army was largely distributed in colonial garrisons.

On the other hand, Germany had used the money raised by the *Wehr Beitrag* (defense tax) to add a great force to her standing army. This force was in being and under arms. Then there were the Zeppelins and submarines and airplanes and the military secrets of poison gas, flame-throwers, and the improved heavy artillery which was to make any fort untenable. To the east of Germany, Russia, recently defeated in her war with Japan, appeared to be occupied by a growing internal revolution. From a military standpoint, if the zero hour of *der Tag* was ever to strike for Germany, 1914 was the year of supreme opportunity.

The conclusions from all this are, of course, quite obvious. When nations compete in armaments, and are constantly thinking about war, there will always come what seems to the military chiefs of one nation to be a favorable moment to begin. Only in common sense, in tolerance and under-standing, and in a carefully supervised disarmament can we find an end of war.

The Kaiser's heavy-handed conceit and his flair for attract-ing unfortunate publicity had one very definite result which, when he became aware of it, must have puzzled him im-mensely. In the minds of all the Allied peoples—and par-ticularly in America—he became the symbol of Teutonic bru-tality. His naïve and astonishing pronouncements and his indiscreet bombast earned for him the blame for the war and the authorship of all the atrocities with which his armies were charged.

For these crimes he was hanged in effigy—and occasion-ally burned—in every Middlesex village and town. Lloyd George, after the war, conducted one of his election cam-paigns on the platform of "Hang the Kaiser." In America, on the Fourth of July in 1917 and 1918, and particularly on Armistice Day in 1918, appropriately dressed straw men labeled either "Kaiser Bill" or "The Beast of Berlin" were hanged and burned. In most people's minds these executions *in absentia* were satisfactory evidence that the master mind of German warmongering had been discovered and laid low, and that with the symbol of war thus eradicated the last threat to world peace had been removed.

Meanwhile, the Prussian military clique remained quietly in the background. They had taken advantage of Wilhelm's vanity to promote the war and encouraged him to take the limelight and the huzzas. In defeat they were pleased and probably wryly amused to have him saddled with the onus of war guilt.

The most remarkable fact about the Kaiser was that a man

of such mediocre talents should occupy the center of the stage in an awesome, world-wide war. He was not, politically, an autocrat—everyone acquainted with German conditions knew this. Nor did he think of himself as an autocrat. He often said to me, "I wish I had as much power as your President." The fact that the Kaiser practically conquered the inconvenience of his shrunken left arm—a congenital infirmity —and became a good shot, shows that from his youth he had ambition and will power. With the same persistence which made him a good shot, he learned to be a good rider. When I was visiting his private apartments in the Castle of Posen I saw a saddle on which I was told he sat when at work. It was typical of his pertinacity.

Since the Kaiser signed the declaration of war technically —but only technically—the responsibility for war rests upon him. But as Count Thiele-Winkler, a prominent German noble, said to me a few days before the war began: "The great armaments and consequent taxes are breaking the backs of the countries of Europe—war is the only solution." There is no doubt that war was looked on with moderate favor by the House of Hohenzollern, which risked its throne, and with avid favor by the great ruling class of Prussian nobles, which stood to gain much. Especially did the General Staff look on war as very desirable—the sole outlet for manly ambition and enterprise. The rich merchant class looked not unfavorably on a war which might give Germany a trade monopoly of the world. Only the working class and a handful of intellectuals were opposed to it, but for the most part their opposition was passive.

My impression is that the Kaiser, even though he acquiesced in the preparations for a war in 1914, wavered at the last moment and desired peace. According to Colonel House, who interviewed the Kaiser in Potsdam in May 1914, the Kaiser proposed an alliance of England, Germany, and the United States for the purpose of guarding the peace of the world. It is true that this proposal may have been made in order to lull international suspicions and add to the surprise of the war's opening attack. More likely, however, it was entirely a little thought of the Kaiser's own. And then there was the marginal note written by the Kaiser himself after the receipt of the Serbian reply to Austria in 1914. He wrote on his copy of that document:

"A great moral victory for Vienna; but with it every pretext for war falls to the ground. I would suggest saying to Austria we congratulate her. There are no further grounds for war."

This brings me to the question of the Kaiser's real character. Certainly no man that I have ever met was wholly anything. We are all a mixture of qualities—of good and bad, of strength and weakness; sometimes one quality predominates, sometimes another. The Kaiser was not what is called a "strong" man. He gave no such feeling of force, of out-thrusting vitality, as I gained from Wilson, Díaz, or Poincaré —men who went to the top by sheer power of will. Neither, on the other hand, did he give the impression of cool reserve and balance which characterized the then King of the Belgians. Wilhelm seemed to be rather a good-natured man, vain of his versatility, who felt compelled by circumstances to put on a fierce front, and doing it with but little success. Coupled with his strong religious feeling was a tendency to loud words which, however, rarely frightened anyone who came in direct contact with him.

An example of the Kaiser's extreme saber-rattling, which

Europe took seriously, was his speech to the German marines about to leave for China during the Boxer Uprising. He said:

Take no prisoners! Kill him [the foe] when he falls into your hands. Even as a thousand years ago, the Huns under their King Attila made such a name for themselves as still resounds in terror through legend and fable, so may the name of Germans resound through Chinese history a thousand years from now.

The time interval of "a thousand years" must be deeply ingrained in the German mind. I doubt if they can recall it without a shudder. In World War II both Hitler and Goebbels took the long view in their exhortations and spoke of their victories as "determining the history of the world for a thousand years to come."

At one period of his career, about 1907, the Kaiser had a number of intimate friends, men of unusual talent, whom he called his Knights of the Round Table. Among them were Prince Eulenburg, Count Kuno von Moltke, and Hohenau. At that time in Berlin there lived a journalist, born Witkowski, who had changed his name to Maximilian Harden. This man, an admirer of Bismarck, published a little newspaper called *Die Zukunft* which appeared at irregular intervals and was sold on the streets by old women and boys. One issue, about 1907, charged that these friends of the Kaiser were homosexuals. A storm broke. Harden was put on trial but was not given the opportunity to prove the truth of his charges. However, the Berlin jury believed that what Harden said was true, and the prosecution failed. In Bavaria, in an action instituted there, the Court intimated that it would allow the truth of the charges to be proved, but that proceeding failed to come off. By public demand, some of these favorites were put on trial, but after a short period the trials were adjourned on the grounds that the defendants were unable to stand trial. Some of them left the country, some retired to their country estates. Every year thereafter, even up to the time of the last war, a commission used to issue from the courts and make a solemn round of the country estates where all these alleged degenerates were living. It would then solemnly report to the Court that they were still unable to stand trial. All this gave Harden an indefinable power which he exercised from time to time through articles published in his little newspaper.

The charge that the Kaiser was surrounded by a group of homosexuals was curiously similar to the situation which existed shortly after Hitler's rise. And nothing could better illustrate the comparative degree of power held by the Kaiser and by Hitler than that the latter could order the cold-blooded murder of Ernest Roehm and others without fear of reprisal either by their friends or the populace.

At the time of the dispute between the United States and Germany on the submarine question, Chancellor von Bethmann-Hollweg was entirely sympathetic to the position of the United States. He complained to me one day that bitter attacks were being made on him because of his desire to keep the peace between the two nations. I suggested that he enlist Harden and his powerful pen on the government's side. He did this, and Harden wrote a pamphlet called *If I Were Wilson* which endorsed the American point of view. I went out of my way to get acquainted with Harden and he came to our house several times.

It became the fashion to despise the Kaiser, but it must be remembered in appraising him that under his rule Germany attained with startling rapidity a tremendous place among nations. The German Army was the most efficient in the world; the German Navy formidable. Commercially, all the gold of the earth was in the process of flowing toward the German coffers. German trading enterprise challenged all nations in the markets of the world. She was supreme in many industries, especially the chemical, optical, and dyestuffs, and the iron and steel manufacture of Germany threatened that of England and the United States. The *Imperator* and the *Vaterland* were the greatest ships afloat, and her numerous merchant ships sailed the seven seas. And, ridicule the German Junker as you will, no country with a political, military, and commercial system so complicated has ever been governed with such a total absence of corruption. Finally, it must be said that the German people at large seemed to be animated by a high sense of patriotism and a rigid devotion to duty and tradition.

Nothing surprised me more after the outbreak of the war than the quick revaluation of great dependence of the rest of the world on German manufactures. For instance, the mining industry of the United States and Mexico almost closed, as I had personal reason to know, for the want of cyanide of sodium, a necessity of modern mining. Only with the greatest difficulty did I finally manage to get out a cargo of this chemical from Germany. With the permission of the Allies this cargo reached the United States and temporarily saved our mining industry until it could find other sources of supply.

In the same way, our production of beet sugar was at a standstill. Almost all of the world supply of sugar-beet seed was produced in the neighborhood of Magdeburg. I managed to get out enough beet seed to save this situation temporarily.

Since, under the peacetime rule of the Kaiser, Germany attained to the greatest power and prosperity in her history, and since the Kaiser to some degree opposed entering the war and was against the ruthless submarine warfare which brought in the United States to compass Germany's defeat, it does seem that this man, despite his manifest weaknesses and his saber-rattling, deserves a somewhat better place in history than that so far accorded him. It has almost escaped notice that the Kaiser had nothing of that hatred of Jews which possessed Hitler to inflict on that race a persecution unequaled even in the most cruel period of the Dark Ages.

Nothing so ill became the Kaiser as his manner of going. If he had placed himself at the head of a handful of cavalry, charged the Allied lines, and survived the gesture, he might have remained the Emperor. It is surprising, with his genius for stage display, that his back-door flight to Holland was ever undertaken. But we must remember the nerve strain from which the man was suffering after the responsibility of four years of war, and the fact that his oldest and best counselors not only advised, but insisted upon this course. Perhaps it was a desire for martyrdom and the German fondness for a tragic ending that were the determining factors in his abdication and flight. After these many years of rumination I see the Kaiser as having been a quiet, vain, ordinary man, little different from the rest of mankind, who made so poor a departure from the stage as to destroy the memory of his better performances.

CHAPTER XXIV

WHEN CONGRESS DECLARED WAR ON GERMANY IN 1917 I thought that my knowledge of Germany, the people, and the language would fit me for a uniform and a post in Intelligence, questioning prisoners, evaluating intelligence reports, and so on. But President Wilson and Colonel House would not hear of this. They urged me to tour the country explaining to the people why we were in the war and what we were fighting for. I had been given a round of this duty shortly after my return from Germany, informing Americans about Germany's war aims and the danger of our becoming embroiled.

Woodrow Wilson had few peers as a phrasemaker. It became something of a vogue, after people began to feel cheated because victory in 1918 had not produced Utopia, to sneer at the rolling periods by which Wilson had once galvanized his countrymen. In the bitterness of their disillusion over the discovery that the war had not solved all international problems, they forgot that Wilson had not promised "To make the world safe for democracy"—forever.

I started out across the country in 1917 to explain the threat we faced.

My speaking tour got off to a splendid start and produced

many memorable experiences. In Harrisburg, Pennsylvania, on my triumphal journey to the meeting hall, I was escorted by a troop of cavalry, amid the rattling of swords and the hoarse orders of the officers. It was stirring, picturesque, and, of course, very warlike.

My experience in Seattle was unforgettable, too, for it was here that—like Saul of Tarsus—I saw the light and truth revealed to me. When my train was about fifty miles from that city a group of its distinguished citizens came aboard to greet me. This was a pleasant gesture and, I thought, quite appropriate to the importance of my visit. In the station the local naval militia were drawn up to receive me. I was escorted to the hotel by horse, foot, and dragoons. The armory where I spoke was jammed, and those who could not get in gathered in churches and refused to go home until I had addressed them too.

A few weeks later I went to Seattle on some private business and couldn't even find a boy to carry my bag. And then I recalled the sage counsel given me by Chauncey Depew. His words now took on meaning: "Don't let this sort of thing get in your blood and expect it always; it's only temporary. If you think otherwise you will be disappointed and embittered." Thereafter I could take a cavalry-and-torchlight escort, or I could leave it alone.

In Los Angeles, Douglas Fairbanks gave a rodeo in my honor, and when he happened, in the course of it, to fall off his horse, he exclaimed, "Everyone falls for the Ambassador!" His intelligent and beautiful wife, Mary Pickford, invited me to watch her work. She was making a picture called *Stella Maris*, and I was amazed at the tremendous amount of hard work the cinema greats endure in order to obtain success.

I never accepted any fees for speaking, and always paid

my own expenses. Once I was offered a thousand dollars a night by a Chautauqua circuit, but that was unusual. Another time I was asked to substitute for ex-President Taft, who was ill. Out of curiosity I asked what he received and was told from four hundred to five hundred dollars. Bryan was said to like to gamble a little and usually asked for two hundred and fifty dollars and half the gate.

In Albuquerque I tried a few sentences in Spanish and a little French in Manchester, New Hampshire. On other occasions I even essayed a few words of the Yiddish I had picked up when I was a judge and had listened to plaintiffs tell the interpreters how the streetcar started before they got aboard.

Of course some awkward incidents occurred now and then. Once I was speaking in Montreal, and to demonstrate to my audience how conservative we were (then) in the United States, I said that Mr. Saklatvala, a Communist or near-Communist member of the British Parliament, had been refused entrance to the United States. The Montreal *Star*, in an editorial the next day, said that I had "mocked and insulted the British people."

I sent the *Star* a copy of my speech and asked that it be published, since a reading of it would show that I had not "mocked or insulted" anyone. The *Star* refused. I then wrote to the advertising department and asked the charges for publishing my speech as an advertisement. The advertising department quoted a price of three hundred dollars. Then I had them; for what the *Star* had refused to do out of courtesy and fairness it was ready to do for money. So I sent a cashier's check for three hundred dollars, but the answer was a nice letter from Lord Atholstan—owner of the paper—saying that they would publish my speech and return the check. I sent it back with another check for two hundred dollars more, five hundred dollars in all, and asked the *Star* to offer that as a prize for the best essay by a Canadian school child on "The Good Relations between Canada and the United States and How Best to Preserve Them."

The five hundred dollars was won by a boy in Revelstoke, British Columbia, and the incident closed tc the satisfaction of all, especially the junior diplomat in Revelstoke.

An invitation to address the Canadian Club in Ottawa on November 5, 1937, led to my meeting Canada's great Governor General, the late Lord Tweedsmuir. After my little speech I went to Rideau Hall and spent a week end with Tweedsmuir and his wife.

Early in 1917 the patriotic Irish in this country (that is, patriotic to the "ould sod") started a fund for suffering Ireland. She was not suffering at all, as a matter of fact, but the idea was to furnish a safety valve for the restless. I was asked to address an Irish meeting in Boston and consented on condition that only American flags be shown in the hall.

I went to Boston with Judge Morgan J. O'Brien, who was probably the greatest diplomat in New York State politics. We had read in the Boston papers that it was being said that I had betrayed Sir Roger Casement to the British and that no Irishman should listen to me. With this in mind, I suggested to the committee that they might not want me to speak. They said, "No, but we hope you don't mind if we have you speak last, as there may be a row when you get up."

With an Irish audience and the prospect of a row, you could not have gotten a knife blade in the packed opera house. I would have been relieved if one of the speakers who preceded me had been thoughtful enough to work in some kindly little testimonial for me. Such as ". . . one of the truly great friends of Ireland such as our distinguished guest, Ambassador Gerard," or some similar reassurance to the unsmiling eyes I felt boring into me. But none of them did, and, as my turn to speak finally came, I experienced a little of that same pre-martyrdom elation that I had felt the evening I stepped out on the balcony with President Díaz when he performed his hit-and-run bong of Mexico's liberty bell.

As it turned out, my martyrdom didn't materialize; there was only a brief flare-up of Hibernian invective. When I got up a woman in the gallery shouted, "Sure an' he betrayed Sir Roger Casement!"

A man near her slapped her face and yelled, "Don't mind her, she's a British spoil!" I made my speech without further interruption.

This Casement story was started by a pro-German American correspondent in Germany, who was vengeful because I had discovered that while he was an officer of the New York National Guard he had accepted money from Count von Bernstorff. I had tried to take away his passport, having received authority to do so from President Wilson. At that time I knew nothing of Casement's proposed expedition to Ireland.

It is the habit of American public characters to collect LL.D.'s, or perhaps, if one is a bookish fellow, or indeed has even once read a book, he may collect Litt.D.'s. I have four honorary degrees. As a rule, the principal speaker at a university or college commencement is given this honor. But in one case, when I had traveled many miles to Nashville, Tennessee, to deliver a commencement address at Vanderbilt University, I got nothing. This indignity was not the result of the mediocrity of my address. It was—I was relieved to discover—because Vanderbilt is one of about three major universities in the country that do not grant honorary degrees. Doubtless a healthy reaction to the widespread practice of practically selling honorary degrees.

When I got back to New York, I telegraphed the university chancellor that I had "Enjoyed my visit to no small degree."

One night in 1917, as I left a hall in Los Angeles where I had spoken, I overheard a woman say to her husband, "I don't think that he's much of an orator. He talks just the way we do."

Rather discouraged, I repeated this later to William Randolph Hearst. "Don't mind that," said Hearst. "I heard two girls talking about me after one of my speeches. One said, 'What do you think of him as a speaker?' and the other said, 'Well, I don't know, but his trousers bag at the knees just like William Jennings Bryan's.'"

I repeated this anecdote to Bryan in 1920 in a New York hotel room while he sat in his shirttail waiting for his trousers to be pressed. He seemed a little nettled. "I don't think that's funny," he said coldly; "not funny at all. I often have my trousers pressed."

When I saw Bryan on this occasion he was engaged in one of his quadrennial efforts to get the Democratic presidential nomination. He had wanted to make a speech in New York, but certain persons arranged it so that he could not get a suitable hall. So I engaged a large room at the Hotel Commodore, gave a supper to about one hundred and fifty of his friends, and arranged for him to speak over what at that time was the largest radio hookup in broadcasting history.

One of the best after-dinner speakers I have ever heard was Lord Derby. I was one of the speakers at a fine dinner given to him in New York by the Pilgrim Society. To emphasize the value of societies for promoting good relations between England and America, I said that the grandfathers of many men in the room were of military age when the British burned the capitol at Washington. "When I was a boy in New York," I continued, "we celebrated Evacuation Day as a holiday, the anniversary of the day the British left New York."

When Lord Derby arose to speak, he said, "If Mr. Gerard wishes to celebrate, I am sailing on the fifteenth of May."

In 1922 I heard that Will Rogers, in the running commentary he gave as he twirled his rope at the Ziegfeld *Follies,* was saying that Otto Kahn and I had gone about Paris making speeches advocating the cancellation of all war debts. I bought two seats in the front row at the *Follies* and attended one night with a friend. As soon as Will Rogers made this statement, I called out in a loud voice, "That is not so."

Will came to the edge of the stage, and we had a colloquy in which I denied having made any speeches at all at the time in Paris or having advocated the cancellation of war debts. Will thereupon very politely retracted what he said.

He had written the same statement for his well-known column for the papers throughout the country, so I wrote to him and said that since he had, like the fine Oklahoma gentleman he was, corrected his statement at the *Follies,* I hoped that he would also correct it in his column. He did, and the exchange led to a fast friendship.

Few personages who have died in the past several decades have been more universally regretted than Will Rogers. Certainly in the time of war and confusion and experiment his sound common sense would have been of great use to his country.

CHAPTER XXV

SOON AFTER MY RETURN FROM GERMANY IN 1917 I REJOINED my old law firm, which had continued its venerable traditions and excellent reputation under the capable direction of John M. Bowers. On the death of John Bowers I persuaded Judge Francis M. Scott, who was then serving in the Appellate Division of the New York Supreme Court, to resign and join our firm. His connection with us was a successful one and most pleasant, but was cut short by his untimely death only a few years after he joined us.

After Judge Scott died in February 1922, I again robbed the bench of the Appellate Division of the Supreme Court and obtained Judge Frank C. Laughlin as a partner to head our firm. This association, which was both agreeable and profitable, lasted until the spring of 1941.

Judge Laughlin was much sought after as a counselor. One of the notable litigations in which he was engaged was the great dispute in the family of the late Jay Gould. Edwin Gould, one of his sons, had been represented by Alton B. Parker, and on Parker's death he retained our firm. Under his will Jay Gould had appointed as trustees his sons George, Howard, and Edwin; and his daughter, Mrs. Finley Shepard. His other two children, the Duchess of Talleyrand and Frank

Gould, were not trustees. Frank Gould brought an action against his three brothers and sister charging that they had not always acted in accordance with the strict rules that govern trustees. The four trustees were eventually compelled to pay large sums back into the various trusts. This refund was heavily to the advantage of those trustees who had children, and, conversely, of disadvantage to those who had none. But childless or not, each of the four trustees had to pay in an enormous sum. It was my belief that all of the trustees had acted for what they judged to be the best interests of the estate, and I felt quite strongly that the return of those large sums was an injustice.

In the period between 1917 and 1941 I was engaged in many, many litigations, some interesting and some dull. In my mind I have labeled the legal turmoil that followed upon the murder of Edward Ridley in 1931 as the most interesting case handled by our firm. This affair had all the elements of a good murder mystery, including a love interest revolving around a beautiful Norwegian, and a number of strange characters avid for part or all of a $6,000,000 estate.

Edward Albert Ridley was a gently bred, well-educated eccentric, who came from a family of old-school ladies and gentlemen. His half-sister, a Mrs. Gerken, was a noted horsewoman. In the dim past Edward's father had founded the Ridley department store on Grand Street, which was at that time in the fashionable shopping district. The store was perhaps the largest in New York; it covered parts of three blocks and housed a thousand employees. When the march of business to the upper part of the city began during the seventies, the Ridleys closed out their business and thereafter Edward Ridley spent his time in the management of his real estate and the placing of his money to advantage in real-estate loans. He was a client of ours for thirty years.

His office was thirty feet underground in the basement of a garage on Allen Street, in what had once been the stable of the Ridley store. He worked there with his male secretary and two part-time accountants who kept his books. He lived in a boardinghouse in the village of Fanwood, New Jersey, and every morning he came to town on the same train. He also made a special trip to New York on Sundays, for his commutation ticket was good for every day and he was concerned lest the railroad get the better of him financially. On these Sunday excursions he returned to Fanwood on the next train.

Winter and summer, in the house and out, he wore his rubber overshoes and his overcoat, and his appearance—with his long white hair and whiskers—was that of a preoccupied and nervous Santa Claus. When he spoke of himself he invariably used the royal or editorial "we," as: "It looks like rain, so we shall take our umbrella."

On January 3, 1931, his secretary, whose name was Moench, was found shot to death on the floor of the little underground office. There were no clues and his murder is still unsolved. Ridley hired another secretary named Weinstein, and the memory of the mysterious killing was beginning to fade when both Ridley and Weinstein were found murdered in the same underground office. This double killing occurred on May 10, 1933. Seven bullets from an automatic had been fired into Weinstein, but Ridley had been beaten to death with a chair. Thus it appeared that the murderer or murderers had come to shoot Weinstein and had been interrupted by Ridley whom they dispatched with a chair because all the cartridges in the automatic had been used in the killing of Weinstein.

Ridley's transactions with our office had been almost alto-

gether with my partner, George A. Lewis, whose specialty
was real-estate law. The police teamed up with Mr. Lewis
and began an investigation. One of Ridley's two accountants,
named Hoffman, said that a will would be found in the safe,
and there, indeed, we found a "paper writing" purporting to
be a will. Its terms distributed the estate among the many
relatives, not, however, in a manner agreeable to all of them.
(A "paper writing" is legal jargon for a document whose
authenticity has yet to be established.)

The accountants, Hoffman and Goodman, were the witnesses to this document and both made affidavits stating that
the paper was Ridley's will, and that all the formalities of
execution had been complied with.

In the meantime, the police began to look into Ridley's
affairs. When they found checks drawn to certain corporations for repairs to Ridley's properties, they—with unusual
acumen—traced the transactions. They discovered that several of these corporations had been organized by Hoffman
and Goodman, and that fake bills for supplies and repairs
were presented to Ridley for payment. The proceeds of this
fraud were divided, 50 per cent to Weinstein and 25 per
cent each to Hoffman and Goodman. These last were arrested
and in due course confessed that the will was bogus. It had
been drawn by Weinstein and handed to Ridley along with
some routine papers that needed his signature. Ridley signed
the will without noticing what it was.

The Central Hanover Bank and Trust Company was named
as executor in the paper writing and there was also a request
that my firm should be employed in the settlement of the
estate. The will gave a legacy of $250,000 to Weinstein, pay-
able only if he should survive Ridley. As was its duty, the
Trust Company presented the paper to the court for probate.

At this proceeding Hoffman and Goodman repeated their confession of their thefts from Ridley and testified that the paper writing was not Ridley's will. The proceedings were then adjourned, and at a conference in my office of all the lawyers for the Ridley heirs, a practical compromise was agreed upon, subject to the approval of the Surrogate.

At this point there called on Mr. Lewis a man named Jens Nelson. He claimed to be a son of Ridley, and, therefore, if the paper writing was not a true will, entitled to the whole of Ridley's $6,000,000 estate. The man who hurled this bombshell into our peaceful compromise camp not only claimed that he was a son of Ridley but added that he held Papa Ridley's note for $125,000. He showed the alleged note to Lewis, and said it had been given to him by Ridley for a patent on a flytrap. The note had the names of Walter G. Baldwin and John B. Mauren on it as witnesses. Jens Nelson showed Lewis copies of affidavits made by these two witnesses, detailing the particulars of the signing of the note, sworn to before two different notaries. Lewis fortunately took copies of the two affidavits.

The Surrogate, the Honorable James A. Foley, when advised of this new claim, directed that proceedings be instituted, and called on Nelson to prove that he was entitled to be heard in the will proceedings, which, of course, was his right if he was a son of Ridley.

Mrs. Gerken, Ridley's half-sister, had also been our client. Since there was a chance that her prospects might be affected adversely by the will, I turned her interests over to Charles C. Burlingham, a former president of the Bar Association and one of the most distinguished lawyers in New York. The lawyers for the other heirs were all legal lights of the first water and made quite an imposing group when gathered

together in one room. It was agreed by all the lawyers for
the Ridley heirs that I should represent them in court and
carry the burden of the proceedings. Jens Nelson was represented by Richard H. Arnold and Alexander C. Dow of
Poughkeepsie, and later he added Herbert C. Smyth, a well-
known jury lawyer.

According to the procedure established, Jens Nelson was
called to the stand and I was permitted to examine him. He
produced two old-looking documents written in Norwegian.
One he represented to be the death certificate of his mother
under the name of Ridley and the other a certificate of his
christening. Both of them were apparently signed by a Rev.
Sebastian L. Geelmuyden, a Lutheran pastor. The story that
Jens Nelson related to the fascinated courtroom was that in
1865 Edward Albert Ridley had fallen in love with and married a beautiful Norwegian girl. He took her to his home,
but strife developed and Ridley's father soon threw her out of
his house. Her husband apparently deserted her and she had
gone to a lumber camp in northern Michigan where her
brother lived. It was there that Jens Nelson (or Ridley) was
born, he related.

The two certificates, both dated 1866, were admitted in
evidence as "ancient documents." They not only had the
signature of the Rev. Mr. Geelmuyden, but two wax seals
with the impression of his initials on each. Right at the start
of my examination of Jens Nelson I was able to show that he
had committed a fraud. Mr. Lewis, in examining Nelson's
claim, had sent someone to interview the two notaries who
had signed the affidavits of the two witnesses, Baldwin and
Mauren, on the $125,000 note. The descriptions of Baldwin
and Mauren given by the two notaries seemed to fit Jens
Nelson himself. When they were shown a photograph of

him, the notaries were perfectly certain that the man who had come to one notary as Mauren and to the other notary as Baldwin, was actually Jens Nelson. To clinch the matter, the notaries identified him in court.

The case went on for days. We called paper experts who testified that the paper on which the certificates were written was not manufactured until long after 1866. The other side called witnesses to the contrary. We called witnesses to show that the Rev. Mr. Geelmuyden had received the degrees of A.B., A.M., and C.T. in Norway, and had been for three years a teacher in the Moss Scientific School there. Therefore he was presumably a man of education, unlikely to make the many mistakes of both spelling and grammar that were in both certificates. The other side then pointed out that in 1866 the Norwegian language was in a state of flux, and that such mistakes might be made by anybody. We called in a celebrated handwriting expert named Stein who testified that the signatures and certificates were not in the minister's handwriting, and the other side called in experts who testified to the contrary. At that point it became necessary to establish whether Nelson had been born in this country or abroad. The Surrogate adjourned the court while each side sent a lawyer to Sweden and Norway (with an allowance for expenses from the estate) to endeavor to find out whether Jens Nelson had been born in either Norway or Sweden.

Nelson was—or pretended to be—almost stone deaf, and although I have a very loud and distinct voice, I was compelled to put every question to him several times, thus giving him time for reflection. He was certainly a quick thinker. I confronted him with an affidavit made at the time of his marriage in which he stated that he was born in Sweden. He answered promptly that American women always preferred foreigners and that for this sensible reason he had put his birthplace abroad.

Nelson's side produced an old gentleman from northern Michigan who related how that once, as a boy of fourteen, he had gone shooting in the woods near his home and discovered the cabin of Jens Nelson's uncle, just as Jens had described it. He had seen, this witness said, a sister of the owner and a little boy who was supposed to be Jens Nelson. Our side then called witnesses who swore that no such cabin had ever existed at the place indicated.

Jens Nelson's case was strongly bolstered by the testimony of one Joseph Collins, who had married Ridley's sister (she died some years before the trial). Collins swore that his wife, Ridley's sister, had told him the story of Ridley's marriage to a beautiful Norwegian girl and his desertion of her. Harry G. Harper, a lawyer and former judge of Poughkeepsie, a vestryman of Christ Episcopal Church in that city (obviously an excellent witness), testified that he had known Ridley during the latter's life, that he knew Ridley's sister, Mrs. Joseph Collins, now dead, and that he had seen Ridley at Mrs. Collins's home.

When Harper told how he had once conferred with Ridley and Ridley's father, his testimony became formidable indeed, for his account of the birth of Jens Nelson and the family situation was strikingly similar to Jens's own story.

His testimony, as well as the testimony of Collins, was admitted as being "a family declaration as to pedigree." To my mind this is a dangerous rule of evidence that should be qualified, because the person who relates an alleged conversation with a person deceased cannot be prosecuted for perjury, since there is no way of proving that such a conversation did not occur.

While all this ancient lore was being carefully placed on the court record day after day, our side had been making a number of quiet investigations. Finally the day came when we had the information we had been searching for—and that day proved to be the last day of the trial. I called a new witness to the stand. He identified himself as a jeweler and engraver who had a shop in Poughkeepsie, New York. Then Jens Nelson was ordered to stand up, and the jeweler immediately identified him as having been one of his customers during 1933, the previous year.

I handed the jeweler the two ancient documents signed by the Norwegian minister. The witness said that he had fashioned out of a ten-cent piece the seal that had impressed the wax which was affixed to these and he added that an examination of the wax impression would probably show the impression of the milled edge of the dime. When the host of lawyers and the Surrogate had all examined the seals with a magnifying glass, they saw the milled-edge impression and this abruptly ended the case. The attorneys for Jens Nelson —one after the other, and one in tears—made little speeches to the Surrogate, saying that they had been deceived by their client, and filed stiff-necked out of the courtroom. Then two Central Office detectives, who had been asked to be present, each took Jens Nelson by an arm, and marched him off to jail. At his trial he received a sentence of seven years, but subsequently he was moved to Matteawan Prison as an insane criminal. Possibly some person had and has an interest in shutting the mouth of Jens Nelson and had him declared insane. He might have turned on those who had backed his excursion for the Ridley millions.

Our side's ability to produce the jeweler and prove the seals to be fakes was the result of laborious and intelligent detective work and good reasoning. At one of our meetings I told the assembled lawyers that a detective of the Flynn Agency, named James C. Dunn, of Philadelphia, had obtained some extraordinary results for me in complicated cases. On my advice he was employed. Dunn proceeded on the theory that if the documents were forged, then the seals were probably forged also. He first went to various seal engravers who told him that the seal had very likely been made by a jeweler and not by a regular engraver. There are hundreds of jewelers in New York. Dunn drew a circle fifty miles in diameter about the city of Poughkeepsie where Jens Nelson had lived, and after going to almost every jeweler and engraver within that circle, finally located the jeweler who had made the seal.

Hoffman and Goodman both served terms in Sing Sing. We succeeded in recovering for the Ridley estate more than $46,000 of the money they had stolen, and the compromise agreed upon by the claimants finally went through. All the elements of mystery seemed to exist in the Ridley case. After the second murders in the basement and not far from the little 14-by-14-foot office of Ridley there was found a secret chamber that had always been kept locked. This was probably constructed by bootleggers in Ridley's absence and used by them to store goods which from inside the garage they could load on trucks and send rejoicing through the city at night.

It remains a little shocking, when you think about it, that so much trouble, talent, and expense should go into settling a man's estate, while the deceased himself was gathered up and buried without any agency making more than a desultory and routine effort to discover his murderer.

CHAPTER XXVI

Cyrus H. K. Curtis induced me to write a book, first to be serialized. Before the first articles appeared containing the story of my German experiences, a young man called on me and introduced himself as Harry M. Warner. He said he wanted to make a picture from the book. From blind legal instinct, in my letter to Mr. Curtis I had reserved motion-picture rights, but I said to Warner, "Why, you can't make a motion picture of a personal narrative." "Let me try," he said. I told him to go ahead.

Harry Warner and his brothers had very little money, but they managed to borrow about $35,000 from a Mr. Dintenfass, which is bad German for "inkstand," and with what additional money they could scrape up they managed to make this picture. Before they started on the filming they came into my rooms one day pushing a man in front of them and shouting, "Look at him! Look at him!"

"I am looking at him," I replied. "What of it?"

They said, "Doesn't he look like you?" On second glance I saw that he did indeed. His name was Halbert Brown. He was an excellent actor, and he resembled me so much that people who had never seen me but who saw the picture would approach me on the street, having recognized me from the resemblance to Brown. The picture was a great success. The Warners got their start as motion-picture producers on a large scale from the success of the film. The picture, *My Four Years in Germany,* was released early in 1918.

Harry M. Warner is today a movie magnate to whom a great many artistic successes are to be credited. Endowed with vision and imagination, supremely patriotic, he produced films which materially aided our war effort in sustaining the morale of our people.

In addition to my other chores and activities in 1917 I found myself suddenly become—without warning—an active champion of Armenian freedom. After 1918 the Allied nations undertook to create an independent Armenia. President Wilson was entrusted with the task of delimiting the frontiers of this re-created nation, which was to be placed under a mandate in the Peace Treaty.

The Armenians occupied a mountainous country in the eastern part of Asia Minor and are a clever Christian race who managed to maintain their religion and their racial purity through many centuries. Many Armenians now occupy high positions in the Turkish administration, but during World War I they, being Christians, were subjected by the Ottoman Government to the most horrible persecutions. About eight hundred thousand were killed and many Armenian women were seized for Turkish harems. At that time Turkey was an ally of Germany. Today there are about two hundred thousand Armenians in this country, the best known of them probably being Michael Arlen, Rouben Mamoulian, and William Saroyan. On the whole they are skilled artists and businessmen; sober, prudent, and industrious.

Vahan Cardashian, an Armenian, was a tower of strength in organizing the Armenian cause. Armenians in America should remember him with gratitude. Bishop Cannon, the "Dry Messiah," as Virginius Dabney calls him in his excellent book so titled, was a power in the United States at one time, his life extraordinary, his fall sad. He once dined with me in a chophouse. I found him most interesting, an example of the queer and changing careers of our country. He was a strong backer of the Armenian cause.

After I had returned from Germany in 1917, the Armenians here decided for some reason that, after Armenia's frontiers had been agreed upon, I was to be the representative of the United States, assuming that the United States were given the mandate over Armenia. I was made chairman of the newly formed American Committee for the Independence of Armenia, and found myself directing the efforts of some one hundred and nineteen American bishops and other clergy of various Christian churches as well as laymen on the committee. Senator King of Utah was also an ardent supporter of the cause.

I attended many Armenian meetings and banquets (held in the neighborhood of Lexington Avenue and Twenty-third Street), and learned to eat the Armenian dishes—which are a far cry from American cooking—and drink their fiery distillations. On one notable occasion we had a great banquet in the Plaza Hotel at which William Jennings Bryan spoke. I introduced Bryan by pointing out that he probably was of Armenian descent since all Armenian names ended in "yan" or "ian."

In the end nothing came of it. The serious illness of President Wilson kept him from the task of delimiting the Armenian frontiers. The Turks on one side and the Russians on the other moved in to what would and should have been free Armenia and the critical moment was lost.

In looking back over one's career, it is always interesting to judge whether any opportunities have gone unrecognized or chances bungled. For instance, in 1918 I could have been nominated for governor of New York. I missed it in the following way. I had told William Randolph Hearst that I was not a candidate. So when William H. Kelley, the Democratic leader of Syracuse, telephoned to say that I could have the nomination, I felt obliged to obtain, as it were, a release from Hearst. Early in the morning, before he was out of bed, I called on him at his apartment at Eighty-sixth Street and Riverside Drive, and he urged me to go ahead and accept the nomination. But in the meantime the forces of Alfred E. Smith had succeeded in obtaining the nomination for him. I agreed to stump the state afterward with Smith but our expedition was called off because of the prevalence of the so-called Spanish influenza.

Of course after Smith was elected I had many bitter hours when I thought that he was on his way to the presidency in consequence of already having won the state of New York. So that, although as treasurer of the National Democratic party I worked very hard for him in the campaign of 1928 when he ran for President, I was somewhat relieved by the fact that he failed. Also if I had been elected governor in 1918, I should probably have been the candidate of the Democrats in 1920 and have gone down to the resounding defeat which met Cox when he ran against Harding.

To my mind the greatest asset one can have for a career in politics is a reputation for always keeping one's word. Both Charles Murphy and Jim Farley are examples of the esteem which that worthy quality can bring.

Speaking of Hearst: when I ran for judge of the Supreme Court in 1907, as I have related, he opposed me violently.

I happened to meet him on the street shortly after my election, and I said, "You know, I am very much obliged to you —you weren't half as hard on me in your attacks as you might have been." The next time I ran for office, in 1914, he supported me just as violently as he had once opposed me, and also expressed enthusiastic approval of my appointment as Ambassador to Germany.

Of all the people I've ever met in my life, Hearst and President Wilson have been the most difficult for me to fathom. I must say that I admire Hearst for his sincere and vociferous Americanism even though from time to time I have disagreed with his policies.

Had I sought public office after the war, I suppose I should have encountered some German-American opposition, for traces of the feelings aroused during the war remained for some years.

In 1919 the term of Judge Newburger on the Supreme Court was to end. He had been an excellent judge. We had become fast friends, and so, when Tammany Hall nominated an opposing Democratic candidate, I joined the Finance Committee of the Bar Association Committee which was formed for the independent re-election of Justice Newburger and Judge Richard H. Smith to the Supreme and City courts.

Shortly afterward a German-language newspaper published this comment:

"Americans of German descent will need only to hear that Bainbridge Colby is the manager of the Newburger campaign . . . and James W. Gerard is financial manager."

On October 25, 1919, the New York *Times* published an editorial denouncing this appeal to prejudice.

Judge Newburger was triumphantly elected. The only other candidate to be elected on the Democratic ticket that year was Surrogate James A. Foley, who made a wonderful record.

The voters of New York City have always been sensitive about their judges and have almost always shown ability to pick good ones whenever the issue of judicial fitness has been properly presented to them.

It is the custom for Democratic leaders to assemble each year in Washington for a dinner in honor of the party's spiritual father, Andrew Jackson. In years when the party is in power it is an occasion for innocent merriment and almost insufferable self-congratulation. During the rather protracted periods when the party has not been in office, the Jackson Day dinner provides an opportunity for the unterrified Democrats to emerge from under logs and stones or wherever they spend their political hibernation, and eat a square meal. At these unhappy gatherings the diners view the Republican administration with alarm and asperity, and profess to see a healthy, nationwide drift of the plain people back to the Democratic party. When it is an election year, any outstanding Democrat who has an inward call to be a successful presidential candidate is invited to make an appropriate speech. The invitation is never turned down. Each aspirant rises in his turn and straddles as many issues as he comfortably can in the time allotted to him, while the assembled sachems study his features and delivery with beady-eyed interest.

The Jackson Day dinner of January 8, 1920, might just as well not have been eaten since, as most schoolboys learn and many adults remember, that year was the first of twelve lean years for the Democratic party. When that long sleep was over in 1932, the Wilsonian Democrats who had survived found themselves ranged alongside the New Deal Democrats—a new and alarming breed of cat. But all went well, and except for a medium-sized abyss between them, the two groups were remarkably cohesive.

Back in 1920, however, there were no prescient Democrats at the Jackson Day dinner, and so the speeches of the prominent contenders were given thoughtful attention. In the guise of a prominent contender I made a speech that night. The other speakers were all outstanding Democrats of the day—William Jennings Bryan, Secretary of the Navy Daniels, Attorney General Palmer, Governor Cox of Ohio, Champ Clark of Missouri—a former speaker of the House; Governor Cornwell of West Virginia, Senators Hitchcock of Nebraska, Pomerence of Ohio, Underwood of Alabama, and Owen of Oklahoma.

A digest of my remarks as printed by the New York *American* gives some idea of the kind of speech that was calculated to captivate the Democratic organization in 1920:

WASHINGTON—Jan. 8—Compromise of the peace treaty fight in the Senate was urged by James W. Gerard, former Ambassador to Germany, and an active candidate for the Democratic nomination for the presidency, in an address tonight at the Jackson Day dinner. He said:

"I have been for the League without change, but a great danger threatens Europe. Without peace the red flag will again be seen in the capitals of the Central Empires—a fire kindled that may spread over the earth. Our country senses this—it is sick of talk.

"It demands that both sides get together, that a compromise be made and peace given to the world—after all the reservations are in favor of America, and if the other powers accept no harm can come to us by adopting them."

Turning to the situation at home, Mr. Gerard said the Republican party today was "confident of success and so its leaders are looking for a candidate warranted in case of election to stand without hitching—while the wicked end of Wall Street is sharpening its knives for the slaughter. . . ."

Referring to the industrial situation, Mr. Gerard said men could not be made to work by threatening them with jail or "by governing the country industrially by injunctions." He said:

"You cannot expect the workers to abandon the unions, but the moment the unions or any other organization seeks to usurp the functions of the Government or to put themselves above the Government they must be put down with a hand of steel. The solution, I am confident, will come in partnership: The admission of the workers to a share in profits and management.

"If we stand by our old ideals and our old friends we can win. I want only to see a candidate named by the people in the party and by no other influence. I myself have no particular delusions of grandeur. There are plenty of good candidates in our party.

"For instance, I understand that when a friend was advocating my name before the proposal men of South Dakota he said:

"'I am for Judge Gerard, but he is not the best candidate. The best candidate is Herbert Hoover.'"

Although I didn't mention the matter to my audience, I had seen to it that my South Dakota supporter would utter this judgment so that I could quote it.

My long-simmering interest in becoming a candidate for President of the United States had become really active about six months before that Jackson Day dinner. The transition from a potential President to kinetic candidate resulted from my reading a newspaper article which described the primary election law of South Dakota.

This novel law provided that in December each party should hold a convention of "proposal men," or delegates, and that the majority of these should choose a candidate to run in the primaries the following March. In addition, the minority could also name a candidate. Further, anyone who received a specified number of signatures on a petition could also be included among the party candidates in the presidential campaign. The state printed and circulated little books containing the photographs of the candidates, together with a short platform and a catchy slogan for each contender. The law further provided that any candidate could challenge the others to a joint debate, and the candidate who refused to debate when so challenged was automatically removed from the primary ticket.

I deduced that the majority of the proposal men would name President Wilson, and that as sure as shooting someone would challenge him to a debate. I thought it most likely that if President Wilson were challenged he would ignore it, which would automatically put him off the ticket. With this in mind, I sent some retainers to the convention of the proposal men in South Dakota to suggest my name as the minority candidate. In due course the minority named me as their candidate. The majority had named President Wilson; and a James Monroe, a well-known Middle West political orator, was nominated by petition. Everything worked out nicely. Mr. Monroe challenged President Wilson to a joint debate. Wilson paid no attention, and his name automatically went off the ticket.

Mr. Monroe then challenged me. The challenge was duly transmitted to me by the Secretary of State of South Dakota, and read—very solemnly—"I hereby challenge James W. Gerard." I answered through the same formal channel that I accepted the challenge of Mr. Monroe and would meet him at any time and place, and with any weapon from machine guns to brickbats.

The Secretary of State wrote and asked me to withdraw this lusty reply and to substitute another more in accordance with the dignified spirit of South Dakota's jealously regarded law. Somewhat chastened, I again wrote the Secretary of State and named the place as the city of Sioux Falls and the time as 8:30 P.M. I don't recall the day, but it was sometime in March 1920.

That evening in the large armory in Sioux Falls, Mr. Monroe and I came out on the stage together and, since we had nothing to debate about, made alternate speeches on the subjects then closest to our hearts. In the following weeks I spoke in several towns in South Dakota, including Aberdeen and Yankton. I won the South Dakota primary election, which obliged the state delegates to vote for me in the national convention at San Francisco, at least for a certain number of ballots. The principal candidates were James Cox, Mitchell Palmer, and Secretary of the Treasury McAdoo. My name was presented to the convention by U. S. G. Cherry of Sioux Falls. I thought that I possibly had a chance of sliding in for Vice-President on a deadlock, but Cox was nominated by the convention with Franklin Roosevelt for Vice-President. With one exception the Montana delegation also voted for me.

During the balloting someone had voted for Irvin Cobb. Since he had a room in the St. Francis, I went up to tell him the good news. I am sorry to say that Cobb didn't prove exactly grateful, for the next day, in an article he wrote about the convention for a newspaper syndicate, he described how, when walking about the convention hall, he had wandered into the hospital. There on a cot, he said, he had seen a poor, sick, pallid thing nervously plucking at the bedclothes. It was, he wrote, the Gerard boom. Ring Lardner, commenting on my candidacy in his news story, said he planned to write a parody of *My Four Years in Germany* which he would entitle *My Four Raspberries in San Francisco*. These were, of course, bitter blows. But my pride survived them, and I was able to enjoy and appreciate Cobb's farewell letter to his friends which was published the day after his death in March 1944.

On my way back East I stopped at Dayton, Ohio, and had luncheon with Candidate Cox and his wife. I went to church with them in the morning (possibly a novel experience for the Coxes, but all candidates must make an appearance in church).

On the fourth of September I received a telegram from Cox asking me to see Senator Pat Harrison and to comply with a request which Harrison would make. When I saw the senator in New York, he asked me to be chairman of the Finance Committee and raise the money for the Cox-Roosevelt campaign. I accepted, and though there was a finance committee, I was never able to get it together.

Raising money for that campaign proved to be hard sledding indeed. Nevertheless, I managed to raise enough so that Cox and Roosevelt could make a decent showing. At the end of the campaign we had raised something over $1,100,-000 and were left with a debt of only about $220,000.

On election night I was delegated to perform the unpalatable task of phoning Governor Cox to acquaint him with the sad news. I could tell from the stunned surprise in his voice that he had not expected defeat. Harding and Coolidge and the Republican party had won the day, and the Democrats drifted into their twelve-year hibernation. Cox would have been a splendid President.

CHAPTER XXVII

I<small>N</small> 1921 J<small>UDGE</small> E<small>LBERT</small> G<small>ARY</small>, P<small>RESIDENT OF THE</small> U<small>NITED</small> S<small>TATES</small> Steel Corporation, and his wife, were stopping with us at Southampton, Long Island, where we had a house for the summer, and I related that President Obregón, newly made President of Mexico, had invited me to come down as his guest and to bring anyone I pleased along. I had had no intention of going, but Judge Gary, who loved expeditions of this kind, argued until I consented.

So in September 1921 Judge and Mrs. Gary and Mrs. Gerard and I headed for Mexico in two private cars. At the border we were met by Colonel Juan Ramos, a most agreeable gentleman, who had been sent by President Obregón to meet us. By the President's thoughtful order Ramos brought along a large supply of champagne, whisky, and other potables. An accompanying note from Obregón explained that he had it in mind that we came from a desert-dry country. Our journey to Mexico City was a stimulating and pleasant one, thanks to this forethought.

Obregón had offered us a house, but as we knew that this meant throwing someone out of it, we went to the Princess Hotel. We discovered, on our arrival, that a national centennial was in progress to celebrate the one hundredth anniversary of the conclusion of the War of Independence. Inasmuch as our government had not recognized Obregón as President, he made Judge Gary and me the unofficial representatives of the United States. We spent about ten delightful days in Mexico. Soon after our return Judge Gary, powerful in Republican politics, used his great influence, and Obregón's administration was recognized by our government.

When President Obregón stepped from the room crowded with diplomats onto the little platform outside the National Palace on the night of September 15, he invited Judge Gary and me to accompany him. And so, for a second time, I stood with a President of Mexico when he rang the bell once rung by the priest Hidalgo to call the Mexicans to arms against their Spanish oppressors. This time we remained for at least fifteen minutes watching the turbulent crowd of big hats in the square below. As we re-entered the room someone called out, "You three with your white shirt fronts made splendid targets."

It was a most unfortunate thing that Obregón was assassinated. He had worked for Americans at the start of his career, and understood Americans and business. If he had lived, I think he would have continued to be an efficient and friendly President.

I have known many of the presidents of Mexico, among them De la Barra, who was President for a very short time after the flight of Díaz, and who held a most important post in Paris in connection with international arbitration. He was a courteous and charming gentleman, representing all that is best in Old Mexico.

When Calles was elected President of Mexico, but before he took office, he visited New York and was given a great banquet at the Waldorf Astoria. On that occasion I made a speech which he liked so much that he had it translated into Spanish and published in the newspapers of Mexico.

Calles had a very attractive daughter named Ernestina, known as Tenina. I used to give her riding lessons in Central Park, since strangely enough for a daughter of a country of horsemen, she was not a good rider. She also stopped with us at Newport. She had a very beautiful sister who had married a physician in New York, but after some years she divorced him. In the winter of 1942–43 I saw her dancing one night in the Hotel Pierre as the leading member of a Mexican dancing team. The changes and chances of political life in Mexico are violent indeed.

In 1922 Mrs. Gerard and I went abroad, arriving in Paris early in May. At the steamer in New York the reporters asked me if I were going to visit Germany, and I replied that I thought I would. But when I got to Paris I found there had been editorials in the German papers urging the government not to allow me to enter Germany. I clipped one of these and sent it to Walther Rathenau, then Minister of Foreign Affairs of the German Commonwealth, with a letter:

"My dear Walther Rathenau: How about the enclosed?"

I received his reply in Paris. He said no one knew better than I did that the government could not control the newspapers and that, of course, there was no official objection to my coming to the country. However, on June 24, 1922, Rathenau was assassinated in a crowded street in Berlin. I discreetly decided that if he wasn't able to take care of himself, his government probably could not take care of me. In any event, if I had gone into Germany and there had been a row of some kind, people in America would have said, with some propriety, "Well, why did the fool want to go where there'd be trouble?"

Walther Rathenau was a warm friend of ours. He had an extraordinary personality, and I believe that his convictions were honest and well-thought-out, although I couldn't agree with all of his socialistic conclusions.

One of the first things the Nazis did when they achieved power was to erect a memorial to the assassins of Rathenau.

I was delighted to be invited to have goûter on May 19, 1922, with the President of France, M Millerand. I sat with him a long time talking, taking refreshment, and nibbling little cakes. He was a strong and sensible man, and talked well—so well, in fact, that his remarks sounded as though they had been designed for a history book or an essay.

As it happened, Millerand and I later were both arbitrators under the Bryan Arbitration Treaty which had been negotiated by William Jennings Bryan when he was Secretary of State. It provides that two representatives from each signatory county shall examine and report on any questions arising which can't be settled through the usual diplomatic means. The job carried no pay, not even the traditional dollar a year. When I wrote President Roosevelt to thank him for the appointment under the treaty with Great Britain, I said that he had given me a job exactly equivalent to picking the flowers off a century plant; that nothing had happened for twenty-five years and probably nothing ever would happen, but that as I was recovering from a severe illness and had adopted the attitude toward life of Ferdinand the Bull, I accepted the appointment. As I predicted, nothing whatever happened that our State Department and Britain's Foreign Office couldn't handle. Nevertheless, I stuck tenaciously to my post until 1940, when I resigned to head the financial committee of the Democratic campaign.

On May 20, 1922, I had an appointment to see Marshal Foch, who had a special interest in my experiences in Germany during the then still-recent war. And for my part I was naturally quite interested in talking to the man who had so successfully co-ordinated the efforts of the Allied armies. In the course of our conversation I reminded him that it was being said that France was currently very imperialistic, and that Marshal Pétain was maintaining a great army for the purpose of conquest. His reply was so full of assurance and conviction that it is perhaps as well he didn't live to see that debacle of 1940. "No," he said, "that's not so. We in France have found that war is a dangerous adventure and we desire only to defend our frontiers."

To my mind, Marshal Foch represented all that is best in France. He was the prototype of a fast-disappearing breed— a gentleman, profoundly religious, a man of family, and an undoubted patriot. What a contrast he presents to those politicians who presided over the fall of France! There was about him the grandeur of simplicity and a deep humility which impressed even the most frivolous observer who came within his influence.

There are two Frances: the old France, the France of the provinces—religious, patriotic, solid, respectable in family life, typified by the men I have mentioned above—the France of the country. And then there is the France of intriguing politicians, allied with crooked big business and a mostly purchasable press—the France of Paris, of Communism, of dirty books and plays, of actresses and loose women who for years have, with the aid of foxy dressmakers, set feminine fashions for the world.

In judging the French we must take their social life and customs and their social handicaps into account. The French are the most thrifty people in the world. A French couple tries to live on a third of their income and save money for the dowry of their children. Boys and girls are usually married into their own class, each bringing an equal sum of dowry or contribution to the joint establishment, and although there has lately been a trend toward greater liberty, the average marriage is a treaty between the parents of bride and groom. In these circumstances—and also because divorce was impossible legally until 1884, and socially impossible even after that—it was inevitable that wives sometimes accepted lovers and occasionally husbands maintained those ladies for whom the Greeks had a word.

The struggle for economic survival in France has always been keen and difficult. A young Frenchman had all his energy focused on his career, always hoping for a secure—if inglorious—place in the world, with early retirement on a fixed and assured income. There is little of that spirit of adventure and change which characterizes the young Britisher or American. The young generation of France greatly admires the American movies which depict the once wild life of our West, and has a romantic yearning to have the same experiences. And yet in the French Colonies adventure beckons. One would think that the fascinating little ladies of Tonkin, the beautiful Ouled Naïl dancers of the Sahara, the fierce Moroccan chiefs, the tireless Arabian horses, the veiled Tuaregs, ruled by their women, and the chance of finding precious minerals and oil in the great, as yet undeveloped, French overseas Empire, all should stir in the youth of France the spirit of enterprise and romance. But they don't. The average French youth is content to get his adventure vicariously by watching American Westerns.

France in 1940 was rotten with Socialism, Communism, even a sort of anarchy. In the South of France in 1937 I myself saw the Red flag and the hammer and sickle. Even the villagers sang the "Internationale" at the annual village fetes, instead of the "Marseillaise." I have been reliably told of regiments marching in 1940 singing the "Internationale" and proclaiming loudly that they refused to fight for "the two hundred families."

For centuries France has gone through recurring cycles of corruption and virtue, and today she is at a low point, the most dangerous spot in western Europe for the infection of Communism to gain a fast hold. Perhaps she will recover her virtue again, and purified by defeat, by sorrow, and by captivity, perhaps a new France will arise—the France of Foch and Lyautey.

Poincaré represented the stern school of Clemenceau. He was the young man of the provinces who sought his fortune in Paris as a lawyer, economist, and politician. I found him an especially close questioner as to the economic conditions of Germany. He has been criticized for the taking over of the Ruhr when Germany failed to pay, but the fault lay with all the Allied nations in their treatment of Germany after the war. It was a mean compromise—neither stern and relentless enough with the ruling class, not sympathetic with the people who, before the rise of Hitler, might perhaps have been returned to civilization by kind treatment and understanding.

In Paris, on May 28, Mrs. Gerard and I lunched alone with

a celebrated statesman, the Aga Khan. I think he wanted to find something out from me but I couldn't discover what it was. I am willing to believe, however, that he probably accomplished his purpose, if he had one. The Aga Khan is, of course, a sort of pope of a sect of the Mohammedans. He is a direct descendant of Mohammed and is the spiritual head of the Ismilihah Division of Mohammedans, probably the most numerous sect in that faith. Even though he has no temporal power, he is very potent politically, especially in Bombay where he lives, and around the shores of the Red Sea. He presided over the League of Nations at one time and earned the gratitude of the British as well as that of the Turks after the last war by pleading for the restoration of Turkey as a powerful country. I have no doubt but that in his quiet way the Aga Khan did splendid work for the cause of the United Nations after the last war, although little was printed about him except for occasional photos of him and his wife at the races until his son's romance with a Hollywood actress qualified him as "news" in America.

On May 29 I motored to Chalons and spent the night there in the hotel with the extraordinary name of the "Hotel of the High Mother of God." The next day was Decoration Day, and I made a speech at the American Cemetery at Romagne.

I met President Poincaré of France twice, once on my way out of Germany in 1917, when he cross-examined me at length about the resources, economic and human, of the German Empire, and again in 1922, when he gave me the decoration of Grand Officer of the Legion of Honor. I was awarded this honor, he said, because of my work for prisoners of war in Germany. The French Prisoners of War Association gave me a gold medal and a bronze statue, and the King of the Belgians, on his visit to this country, gave me the Grand Cross of the Order of the Crown. Three years later, in 1925, Mrs. Gerard and I were again in Paris. The President of France gave us his box for the races and we dined with Mr. Cerf, the well-known French banker, whose wines and dinner were something to remember. At that dinner the Chief Minister of France, Painlevé, was present, and after dinner, as the climax of a nice little speech, he made Mrs. Gerard a Chevalier of the Legion of Honor.

I met Aristide Briand in Paris several times and found him to be a politician who took political life not too seriously. He told me that he had been Premier of France eleven times because he knew exactly when to resign and just when to pick the hour for a comeback. Once he explained to me that in an election one must "promise the voters everything, but be very careful when elected not to carry out all your promises, because you would have nothing left to promise next time."

Early in June we went to England, where Ambassador Harvey, who represented us then in London, had invited Mrs. Gerard and me to a dinner which was to be given to King George V and Queen Mary on the twenty-fourth.

At the dinner for King George other American guests were President Taft, Frank Munsey, and Mr. and Mrs. Marshall Field. The men were requested to wear knee breeches—a part of the British Court costume that has at times become a matter of controversy among Americans—and I must say that President Taft, in spite of his great weight, made a very fine appearance. Frank Munsey, Marshall Field, and I showed well-turned calves, and each of us was, I suspect, secretly a little vain of them.

At this dinner I suggested to the Dean of Westminster Abbey who was present that I should like to give to the

Abbey a window in memory of those of my wards, the British prisoners who died in German World War I prison camps. Later the Dean and Chapter accepted this offer and two beautiful windows were installed in the Abbey near the tomb of the Unknown Soldier. I could not be present at the dedication ceremonies and the windows were presented on my behalf by Ambassador Houghton at a solemn memorial service attended by many of the relatives of the prisoners who had died.

After dinner I had a talk with Lloyd George, and he told me that he thought the Communist domination of Russia was only a phase and that the rule of the Bolshevists would someday come to an end. Then, he said, the old regime or something like it would be re-established. I have since been afraid that, even though he was a shrewd politician, on this occasion he guessed wrong.

Later I talked with King George and described to him an interview I had once had with the German Kaiser in which the Kaiser had said, "If the British blockade injures the health of any of my grandchildren, before I will allow them to starve, I will send a Zeppelin over and blow up Windsor Castle and the whole royal family of England."

King George—who was known to have a short temper on occasion—was visibly affected and said several times in a very loud voice, "He said *that*, did he? He said *that*, did he?" Queen Mary, who had been sitting at the other side of the room, came over to see what the trouble was about.

On June 18 Mrs. Gerard and I lunched at Ambassador Harvey's country place with Earl Beatty, the British naval hero of Jutland, who had married the widow of Marshall Field II. After luncheon there was a tennis tournament in which a lovely English girl and I played against the seventy-three-year-old Lord Balfour and his partner. On another week end we had lunch with Lord Beaverbrook at his country home near Leatherhead, and there I played tennis with ex-Prime Minister Bonar Law, who was then about sixty-six.

On the twenty-first we lunched with Lord Balfour at his house in London, and met, among others, the Earl of Birkenhead, better known as the celebrated barrister, F. E. Smith.

CHAPTER XXVIII

IN 1924 I WAS AGAIN A DELEGATE TO THE DEMOCRATIC CON-vention, held in New York, and witnessed the bitter fight be-tween Al Smith and McAdoo, in the course of which Franklin Roosevelt proposed the nomination of Smith and hailed him as "the Happy Warrior." After much shouting and tumult, the convention nominated John W. Davis.

Because Davis was put in nomination by the delegates from West Virginia, everyone assumed that he was a citizen of that state. The New York City delegation decided in cau-cus to vote for me for Vice-President, but shortly after Davis was nominated he disclosed that he had become a citizen of New York. This change of heart automatically cut me out of the running since, under the Constitution, the President and the Vice-President cannot come from the same state. Never-theless, I was put in nomination by W. W. Howes of South Dakota. His speech was as follows:

Mr. Chairman, ladies and gentlemen of the Convention:

We have placed in nomination today for first place on our ticket a great Ambassador. I offer another great Ambassador as a candidate for the second place on the ticket, one who served with great distinction abroad during very trying times, one who is a close student of affairs at home, and understands the needs of our great Northwest as well as the needs of the other sections of this country; one who did great service to the Democratic party in the campaign of 1920, when he became chairman of the Finance Committee and raised the funds that were needed so badly to carry on that campaign; one who, running for a great office in the city of New York in 1916, ran over fifty thousand votes ahead of his ticket. South Dakota takes great pleasure in nominating for the office of Vice-President the Honorable James W. Gerard, of New York.

During the convention several of the New York delegates agreed to take charge of the entertainment of other delegations. I chose the South Dakota delegates because they had voted for me in 1920, and because I had many friends there. My brother Sumner took Utah, and my brother Julian, Nevada.

In the convention the New York delegation was seated behind the one from Ohio, and directly in front of me sat a fine-looking young chap with whom I conversed daily and who told me that his name was Wendell Willkie. A few years afterward Willkie appeared in my office in New York. He said, "I have come from Akron to ask your advice, to consult you as an older man. I have been offered the position of counsel to the great Commonwealth & Southern Corporation. This involves moving to New York, and I hesitate to accept. I am very pleasantly situated in Akron, where I have a good practice, many friends, and a pleasant life, and I am a little undecided about making this radical change in my life and coming to this great cold city of New York."

I said, "I can only give the same advice I would give myself in a similar situation: take a chance and come on."

Willkie took a chance, accepted the position, and settled in New York. When he became the Republican candidate for

President, I read in the newspapers that the reporters, looking over his office, found two photographs, one of Newton D. Baker, one of me. I suppose that Baker and I were two who had counseled him to leave Akron and come to New York.

The morning after Willkie's defeat in the 1940 presidential election, I sent him a note (he lived next door to me), in which I said that I hoped that he did not now regret taking my advice and moving to the relentless city of New York, and I wrote further, "Remember that if you had stayed in Akron you might have gotten in a row with the pastor of the Second Presbyterian Church which would have been just as hard on your nerves as being defeated for President."

Willkie's answer some days later included these paragraphs: "I appreciate your note very much, as I always appreciated your advice to come to New York in the larger fields of action. God bless you, and when I am back in New York I will give you a ring." Willkie's death on October 8, 1944, occasioned genuine regret throughout the nation which had learned to respect his sincerity of purpose.

After the 1924 convention, the National Committee elected me treasurer of the Finance Committee, of which Jesse Jones was chairman. We worked very well together but raised only about $700,000 for the campaign.

In this campaign Davis and Charles Page Bryan, the candidate for Vice-President, represented somewhat divergent political and economic views. Bryan had been put on the ticket as a compliment to William Jennings Bryan. Davis, who had been Ambassador to the Court of St. James's, was not very well known throughout the United States. Polished gentleman, fine leader, and graceful speaker though he was, the cards were stacked against him, and the silent Coolidge, who was supposed to have stood out nobly against the police strike in Boston and who represented the continuance of what Harding had called a return to normalcy, won easily.

I, of course, saw much of Davis during the campaign and learned to admire him, and I bitterly regretted his defeat and the fact that a man so well qualified had not won the presidency. I have learned, often to my disappointment but sometimes to my happy surprise, that the public reputations of men form a very inaccurate guide to their true nature and behavior. King Carol of Romania, for example, enjoys a dubious niche in the estimation of the general public, largely because of his celebrated romance with Magda Lupescu. Yet he displayed courage in facing the Nazis, and his administration of his country's affairs, prior to his abdication, was marked by considerable strength and wisdom. I entertained Carol and saw much of him during his visit to this country in 1920. He reminded me much of his cousins, the Prince of Wales (as he was then) and the Crown Prince of Germany, although he was stronger and huskier than either of them.

The story of Carol prompts the reflection that the historian writing one hundred years from now will fill many pages with accounts of the "fatal women" of our epoch. Because of Mrs. Simpson, King Edward VIII gave up one of the greatest empires the world has ever seen. Only slightly less spectacular are the stories of Manuel of Portugal and the French dancer Gaby Delys; Hitler and Mussolini facing death with their mistresses; and the cause of Irish Home Rule temporarily lost because of the affair of Parnell, the uncrowned king, with Mrs. O'Shea.

After World War I King Edward, then Prince of Wales, visited New York on the battleship *Renown*. He invited Mrs. Gerard and me to lunch on board. The prince was then a quiet, earnest, hard-working young Ambassador of Empire, taking his position most seriously. Subsequent visits to America were on pleasure bent. I attended one party given for him by Averell Harriman's sister, Mrs. Rumsey. She had hired a whole restaurant, all the chorus of some musical show, and the renowned Dolly Sisters.

When I was in London as Special Ambassador to the coronation of George VI, the various prime ministers of the British Dominions told me that their people would never have countenanced his proposed marriage. After that marriage I have had the pleasure of sitting next to the Duchess of Windsor on several occasions and of finding her clever and most attractive when she chooses to turn on her undoubted charm. So far the ducal pair seem to enjoy a perpetual honeymoon—"All for love and the world well lost."

Somehow, perhaps because of her poise and quiet determination, the duchess makes me recall the famous woman flier Amelia Earhart. Once at dinner at the house of Ogden Reid, publisher of the *Herald Tribune*, and his wonderful wife, Helen, I sat next to Amelia. I told Amelia that there was something I wanted to do and only she could help me. "What is it?" she asked. I confessed that I wanted to rumple her hair. "Go ahead," she said, and I did.

CHAPTER XXIX

Every time I've taken a place in Scotland I have looked forward to fine weather and lots of birds to shoot, but in almost every instance I encountered long days and nights of chill rain. As a result I have spent much of my Scotland vacations indoors huddled by the fire with my guests, so that what I missed in shooting I gained in stimulating conversation and memorable dinners.

In the summer of 1927 my brother-in-law, Marcus Daly II, and I took a place in Scotland called Dunalastair, situated on a promontory overlooking the valley of the Tummel. As usual the shooting was bad and the rain poured down on us. After twenty-eight days of rain, I ordered a motor and told the chauffeur to drive toward the village and whenever he saw gates to estates to drive in. When we reached a house I got out and rang the bell and asked the butler who lived there. The butler would tell me Mr. Snooks or Mr. James, and I would then say, "Tell Mr. James I want to see him." When he appeared I would introduce myself and in this way I met the neighbors. On the last day of my stay I invited a number of the neighbors to a shooting party, and one of them said, "You Americans are a most extraordinary people. If it had not been for you, we neighbors never should have met each other."

The Scotch and English are sure in their minds that they know a good deal about America. I became aware of this when one of my visitors that summer told me how he had attended the dedication of a statue given by American Scots to the city of Edinburgh as a war memorial. "I do not understand it at all," he said. "Someone from each of your states was supposed to lay a wreath and they kept coming and coming and coming. I can't understand it, because of course you have only thirteen states."

Shortly before we went to Scotland in 1927 I told a friend of our proposed expedition. My friend, knowing that some of my ancestors had come from Aberdeen or its vicinity, wrote to the Secretary of Marischal College, Aberdeen, suggesting that it would be a graceful thing to give me a degree in view of the work I had done for the English and Scottish prisoners during World War I. The first I knew of this was when he showed me the wonderful letter he received in prompt reply.

The Scotch are a proud and hardboiled race, and the Secretary undoubtedly felt it to be his plain duty to keep the American Philistines at a distance. Here is his letter to my friend, which, while it could hardly be termed graceful or polite, has the virtue of calling a spade a spade.

Marischal College,
Aberdeen.
21st April, 1927.

Dear Sir:

I am in receipt of your letter of 12th, April. Honorary Degrees are granted under Ordinance No. 41; General No. 13; made by the University Commissioners of 1889. Such ordinances have the force of an Act of Parliament. By Section II, sub-section (2) it is provided that the Committee who selects persons to be recommended to the Senatus for the Degree "shall not entertain applications from, or on behalf of, persons desirous of receiving the Degree." I shall however lay your letter before the Principal. I may add that the degrees are conferred only once a year and that the Committee will not now meet until November, 1927.

I am,

Yours faithfully,

H. J. Butchart.

Secretary.

I returned to the United States in time to take part in the political preliminaries that preceded the 1928 Democratic National Convention. The maneuvering was fraught with conspiracies and cabals. During the winter of 1927–28 a number of New York Democrats met in the Vanderbilt Hotel for dinner about once every ten days or oftener, to devise means of promoting the nomination of Governor Alfred E. Smith. The dinners were mysterious and secret; we went in by the side door of the hotel in cloak-and-dagger style.

At one of the first meetings, held July 5, 1927, the conspirators were John Curtin, John F. Gilchrist, Norman E. Mack, Henry Moscowitz, George W. Olvany, Robert F. Wagner, George R. Van Namee, and myself. At later meetings were added James J. Hoey, Herbert H. Lehman, William F. Kenny, Joseph M. Proskauer, James J. Reardon, James A. Foley, and Mrs. Henry Moscowitz. Franklin Roosevelt dined with us on December 15, 1927, and December 28, and on the following March 19 Jouett Shouse of Kentucky was present. Eventually George R. Van Namee was selected as pre-convention manager and carried out his task most efficiently.

We made a careful survey of the party primary elections in the different states, and as soon as the delegates were elected, we arranged for private investigators to give us reports on each of them—such things as their business affiliations, religion, and so on. It was curious that on many of these reports, under the head of religion, would be entered "Knights of Pythias." At first I judged this specification to be a fancy of the detective agency, but at times during the convention I had reason to suspect that it may actually have represented the religious convictions of some of the delegates.

I had known Al Smith, of course, for many years. He was a picturesque son of the sidewalks of New York and cultivated that appearance. On one occasion, before the 1928 campaign, Mrs. Gerard and I were invited to dine with him in a private room in the Biltmore Hotel. It was quite hot, and during the cocktail half hour Smith removed his coat. When Charles Mitchell and his wife, late-coming guests, entered the room they found Al Smith in his shirt sleeves, a huge cigar in his mouth, playing a hand organ which was on the table. The Mitchells managed to mask their surprise, but it took considerable effort.

Before I attended the 1928 Democratic Convention in Houston I went to Fort Worth to make a speech at a Chamber of Commerce convention. The city was full of marching delegates and brass bands. I was met at the station by my wife's cousin, Horace Durston, and the Brownsville Cowboy Band—led by a gorgeous young lady on a white horse, who later rode it into the convention hall and up to the speaker's desk to promote the fortunes of Jesse Jones. Senator Robinson, who was presiding, quite visibly did not approve of this incursion, and said in a loud, cold voice, "If the cavalry will now withdraw, we will proceed to the business of the convention."

It was so hot in Houston that from curiosity I looked at the map to see where Houston was situated latitudinally in relation to the steaming cities of the Orient. I found that it was one hundred and fifty miles south of Baghdad, a city which no one would choose for a convention place in July.

As soon as Smith had won the nomination, the party leaders had to deal with the problem of financing the campaign. I was continued as treasurer of the Finance Committee and Herbert H. Lehman, later governor of New York, was made its chairman. Lehman soon left the campaign, however, to run for Lieutenant Governor, so I had to be both chairman and treasurer of the Finance Committee. I raised an enormous sum of money, about four million dollars or more, but John J. Raskob, who was chairman of the Democratic National Committee, which he managed with great knowingness and ability, spent something more than six million, leaving the party in debt about two million dollars. Raskob, by the way, made quite large contributions from his private purse.

It is not possible to say with assurance just what changes there would have been in the nation's history had Al Smith, a Roman Catholic, instead of Herbert Hoover, been elected President in 1928. The economic forces which created the crash of 1929 were unleashed and rampant, and it seems improbable that a different administration could have prevented the reaction. The effect on our democracy of a Smith victory would have been considerable, however, for it would have signified a victory over the ugly prejudices that were raised by his candidacy. Certainly if a Democratic President had been in office when the depression began, the effect on the 1932 election might well have been to return the Republicans to office.

It is almost impossible to exaggerate the story of the Stock

Exchange boom that flourished just before the crash of 1929. Unbelievably large paper fortunes were made overnight, and the moral and physical effect of this game on people was startling. I recall no better proof than the case of a man who had been secretary to my partner John Bowers. After the death of Bowers, he did practically no work except to attend to some small matters such as the registration of stock. One afternoon he came into my office and said, "Do you mind if I go abroad? I've made enough money on the Stock Exchange to take a holiday." I asked him, "How much did you start with?" He replied, "$2,500." "How much have you got?" The answer, for which I was not prepared, was "One million."

After a short trip abroad he continued his speculation. If he had sold out his holdings in September of 1929, he would have had $11,000,000, all run up from the initial $2,500. It seems unbelievable, but I know that it was true. I begged him to put some of it in trust, but he refused, asserting that he was going to make a hundred million. He continued his speculations with such intensity that his health broke. He could talk nothing, see nothing, or read nothing but Stock Exchange reports. He died and most of his winnings were lost, of course. Even so, he left about a million one hundred thousand dollars to his son. There were many cases of heroic speculation as extraordinary as this, and in almost every case the mind, nerves, or general health of the speculators were affected. Domestic troubles were commonplace, and either premature death or suicide was the end of not a few.

The moral aspect of the orgy was bad from several points of view. One of the worst stratagems developed and exploited by the less responsible elements in Wall Street was the practice of "short selling." This device, even though it has been "justified" as beneficial to market values under certain conditions, is one of dubious honesty, and has been the means of building up many fortunes and—at the same time— impoverishing thousands of innocent investors.

I became so upset at cynical exploitation of investors through this device that I delivered a radio speech over WJZ on October 12, 1930, on a coast-to-coast network. It was a short, clear description of the mechanics of some of the financial practices that marked the twenties.

Since I made that protest many stockbrokers have told me that had the Stock Exchange taken some measures to curb short selling at the time of this agitation, prejudice would not have been so aroused against the Stock Exchange as to lead to the drastic regulations made by the Securities and Exchange Commission.

Many heads of great corporations encouraged me in my campaign. For instance, Walter Teagle, then head of the Standard Oil Company of New Jersey, and Thomas J. Watson, head of the well-conducted International Business Machines, not only patted me on the head, as it were, but Watson told me how the short sellers had had the consummate nerve to send him word that they were going to break the price of his stock and had promptly proceeded to do so.

Surveys of "conditions" with an eye to eliminating economic and social problems are commonplace nowadays, recognized as valuable, and obtain wide publicity and discussion. But from 1926 to 1929—in the alleged golden age of prosperity—I took part in such a survey, the results of which were quite important, and its coverage by the press consisted of a lone paragraph between two patent-medicine ads on the last page of the real estate section.

In March 1926 the New York Legislature created the New York State Industrial Survey Commission to investigate the condition of manufacturing, business, and labor. The committee consisted of three senators and five members of the Assembly and one representative each of workers, business interests, and the general public. I was appointed as the public representative. The committee sat for three years. As a result of its work many good laws were adopted, and its investigations aided the state in improving several bad or outmoded industrial and labor conditions.

The committee considered the Workmen's Compensation Law and frauds connected with it; state and mutual insurance; the curbing of "runners" for accident lawyers; employment agencies; the New York State agricultural situation in which at the time was leading farmers to abandon about 300,-000 acres every year; the depression in the textile industry; compensation for occupational diseases; and the very important question of unions, which were then so restrictive in membership that contractors in need of workingmen were often unable to obtain any at all; and a study of the transportation rates in the state. We also made a study of the cost of the distribution of food, particularly the factors that affect the price paid by the consumer.

During our existence we had, as I have said, recommended many good laws which were adopted, and I think we succeeded in curing many abuses in the labor, insurance, and on employment agency laws of New York. Nevertheless, when our final report was released, it was given only a short, nondescript back-page paragraph in the press. Shortly after we had presented our report, I spoke at a banquet in Utica given to one of the members of our commission. In my speech I referred to this lack of newspaper interest as indicative of the

small recognition for public service in this country, at least as
far as the newspapers were concerned. I added that if I had
gone to Palm Beach and given a dinner to thirty people
there, the newspapers would have given half a column to it,
and that if I had had a monkey at the dinner, it would have
made the first page.

During a trip across the Atlantic in 1930, after two or three
days on shipboard with nothing much to do, I felt so full of
energy that I wrote an article called "The Great Empire and
Imperial Free Trade." In it I advocated, simply as an economic study, free trade among the various members of the
British Empire. This idea was more or less carried out at the
Ottawa Conference at which the British Commonwealth of
Nations was formed. When I got to Paris about a month later,
I had typewritten copies made, and sent one to Lord Beaverbrook. He liked it so much that he had it printed as a
pamphlet, and placed it on sale on newsstands throughout
England, "price sixpence." From time to time thereafter, especially during by-elections, he distributed free copies of it as
a campaign document, for he himself was an advocate of
the economic principles that I had set forth.

The article had still another result which surprised me at
the time and has haunted me pleasantly ever since. It was
caused by an innocent reference to the United States which
read as follows:

It is unnecessary here to enumerate all the many and largely
developed resources of the Empire: the waving grain fields of
Canada, the cotton of Sudan, the oil of Mosul, and the rubber of
Malaysia—why, give the forty men who rule the United States
ten years for the development of this industrial empire, and no
country of this earth could approach it in per capita wealth.

Shortly after our return to America the New York *Times* sent a reporter to ask me the names of the "rulers of America." Sitting in my office that afternoon, I gave the reporter a list. They amounted finally to fifty-two, and of course, as Ferdinand Lundberg says in his book *Sixty Families*, it was quite evident that I added some personal friends to the list. When I returned from another European trip two or three years later, during the depression and the first term of Franklin Roosevelt, the reporters at the ship asked me about the forty men. I told them that the number had been reduced to one—Franklin Roosevelt.

Of course my list of "rulers" referred to economic headship, but it was taken generally to mean the men who ruled America not only economically but politically. It seemed to create quite a sensation. Mr. Lundberg's book came out at a time when it was fashionable for the hall-bedroom economists to challenge the morality of capitalism. He added eight names to my list, compiled some terrifying statistics and facts, and produced a book of impeccable social significance. I have always thought of the *Sixty Families* as being a sort of literary by-blow of mine, and cherish an inward fondness for it in the same way that a man might be secretly proud of an illegitimate son who has distinguished himself in the world.

CHAPTER XXX

Men PROFESSIONALLY ENGAGED IN POLITICS CANNOT afford to be altruistic in their loyalties, for their careers and livelihood often depend upon correct analysis of a candidate's chances. Consequently, a delicate problem faced the delegations of politicians at the 1932 Democratic National Convention in Chicago. It was quite evident to all that the next President was to be a Democrat, for the country had firmly fastened the blame for the crash and depression onto the Republicans, and demanded a change. The momentous question for the party armies, however, was which Democrat will it be? Those who guessed right on this point were in general rewarded, and the fact that he was "for Roosevelt before Chicago" was the sole reason for the government career —usually brief—of many an otherwise unlikely appointee.

The 1932 convention presented the spectacle of a number of candidates, all more or less evenly matched, trying desperately to woo the enthusiasm and votes of the delegates— a situation bound to bring out everything maudlin and silly in the so-called "democratic process." Manufactured "spontaneous demonstrations" have rarely been carried to more ridiculous extremes.

Behind me, among the New York delegates, sat a man who

from time to time blew ear-splitting blasts on a whistle. Exasperated, I finally asked him why the devil he made such a racket. It turned out that of all those present he, at least, had a serious purpose in his noise. He replied that his wife made him blow it at designated intervals. It seems that when he blew the whistle, she could hear it over the radio, by which she was following the proceedings. As long as she heard his whistle blasts she knew that he was safe inside the convention hall and not the prey of some Chicago blonde. Of course I suggested that some friend might blow in his absence—and, indeed, I made a sportsmanlike offer of my services—but he showed me a card on which his wife had worked out a code of blasts so complicated that some concentration was required in blowing the signals. I realized then that because of the distraction caused by the selection of a President of the United States I might easily miss a cue and break up a home, so I regretfully withdrew my offer.

Before the Democratic convention of 1932 I was for Roosevelt and, as I have said, contributed money whenever he needed it for his payroll, giving it to Louis Howe, Roosevelt's grand vizier. I even shelled out eight hundred dollars on the floor of the convention to a western delegate to help him entertain his delegates and keep them happy and loyal.

James A. Farley, who is undoubtedly one of the most honest men ever to enter politics, was for Roosevelt, and the Tammany delegation was for Smith. At a Tammany parade in New York City shortly before the convention, Farley and I walked together apart from the supporters of Smith; and when we arrived in Chicago I voted with Farley on the naming of a chairman and other matters. It was agreed that that unity should always stand on questions which might arise in our New York delegation.

However, Mayor James J. Walker demanded a roll call of the delegates on the first ballot for President, and the Tammany leaders demanded my vote for Smith. Accordingly I cast my vote for Smith, being additionally moved thereto by the fact that I had been the treasurer and chairman of the Finance Committee during his campaign. It seemed then that there would be plenty of opportunities later to change. However, Roosevelt was nominated on the first or second ballot after I had gone to my hotel.

Just after the 1932 convention I had a serious operation, and during the greater part of the subsequent campaign I was in the hospital. As a result, I gave but little time, although I contributed heavily to the party war chest, and remained throughout the campaign a member of the Democratic Executive Committee.

After his election in 1932 Roosevelt offered me, through Secretary of State Hull, the post of Ambassador to the Argentine Republic. This I was forced to refuse because my mother-in-law, Mrs. Marcus Daly, then growing very aged, was entirely dependent on my wife, who spent practically every day with her. As Mrs. Daly refused to go to the Argentine, and since we couldn't leave her, I had to decline.

In June 1930 I sailed for Europe. On board was Dr. Sirovitch, an intellectual member of Congress from East Side New York. He was a faithful admirer of Mr. Justice Frankfurter. Dr. Sirovitch succeeded in persuading me to come out for the recognition of the Soviets on my return to the United States.

It is my belief that nations, no matter what the circumstances, should be recognized as long as we are not at war with them. As Sumner Welles wrote in a letter to me, "I am a convinced believer in the continuation of diplomatic relations with every government as a means of procuring information and exercising our national influence. I believe in the withdrawal of recognition only as a step short of war."

Later on, by a letter from Secretary of State Hull, I was offered the Ambassadorship to Russia. In replying to him and to President Roosevelt, I thanked President Roosevelt for the offer and then said, "as a hard-boiled realist I advocated the recognition of the Soviet but as for the last few years and publicly I have been calling these people thieves and murderers, I do not think that I could be of any use to you in that country."

This, of course, turned all the Russia-lovers who surrounded Roosevelt against me, and I was never offered anything formally again except the post of Special Ambassador to the coronation of George VI although at different times I was promised the ambassadorship to Italy and to Great Britain by Roosevelt—promises which he had not kept.

When Roosevelt took office, in 1933, the Democratic party funds were extremely low. To overcome this, Roosevelt asked me to become chairman of the Finance Committee again. I worked hard for some time and managed to keep the party's head above water financially. Associated with me, as treasurer, was the great financier Walter J. Cummings, head of the Continental Illinois National Bank and Trust Company of Chicago.

It is no small job to run the financial end of a national campaign. I had given an enormous amount of time in 1920, all of the summers of 1924 and 1928, and several months each year since 1934 to this work. I employed skilled accountants, and in 1928, for example, no check was signed by me unless it had been passed on by the head of the particular department involved, the comptroller, the accountants, and myself.

Obviously a contribution received and credited to a notorious gambler or bootlegger, for instance, might seriously embarrass the party, and I often refused large contributions because of their suspicious source.

I functioned for some time as chairman after 1934, but finally I told the Democratic authorities that I couldn't give the necessary time to the job, so Forbes Morgan, whose first wife was a niece of Mrs. Roosevelt, took up the job. In the 1936 campaign I was made the honorary chairman of the Finance Committee, instead of chairman. I think the reason for this was that the boys feared that if I had been chairman I would have refused the $500,000 contribution given by John L. Lewis on behalf of his labor organization. The ready acceptance of that contribution by the party constituted, in Lewis's picturesque language, an obligation for having "supped at Labor's table." I have never met John L. Lewis.

It is always instructive to study the machinery that brings about political coups. The Democrats' capture of the Negro vote is a case in point. Particularly in the 1936 election the nation was surprised to learn that the Negro voters had, in the main, abandoned their historical allegiance to the Republican party. This change came about as the result of the perspicacity of one Negro manicurist and an organization called the Good Neighbor League.

The political and historical background of the Negro vote is worth a brief review in order to appreciate the Good Neighbor League. By the 1930s it became evident that the Republican voting habits of some millions of Negroes—especially those in the northern industrial states—could be, and occasionally were, a serious threat to Democratic candidates. Obviously, the logical thing for the Administration to do was to convince the Negroes that their best interests lay with the

New Deal Democratic party—if not with the Southern Democratic party. It was necessary to demonstrate to the Negro voters that there was a considerable difference between these two brands of Democrat, and the Good Neighbor League under Stanley High (who afterward fell from grace and deserted the New Deal) did excellent work in presenting the New Deal's bid for their allegiance.

I remember the day that High came to me and asked me for money for what he called the Good Neighbor League. He explained its purpose and told me it was particularly favored by the White House. When I said that I did not know this, he suggested that I call up the White House. I did, and was urged to go as far as I could in giving financial aid. I gave him a large sum and also collected contributions from others. We had a great Negro meeting of the League in Madison Square Garden.

It is remarkable that the Democratic party has been able to swing as many Negro votes as it has, for in regard to the Negro the party had been carrying water on both shoulders. The southern section bars the Negro from voting in Democratic primaries, and in many places does not allow Negroes to vote in the elections. At the same time, the northern section is cultivating the Negro vote and making every effort to encourage the Negroes to quit the Republican party permanently.

The result of the League's activity was a sort of historical paradox, for the majority of the Negroes voted for President Roosevelt as also did the old-fashioned Democrats of the deep South, descendants of the Knights of the Invisible Empire and of the Knights of the White Camellia. Politics, as they say, makes strange bedfellows.

After the election I received the following letter from President Roosevelt:

THE WHITE HOUSE   November 14, 1936.
WASHINGTON

Dear Jimmy:

Before I leave on Tuesday I do want to send you this line to thank you for all that you did during the campaign. You were more than generous.

I want to tell you, too, of my interest in the Good Neighbor League and to express the hope that you feel about it as I do and will occasionally give it some of your time and thought.

My best wishes to you. I hope I shall see you sometime soon.

Always sincerely,
Franklin D. Roosevelt

Honorable James W. Gerard
40 Wall Street,
New York City,
New York

The careful campaign to wean the Negro vote away from the Republicans began with the following incident.

Mrs. Emma Guffey Miller is a Democratic national committeewoman from Pennsylvania, a sister of Senator Guffey, and a very clever woman. In 1936 her nails were manicured by an intelligent Negro woman, Eva DeBoe Jones, who broached to Mrs. Miller the possibility of securing the Negro vote for the Democratic party. Mrs. Miller immediately acted on the suggestion and soon the movement got under way. She wrote this account of her story for me:

The gist of the part concerning the colored manicurist is as follows. She is Mrs. Eva DeBoe Jones. . . . She proved to be an excellent manicurist and for years had a large and "important" clientele. Though a Republican, Eva was very intelligent and in 1928 told me that she intended to vote for Smith because if religious intolerance prevailed, it would mean more racial intolerance. By 1932 she was openly for Roosevelt although I believe my sisters and I and perhaps one other family were the only Democrats among her patrons.

In April 1932 she asked me if I would meet Robert L. Vann, owner and editor of the Pittsburgh *Courier,* a colored weekly which was sent all over the country. I said I would be very glad to see him, and a day was arranged for him to come to our house. He told me that he had wanted to be for Smith in 1928 and that Jim Farley had taken him to see Mrs. Moskowitz but she told him some man in Massachusetts was heading the Negro committee and they got nowhere. . . .

We went to Chicago and you know the rest, but the aftermath was both tragic and amusing. Joe had Vann appointed a special assistant United States attorney in Washington, the first Negro ever to hold such a high job.

Eva Jones has stuck by the Democrats though it has practically cost her her living, for when the articles came out giving her so much credit, her Republican patrons were furious and refused to employ her.

Sincerely yours,
Emma Guffey Miller

Relatively few people in the North understand the historical background of the Negroes' political outlook. With the assassination of Lincoln, the so-called "era of good feeling" came to an end. The newly enfranchised slaves of the South were encouraged to vote under the protection of northern bayonets, and from the North came miserable beings called "carpetbaggers," ready to exploit the situation and to attain office by Negro votes. At the same time other low types in the South called "scalawags" joined with Negroes and carpetbaggers to oppress the white population.

The Negroes' social and political problem is still dominated by the events of the Reconstruction era. This unfortunate situation is made quite complicated by the fact that the great majority of non-southerners can't understand why those events of eighty years ago are still important in the South. This northern view is understandable. Practically all of the Civil War was fought in the South, and there the scars of battle and humiliations of the Reconstruction remain a strong memory. The North not only had few scars to remember but today a great part of its population are people who immigrated and settled here since the Civil War. Beyond a generation or two, their traditions are more European than American. To the mass of northerners it seems absurd of the South to keep flogging a dead mule. Every second northerner who returns from a visit to the South makes the stock, smiling comment: "They're still fighting the Civil War down there." And they are too. Many of the elder statesmen of the deep South were brought up surrounded by evidences of the chaos and poverty that the Negroes and their white carpetbagger leaders wrought on a proud people already impoverished by a long and exhausting war. It is not unnatural that the whites thereafter rigidly excluded the Negroes from the polls and from public life. They regarded it as the only way to insure their own economic survival. All of the foregoing is what a southerner has in mind when he refers to "white supremacy."

Mixed in with the "white supremacy" invokers is another section of southerners. These are descendants of the artisan class who were economically disfranchised as far back as the eighteenth century by the fact that the Negro slave could be trained to do the same work much cheaper. These people—

blacksmiths, field hands, gardeners, hostlers, and the like— were thus driven out of their niches early by the presence of the Negro, and were forced to make their living on marginal lands or hillside farms. These people hated the Negro, and their descendants today—even those who are rich, "aristocratic," and unaware of their lowly ancestry—have inherited their forebears' antagonism for the Negro. The inhabitants of the mountainous sections, where there have never been many Negroes, also resent the Negro.

Accounts of the depredations wrought by the freed Negroes, the local scalawags, and the carpetbaggers, are as carefully documented as the present-day records of the misdeeds of the Germans in Poland, and most southerners are familiar with them and not inclined to dismiss them as ancient history.

In the ten years that followed the Civil War the people of the South lived in a reign of terror. Many Negro legislators and public officials were elected, some of whom extravagantly abused their power, selling legislation to the highest bidder, while their white colleagues plundered the treasury. Few of us realize, for instance, that until 1877 the militia of South Carolina was all Negro.

Thus from the awesome days of the Reconstruction the Negroes had always, when they could, voted Republican, while the whites, with the ever-present memory of those days of race war and extravagant Negro government, always voted the Democratic ticket.

During the last thirty years great numbers of Negroes have migrated from the South to the North. In New York City alone there are now upward of four hundred thousand. In a state which has been carried by as few as a thousand votes, this constituted almost the balance of power. Other industrial states and cities in the North also have great numbers of Negroes, all of whom are permitted by the localities to vote as they choose. It was in this fallow field of votes that the Good Neighbor League operated so successfully.

While I was in London in the early summer of 1935 I felt a growing desire to meet and talk to Italy's dictator, Benito Mussolini, who, it may be recalled, was then at about the height of both his physical and political powers, and quite a figure. So I wrote to Alexander Kirk, who was then Chargé d'Affaires in Italy, and asked him to arrange an audience for me if possible.

Kirk had been one of my secretaries in Berlin and turned in a first-class performance. He was afterward in Italy for a long time, and then was Chargé d'Affaires in Russia, Minister to Egypt, and Ambassador to Italy.

Kirk wrote me that because of the preparations for the Ethiopian campaign all audiences were canceled, but when I reached the South of France I received another message from him saying that my audience with Il Duce was set for August 10 at 6 P.M. About five o'clock someone from the Italian Foreign Office telephoned me at my hotel and asked if I could speak French. I said, *"Oui,"* and he seemed satisfied with the sample. I arrived at the Palazza Venetia shortly before six, and promptly on the stroke of that hour was ushered into a room almost as long as a bowling alley. At the far end sat the Duce, erect and expressionless behind a table, his arms akimbo. As Il Duce's device of having his visitors make a sixty-foot approach under his scowling scrutiny has been given a paragraph in all the foreign-observers' books, I dare not fail to mention it.

When I finally arrived in front of him, he stood up and shook hands with me across the table. He was dressed in a white uniform trimmed in black and gold. I told him that I had had interviews with many distinguished people—like himself—and had never disclosed what was said, whereupon he invited me to sit down. We had a long and intimate conversation in French. When we had finished, he accompanied me to the door and asked me to come again, something which I understand he seldom did.

I congratulated him on having accomplished two things which had stumped the rulers of Italy for centuries—the accord with the Vatican and the draining of the Pontine Marshes. He himself commented favorably on the fact that he had made the Italian railroads run on schedule. I suspect that he accomplished that mainly by browbeating the workers into faithful performance of their duties.

In the course of the interview I predicted so correctly the march of subsequent events that, a year or two later, I believed that he would pay some attention to my views and that perhaps I could persuade him to stay out of the coming World War II.

So I sought the Ambassadorship to Italy. Breckenridge Long was then the Ambassador but in poor health.

President Roosevelt solemnly promised Senator Wagner and James A. Farley that when and if Long resigned I should have the Italian mission. But when Long resigned, Roosevelt appointed William Phillips without a word to me, to Wagner, or to Farley. I was sorry because I really think I might have had some success in keeping Mussolini among the neutrals, although it may be that he had little choice.

On my return to Antibes next day I dined with Sir Charles Mendl, skillful press representative of the British Embassy in Paris, and lunched the following day with Sir Robert Vansittart, then British Under-Secretary of Foreign Affairs.

I told them both that I could not, of course, repeat what Mussolini had told me, but I said, "I warn you that you are dealing with a desperate and determined man."

I wish I could record my belief that the miserable fate of this vainglorious mountebank and his master confederate, Hitler, improved the probability that the world will see their like no more. But the lust for power is a cancer of the soul, and civilization must stagger a long way forward if, indeed, some maniacal despot does not, as Hitler threatened, carry the world with him into dust, before that curse is tamed.

CHAPTER XXXI

ONE SUNDAY NIGHT IN DECEMBER 1936 WALTER WINCHELL, in one of his bursts of radio oracularity, announced that I was to be the President's representative at the coronation of King George VI. I took the skeptical course and before booking my passage waited until I had received verification from the President. In due course the prophecy proved correct.

The coronation was the occasion and excuse for one of the most brilliant social seasons that has ever occurred anywhere in modern times. All of British society—which in this case meant all of world society—was concentrated in London, and the entertaining was at a pace and on a scale that could not conceivably be maintained for more than a short period. All of Britain's beauty and chivalry and jewels and country houses were on display, and all her incomparable hostesses were on duty. Superimposed upon the inimitable quality of English hospitality and the opulent pageantry of the occasion was a vague atmosphere of unquiet and urgency—a reflection of the feeling that war was not far off, and that this might well be the last full dress parade of the Empire for a long time.

To my mind the coronation was comparable, in a vague

way, with the Duchess of Richmond's Ball in Brussels on the eve of the Battle of Waterloo. The comparison cannot be pushed too far, but in a sense the coronation activities were an almost conscious effort of a regime and a way of life to make a last display and tread a final measure before the dread calamity. There undoubtedly were some who thought —and perhaps correctly—that the coronation would turn out to be the swan song of the Empire.

In any event, I have thought that some notes on my experiences as Special Ambassador would be an interesting record of the social life produced for the occasion.

We crossed on the *Queen Mary* and arrived in London at the end of April 1937. Among my fellow passengers were the Ranee of Sarawak, J. P. Morgan and his bodyguards. During the crossing we had tea several times with J. P. Morgan. He had none of the force and grimness of his celebrated father. In fact, he had been so overshadowed all his life by his forceful parent that his appearance was timid and shy. He lived very quietly in New York, at his estate in England and at his place on Long Island, surrounded by a very few intimate friends. Indeed, having been the intended victim of the famous Wall Street bomb explosion, and also having been shot in the groin by a would-be assassin on another occasion, he might well be shy.

The Ranee of Sarawak was a daughter of Lord Esher, who, in 1917, had taken me to see Marshal Lyautey, the French Minister of War. She was a charming little lady, the wife of Sir Charles Vyner Brooke, the white Rajah of Sarawak and mother of his three daughters. These girls were known as Princess Gold, Princess Pearl, and Princess Diamond. One of them married a popular orchestra leader, one a British lord, and one a professional wrestler. The Rajah, his fabulous domain, and his antic daughters have been standard subjects for the Sunday-supplement writers.

In the American delegation to the coronation, General Pershing represented the Army, Admiral Rodman represented the Navy, and Judge Curtis Bok of Philadelphia (grandson of Cyrus H. K. Curtis), whose pretty wife accompanied him, was secretary.

Among the Britons assigned particularly to look after us were Lord Gage, a descendant of that General Gage who commanded the British at the battle of Bunker Hill.

Even before landing there arose the great question of my legs. I had said on sailing that I would wear the costume prescribed by our hosts whatever it was, breeches, pajamas, or gunny sacks. The American newspapers were full of debate over this great question, unmindful of the fact that, as I have said before, Americans are the greatest dressers-up in the world. Think of the processions down Main Street of Knights Templars, Knights of Pythias, and gentlemen from Mecca Temple with little red fezzes and Zouave trousers! The great Chicago *Tribune* published a long editorial attacking me violently because I conformed to age-old custom, and declined to affront my hosts. The *Tribune* trumpeted that in wearing breeches I was wearing the garments of servility that America had renounced in 1776, and so on. American representatives abroad, the editorial said, should dress like Americans. Colonel Robert R. McCormick, the editor and principal owner of the *Tribune,* is a good sport and a mighty crusader whose chief foible is a slight bias against the British Empire. I immediately recalled that his father had once been our Ambassador to Russia. So, at great trouble, penetrating the red tape and confusion in Russia, I obtained a photograph of Father McCormick in his ambassadorial court robes.

It is an interesting document. His chest is plastered with gold lace, his cocked hat, so jaunty, is crowned with ostrich plumes. By his side is his faithful Toledo blade—an implement no American should be without!—with which, possibly, he speared roasting marshmallows to while away the dark winter days in the cold embassy in Petrograd. Perhaps Colonel McCormick would like a copy to show to his rugged Middle Western admirers. Knowing something of the colonel, I feel sure that he didn't examine and approve the *Tribune's* editorial. He was probably playing his favorite game of polo, with his legs encased in his super-English white riding breeches and yellow boots.

Before I had been fifteen minutes in London our regular Ambassador, Robert Bingham, a tactful and successful diplomat, called on me and begged me to wear the breeches. He had been thus attired on all occasions of ceremony, and he made it clear that if I stuck to conventional trousers the newspapers at home might make sport of him.

As a matter of fact, there is nothing startling about the required dress: an ordinary dress coat and waistcoat, knee breeches of the same black material as the dress coat, black silk stockings, and ordinary plain patent-leather pumps. There is a reason for this unexciting costume: the most cherished decoration in England is the Garter, an order founded by Edward III. One of Lady Salisbury's garters had fallen to the floor at a court ball, and the lords and ladies present leered at her embarrassment and waited to see what the King would do. He did the chivalrous thing: he picked it up and handed it to her, and remarked for the benefit of the smirkers, *"Honi soit qui mal y pense* [Evil be to him who evil thinks]"—a sentiment which became the motto of the order which grew out of this incident. The King on state occasions always wears the garter just below his knee. It is blue, about an inch wide, and has the motto on it in letters of gold. Naturally, he and the other knights cannot wear their garters outside one leg of a pair of long trousers.

The coronation in Westminster Abbey was an unforgettable spectacle. The rich vestments of the clergy; the robes and coronets of the peers and peeresses; the uniforms of the yeomen of the guard; the sultans of Malaysia and Zanzibar and the Maharajahs of India in their wonderful dress afire with precious stones; the colorful uniforms of guards and Highlanders; and little pages with their daggers, all combined to make a rich and dazzling scene. The deeply stirring effect of the occasion was heightened by the extreme solemnity of everyone concerned. The dramatic events of Edward VIII's abdication were still fresh in everyone's mind.

To me the most impressive part of the ceremony was that in which the Archbishop led the King successively to each of the four sides of the platform and presented him to the people, intoning, "Sirs, I here present unto you King George, your undoubted King: Wherefore all you who are come this day to do your homage and service, are you willing to do the same?" Whereupon, on each presentation, there was a great shout, "Long live King George," and a flourish of trumpets.

A member of the Court assured me that the smaller princess said to her sister, "But where is Uncle David?" (David was the home name of Edward VIII.) My informant said that Princess Elizabeth replied, "Why, don't you know, he made love to Mrs. Baldwin so Mr. Baldwin wouldn't let him come."

The state dinner in Buckingham Palace was a great sight with the same costumes and uniforms. I took Princess Helena Victoria, a daughter of Queen Victoria, to dinner, and on my other side was the beautiful wife of the Portuguese Ambassador. We were at the King's table, which seated about twenty-six. Mrs. Gerard was in an adjoining room at the Queen's table, where she was taken to dinner by Prince Ernst of Brunswick, a grandson of the German Kaiser. Toward the end of dinner twenty-five pipers in full regalia marched piping about the tables in the ancient Highland fashion.

Those who consider democracy a matter of dress would perhaps be interested in knowing that the wife of the German Ambassador, Joachim von Ribbentrop, did not follow the regulations as to dress at the state dinner and other ceremonies. She omitted the tiara and plumes called for by the regulations and was very simply arrayed.

At the various dinners I had the opportunity to talk to the King and Queen. The system was for an aide to approach and take you to the King and Queen for a brief conversation, Their Majesties always standing. All the royalties I have met seemed to have iron legs. I shall always cherish the memory of old German Chancellor von Bethmann-Hollweg who, after hours of mild exhibitionism by the Kaiser on such an occasion, used to murmur to me, "I wish to God the Kaiser would sit down."

President Roosevelt gave me one specific task to do at the coronation. That was to invite the King and Queen to visit him. I spoke to Anthony Eden and Baldwin and was told to speak to the King. So, after the Foreign Office dinner, I proposed the idea to him, and he immediately promised to come. Later the details of the visit were arranged by President Roosevelt and Premier Mackenzie King, when they met at the opening of the Thousand Islands Bridge.

During the week of the ceremonies I had long talks with most of the high officials. Stanley Baldwin was a great surprise. I saw him in the historic No. 10 Downing Street. I had pictured him as a stodgy pipe-smoking Englishman. He did smoke a pipe, but he is certainly not stodgy, for a better informed, more cosmopolitan, and more agreeable man it has never been my fortune to meet.

Neville Chamberlain told me that he had spent six years of his early life on Andros Island in the Bahamas—an all-Negro island. He was sent there to superintend the growing of sisal by a family company, but the venture was a failure—not enough good soil. Chamberlain said he was allowed a few weeks' vacation every year. I said his life on Andros must have made him a contemplative philosopher, and he agreed that it had.

One of the most interesting affairs was a men's lunch at the house of Lord Camrose, proprietor of the *Daily Telegraph*. This lunch resolved itself into an oral duel between Winston Churchill and J. L. Garvin, editor of the *Observer*. Garvin wanted to let the Germans take Austria; Churchill was opposed.

An old acquaintance whom I saw at the coronation was the Aga Khan, who remains probably one of the most talented statesmen in all Europe. He and his beautiful wife and little son, then seven years old, were in the rooms next to us at the Ritz. The British had sent me a magnificent red-coated guard who waited in the corridor outside our rooms, and the little son of the Aga Khan was inconsolable until he was given a red coat and could mount guard before his father's door. The Aga Khan gave me a book of verse by Indian poets as a parting gift.

At a dinner the Pilgrim Society gave during the coronation to General Pershing, Admiral Rodman, and me, the redoubtable Archbishop of Canterbury, Cosmo Gordon Lang, spoke just before I did. He said that above all things he hated the American habit of interlarding a funny story in every speech. I felt that the honor of the hundred thousand American after-dinner speakers was in my keeping, and when I rose to speak I said that I hoped that the Archbishop would not imprison me in the Tolbooth if I told a story. I included an anecdote in my speech, and when I sat down the Archbishop invited me to lunch: possibly he wanted to hear some more. The Archbishop was a splendid man and a reincarnation of the powerful churchmen of the Middle Ages. He had started in life as a lawyer, a fact that gave us a special bond.

Winston Churchill included in his book *Step by Step* a quotation from my speech that evening. It was:

When you are armed, then armed Britain will be the greatest guarantee of peace on earth . . . We in America—I think in this one thing I can presume to speak for my country—are firmly de-termined on three things. First, we are against war; secondly, we are against any alliances; and, thirdly, we are against meddling in the muddled affairs of Europe. But we and you, the great British Empire, are bound by something more binding than alliances and treaties. We are bound together by a mutual trust, by mutual understanding, by a common desire for stability and peace, and especially by the feeling that at this moment, with Fascism on one side and Communism on the other, the three great democracies, Great Britain, France, and the United States, stand as the sole hope of liberalism and of the freedom of the world.

Mr. Churchill commented on this part of my speech as follows:

There certainly has not been any occasion either before or since the Great War when the views of the United States Government have been so clearly and weightily expressed upon European affairs . . . One may say that throughout the United States there is a keen abhorrence of the doctrines and practices both of Nazism and Fascism, and a strong current of sympathy with the countries great and small who are faithfully endeavoring to preserve their parliamentary institutions, and to maintain the conditions of law, freedom, and peace.

A few days before I left London, early in June, I was notified to go to Buckingham Palace for a private audience with the King. I presented myself at the designated hour, and was shown into a small sitting room where the King awaited me, and had about an hour's conversation with him alone. There was no hesitation in his speech, and in the short time since I had first spoken with him at the coronation ceremonies he appeared to have matured to a noticeable degree. The King is not only a most agreeable and fine-looking man, but he also has a great depth of character and other attributes that have been manifest during the stress and strain of the war and its aftermath.

On June 4, 1937, I saw the Minister of Air. When I suggested to him that the British might buy planes in America, he tartly remarked, "We don't need to buy anything in America, or anywhere else." When I observed to him that the Germans were far ahead of the English both in the number of planes on hand and in monthly production, he said, with an airy wave of his hand, "We can make all we need."

It is difficult to describe all the rewards of my experiences at the coronation and my other activities during that European stay. The events themselves were stirring and provocative, but there was a great deal more that gave me satisfaction. For a person such as myself, who had had many contacts with Europe over the past seventy-five years—in the various roles of schoolboy, ambassador, and traveler—and who has both a long memory and a well-kept diary, such a trip was a fuller experience than it is possible for me to tell.

Following the coronation we went to Paris for a short visit. William Bullitt, then our Ambassador in France and one of the few who understand Europe, helped to arrange for me to meet the then President of France, Lebrun. He received us in the garden of the Elysée Palace, where we had tea. I had a long talk with Lebrun while we walked around the gardens. One matter about which Lebrun made no secret was his bitter opposition to Communists, to whom he ascribed many of France's troubles. He accurately predicted their activities in the event of war, and their part in the internal collapse of France during the German invasion in 1940 bore out his judgment.

Bullitt also arranged for me to meet Premier Blum, who was then in office. I had an interesting and far-ranging conversation with him, and while I understand his striving for the social ideal, many of his reforms, good as they were, struck me as curiously at odds with the fixed pattern of the French national life. I think that many of the things he and his followers stood for and promoted resulted in making the invasion much easier for the Germans in 1940 than would have been the case had France been more nationalistic and cohesive.

After our short stay in Paris, we tapered off our diet of excitement with a visit to the delightful Antibes in the South of France. I convened there with some comrades in arms, so to speak. I had been made an honorary member of the *Chasseurs Alpins,* popularly known as the "Blue Devils." On the Fourth of July a number of their officers brought a band of the Chasseurs to serenade Mrs. Gerard and me, and we entertained them at the competent bar of the celebrated Hôtel du Cap.

I have another pleasant memory of Antibes. In a previous summer the great Churchill, accompanied by his wife and daughter, were in nearby Cannes and came often to Antibes, where the swimming was more inviting. On occasions they lunched with me.

CHAPTER XXXII

A MAN COULD HAVE NO MORE REWARDING HOBBY THAN TO study England and its intriguing inhabitants over the years. I have been intrigued all my life by everything about Great Britain—its people, customs, prejudices, accents, habits, clothes, food, history, and literature. The subject has never cloyed or grown tiresome, because it is not all sweetness and light. There are many things about the English that can drive an outlander to distraction; for every British virtue has a complementary and often irritating foible, and the British display both of them with assurance that can itself be infuriating. In general, it is their sublime insularity, their almost offensive moral rectitude, and their ability to endow their rudest acts with "good taste" that excites the foreigner to either irritation or admiration, or both. No matter what the British do—or what other people think—they perform no act that they are not convinced is "fit, right, and our bounden duty so to do."

The English system of education has helped to perpetuate class lines. The average English boy of good family goes to such a preparatory school as I attended some seventy years ago. In my day his sisters were educated by governesses and, unlike the custom in America, never appeared at all family meals. The boys, after the preparatory school, went to a so-called public school, such as Rugby, Eton, Winchester, or Harrow. The public school system was an excellent one except for the "fag" custom under which each older boy in the top form had a younger boy as his "fag" to look after his belongings and act as a sort of slave. I suppose the idea was to impress young gentlemen that they were not everything on earth, but from another side this system seems to me pernicious. Happily, the more brutal aspects of the fag system have been dropped.

After a time at Eton or Harrow or another public school, the boys went either to Oxford or Cambridge.

In this country, when a man makes a fortune and acquires a beautiful country place and then dies, there is usually no one to maintain it because the estate as a rule is divided between all the sons and daughters. But in England, by custom —and until recently by the law of primogeniture—the estate descends to the eldest son. Because of this system there were very few heiresses in England and this, in turn, made for a finer race. Instead of young people marrying, as they did in France, because of a carefully thought out financial scheme, the young English people of good family were able to marry for love and produced strong and beautiful children.

In this country members of Congress are elected from the districts in which they live. This is not necessarily so by law but has been made so by custom. But in England the political parties select the candidates for the various constituencies regardless of residence. Any man desiring to enter politics, and having influence enough to be named as a candidate, is at first entered in a constituency where there is little chance of success. Gradually he is promoted to easier districts. This means that for a long time the ruling class in England held control of Parliament, sitting either as Conservatives or Liberals, or even as Radicals.

When I was treasurer of the Democratic party, I had to report the name and address of everyone who contributed more than one hundred dollars to the party. This rule does not hold in England, and it has been often charged that ambitious individuals have obtained a knighthood or a peerage in exchange for a heavy contribution. On one occasion a friend of mine—a noble lord—invited me to the House of Lords to hear a debate on the propriety of offering a peerage to Sir Jeremiah Robinson, a rich mineowner from South Africa who was reported to have contributed three hundred thousand dollars to his party's funds. My friend told me that he and other noble lords had decided that if this mineowner was given a peerage they would give him what is known in America as the "bum's rush" and physically throw him out of the House of Lords. However, on the occasion of the debate the Lord Chancellor rose from the sack of wool on which, by old tradition, he sits, and defended the elevation of the South African "angel" by charging that the other party had handed out fully as many peerages and knighthoods as his own. He concluded by saying, "But all this is of only academic interest in view of the letter which I shall now read you, in which Sir Jeremiah says that he is an old man, that titles and honors mean nothing to him, and that he refuses the peerage which has been offered to him." This Lord Chancellor was F. E. Smith, who had risen by his talents to a high place, and had been created Earl of Birkenhead.

There is a belief abroad that the average Englishman is rather stupid. This is a slanderous error. The English are the foxiest, craftiest people on earth. Taking them all in all as a people, the English are distinguished by courage, pertinacity, and honesty. The British system of rewards and decorations does much to maintain the national honor.

In unusual cases British honors are conferred on foreigners.

Because of the work I did for the British in Germany during World War I, I was given the Grand Cross of the Order of the Bath. For a while I was the sole American to be so honored, but I was soon joined by General Pershing, and twenty-five years later we were reinforced by Generals Eisenhower and MacArthur.

In 1948 I addressed the annual meeting of the Pilgrims of the United States, officiating as vice-president in the absence of President John W. Davis. I was introduced by Gano Dunn, chairman of the executive committee, who remarked:

"If he were a British subject he would be *Sir* James, for he is a Knight Grand Cross of the Bath." To which I replied:

"I am sorry that Mr. Dunn brought up the fact of the Order of the Bath. I understand that after receiving it I was known in Tammany Hall as 'Saturday Night Jim.'"

The Order of the Bath is really the oldest order in England, but because it was reformed and re-established by George IV, it is made to rank below the Order of St. Patrick and the Order of the Thistle, which are orders of the high nobility of Ireland and Scotland respectively. In English history you may read of the Knights of the Bath as far back as the fourteenth century. They were called Knights of the Bath because a prospective knight, on the night previous to his reception into the order, was actually required to take a bath—something unusual in the Middle Ages—after which he had to spend the night in prayer in some chapel. Thus, when he entered the order, he was both physically and spiritually clean.

These orders of chivalry, as they are called, exist in all countries of Europe. I am also a Knight of the Grand Cross of the Order of St. Sava of Yugoslavia; of the Star of Roumania; of the Crown of Italy; of the Crown of Belgium; of the Paulonia Flower of the Rising Sun of Japan; of the

Dominican Republic, and am Grand Officer of the Legion of Honor of France created by Napoleon to reward civilian and military merit. It is unfortunate that in America we have created recently no respected symbols of reward of public service, and that up to this moment it has been the fashion to regard the acquisition of a large sum of money as the supreme achievement in any man's life, regardless of how that money was obtained.

All in all it is much easier for us to live in a world where the English are powerful than in a world dominated by either the French or the Germans or the Russians. The English have been very wise in permitting other nations to go into their empire and operate enterprises on the same terms as their own citizens. In operating mines in Canada, for example, I have always felt that I would receive exactly the same fair treatment as any citizen of the British Empire. I must say that I have the greatest admiration for the British, their skill in colonizing and bravery in war, and the honesty with which their government and business is conducted.

It is very difficult for an American Ambassador in England to stand out against the blandishments of British society. Lord Grey, who was Sir Edward Grey during World War I when he was Minister of Foreign Affairs, relates in his memoirs how the American Ambassador, Walter Hines Page, called on him to present a stiff note from America relating to the British sea blockade. This interview is described as follows in *Twenty-five Years, 1892–1916*, by Lord Grey of Fallodon, page 110:

Page came to see me at the Foreign Office one day and produced a long dispatch from Washington contesting our claim to act as we were doing in stopping contraband going to neutral ports. "I am instructed," he said, "to read this dispatch, but I do not agree with it; let us consider how it should be answered."

In the book *Grey of Fallodon,* written by George Macaulay Trevelyan, it is stated that Lord Grey "made the conquest of the private affections of Colonel House and Ambassador Page, which proved of no small public importance."

It is a great temptation for an ambassador to seek popularity in the country to which he is sent. As Bismarck once said, an ambassador should not be too well liked in the country to which he is appointed, for if he is, it means that he is giving away some of the interests of his own country.

Grey, a man of deep learning and gentle manners, found a way into the heart of Colonel House, who was a nature lover, by discussing with him such subjects as birds and flowers. When Lord Grey came to America as British Ambassador, President Wilson, for some reason unknown to me, refused to see him. The unfortunate Grey, after a short and embarrassing residence here, returned perforce to England without having once been admitted to the presence of our President.

At various times I have met some of the grandchildren of Queen Victoria, each one with his or her memories of Grandmother. One of them told me that Queen Victoria was not the prim and stern individual she appeared to be. The fact was that the monarchy of Great Britain had so fallen into disrepute through the immoral doings of the Georges and William IV that she felt that only the utmost show of puritanism could restore the prestige and the moral leadership of royalty.

For instance, the immediate predecessor of Queen Victoria was William IV. As the Duke of Clarence he kept a Mrs. Jordan, a beautiful actress, wife of a bricklayer. He stole her from one Ford, a theatrical manager by whom she had had four children. By the duke she had ten—five sons and five daughters. Think of it! Ten little illegitimate Fitz-Clarences, children of a king, trotting about London. By today their demi-royal descendants must be legion. Mrs. Jordan was very successful as an actress, earning a large salary which the duke, accompanying her to the theater on paydays, used to take from her and lose in gambling. In spite of his promises to her and a bond which he gave her, he allowed her to die in poverty.

A brother of William IV, the Duke of York, was once commander in chief of the British Army and was well walloped in Holland by the French in 1793. When he was six years old he had become Bishop of Osnaburgh in Hanover so that he might enjoy the large revenues of the bishopric—thus becoming a Right Reverend Father in God. For a time he was forced out of his army command over a great scandal in the sale of army commissions. Mrs. Clarke, the duke's mistress, who was compelled to testify before Parliament, was found to have an office in London for the sale of army commissions, promotions, and influence generally. The duke was certainly a novel Right Reverend Father in God! Is it any wonder that, as her grandchild told me, Victoria felt compelled, by over-austerity, to restore respect for royalty and the Crown?

Another grandchild of Victoria told me once of being present at a luncheon when Queen Victoria opened her mail, or rather had it opened for her by this grandchild. At one point Victoria said, "Here is a letter from dear Christa," by which name she referred to the Queen Regent Christina of Spain. "Dear Christa," Victoria mused, "wants permission to fortify Ceuta, but we cannot grant that." Ceuta is a town in Spanish Morocco opposite Gibraltar. The incident shows not only the power of England at that time but the interest Victoria took in empire foreign policy.

When another grandchild told me of having seen Helen Hayes's charming impersonation of Queen Victoria in the play *Victoria Regina,* I asked whether the play was entirely factual, chronologically or otherwise. This grandchild said there were two small things wrong: that the place stated as that where the then Prince of Wales had been educated was incorrectly given; and that the characters in the play, when talking of the marriage of Victoria, spoke of the blood disease which apparently is a heritage of the Coburg family, transmitted by the female who does not have it to the males who do. This grandchild said this reference was incorrect because at that time the disease or the method of its transmission had not been identified or understood.

It is fascinating to speculate on all the factors which prompted the British people to accept the socialistic program of the post-World War II Labor government. Prominent among them must have been a simple desire for a change after the hardships of the war, and a reaching for some of the promised fruits of victory. But underlying these was a class consciousness of the uneven distribution of wealth and privilege.

I view this adventure into Socialism with strong misgivings, principally because it narrows the field of individual initiative. Womb-to-tomb security seems desirable to the average worker, but the price exacted for it may well be national mediocrity. The Roman Empire flourished until the chief occupation of its government became the providing of bread and entertainment for the populace, paid for by taxes on the productive classes. Then it succumbed to the assaults of a hardier and more virile people. The goose in his wild state is a most admirable bird, with magnificent endurance, cunning, and resourcefulness. Domesticated and fed without risk or effort, he becomes a very synonym for dull wit and easy prey.

CHAPTER XXXIII

I FIND THAT THE OLDER I GET THE BUSIER I AM. EVER SINCE the coronation both my business interests and my various other projects have become greater and demanded more and more attention. Even when, in 1941, I retired from the practice of law, I found that I was still too busy to relax. Fortunately, this was just as well, since I have no inclination or desire to relax.

During the past dozen or so years—since I was seventy—I have had my time filled with politics, speechmaking of many kinds, running my various business interests, planning new business activities, and writing these memoirs. I have also found time to keep track of a host of friends—old and new— and to do a great deal of entertaining.

One of the occasions in recent years that have given me great pleasure was a dinner given by the Society of the Genesee in honor of my old friend Louis Wiley in 1937, just a short time before his death. For this event I made a speech from which I quote here because it gives some account of one of the most delightful and valuable citizens that the country has produced, who had a myriad of friends all over the world. Of Wiley I said:

No social gathering is complete without him and from the humblest shop to the White House his wise counsel is sought on those economic questions which today insistently face everyone who has either a job or a dollar.

His earlier life, his progress from his birthplace to New York, is an Odyssey of hard, unremitting work varied only by a stay in the enchanted Valley of the Genesee, where dreaming under the oaks of that lovely countryside he conceived the idea of founding this immortal society.

And then Blind Fortune took him by the hand and led him to the workshop where Adolph S. Ochs was in process of changing the New York *Times* from a weak, struggling sheet to that powerful engine of public opinion which it is today, and Louis Wiley was given the privilege of assisting Mr. Ochs, of becoming one of his most efficient aides in this transmutation.

So Louis Wiley also seized opportunity defined as "the jade who waits without, intent on favors granting, when we are deep in witless sleep or absent gallivanting," and won to the front in this relentless city by the force of undoubted talent, rare diplomacy, and personal charm.

Years ago I wrote some verses which began, "For man is ruled by passions three—war, hunting and polygamy." I was wrong. Next to that sacred love which itself has been defined as "friendship set on fire," the greatest thing in the world is friendship, and our guest tonight is the very incarnation of friendship. His friends are legion. They are to be found in every country.

If you were to take the wings of the morning and fly to the uttermost ends of the earth and land in a desert oasis or a lovely tropical isle, the local chief would be sure to say, "You come from New York? Yes? And how is my friend, Mr. Wiley?"

In 1937 Jeremiah T. Mahoney, former judge of the New York Supreme Court and active for many years in Democratic politics in the city of New York, was put forth as candidate for the mayoralty. In the primary election he was opposed by Senator Royal F. Copeland, who represented the so-called Old Guard of Tammany Hall. In these primaries Mahoney won over Copeland and became the candidate of the Democratic party. I was his campaign chairman in this primary and after he won I became chairman of his mayoral campaign. He was opposed by Fiorello La Guardia, running for a second term and nominated by the Republican party, American Labor party, and Progressive party. Against this array Mahoney went down to defeat, and La Guardia entered his second term.

I had worked hard for Mahoney, and regretted his defeat, as I am convinced that he would have been a splendid mayor.

The late Sara Delano Roosevelt, the President's mother, was a delightful *grande dame* of the old school. One day in New York she and I and a friend of hers went together to see an exhibition of pictures. She talked a little about politics and I criticized several measures of the New Deal. She said, "You write to Franklin and tell him that he is to invite you to lunch so that you can tell him these things." I did this, and had lunch with Roosevelt in the White House, then and many times later but his mother's admonitions and my own infallible advice did not turn him from his course.

When I lunched with Franklin Roosevelt from time to time it was at his desk in his White House office. Two waiters spread napkins in front of Roosevelt and his guest, who sat at Roosevelt's left at the end of the desk. First they served a good soup, and placed bread, butter, and coffee on the desk. Next, a high contrivance, a metal warming oven, about five feet high, was wheeled in and placed at Roosevelt's left. The waiters then left the room and Roosevelt extracted the next course—maybe chicken hash and a vegetable—from the contrivance, and later a simple dessert. Lunch lasted about an hour. If the visitor did not depart in time for the next appointment and Roosevelt remained interested, a reminder from a tactful secretary, usually General Edwin Watson, sufficed to speed the parting guest.

I lunched with Roosevelt on May 7, 1940, and when I came out of his office the reporters asked me for a statement. I said that of course I was not at liberty to quote the President. When I was then asked what I would say on my own responsibility, I replied, "If we do not get into this war, we are cooked."

On one occasion when I was having lunch off one end of the President's desk, Bernard Baruch was also present, eating at the other end. I have always liked and admired Bernie. For a long time he and his well-tempered wisdom were ignored by Roosevelt and his advisers. Nevertheless, many leaders in both business and politics sought him out in his office and listened to his counsel. His office, during the early war years, was a park bench in Lafayette Square, facing the White House, where it was convenient for many a man coming from or going to the White House to stop by the Baruch bench and enjoy the sunshine for a few moments with him. I have often sat with him on a bench in Central Park, not far from our respective homes in New York. This bench he called his "New York Office," and he admitted me into full partnership in it. Several times Baruch has reprimanded me for not being present and at work and has threatened to close up the New York Office and liquidate the affairs of the firm.

In any event, on the occasion when Baruch and I were lunching with the President, I made so bold, as the British say, as to suggest to Roosevelt that he give Bernie back his old Wold War I job, and put him in charge of the economy of the nation. Both of them fell silent and looked a little embarrassed, and the President smilingly led off into another subject. I realized before I spoke that this question would be a species of break, but I was not troubled by the thought. Sometime afterward, when Baruch was finally entrusted with the job of solving economic complexities of World War II— complexities that had baffled the clever young New Dealers —I was delighted.

When Edward F. Flynn, that wise man of politics, who was Democratic national chairman, asked me again to become honorary chairman of the Finance Committee of the National Committee to help raise money for the 1940 campaign, I found on examining the Hatch Act that I couldn't engage actively in the campaign and still retain my position as one of the American members of the International Arbitration Commission, so I sent in my resignation, which Roosevelt accepted with a gracious and complimentary letter.

In addition to my work of raising money for the 1940 presidential campaign, my services as a fund raiser were sought by many other political candidates.

When I decided to retire from the active practice of law in May 1941, I was melancholy, for the breaking up of the firm not only marked the end of my long and pleasant professional career, but also ended the existence of a law office which had been continuously active ever since my grandfather founded it in 1812.

It is not usually realized that the practice of law involves great responsibilities and risks. For instance, if your managing clerk should fail to file, within the period allowed, a notice of appeal from a judgment of hundreds of thousands of dollars, you would be sued by a justly indignant client. Of course in a large office it is practically impossible for the heads of the firm to oversee every act and read every paper that is prepared.

Chief among my reasons for retiring from my law practice was the increasing attention required by my private business affairs and investments and to the various trusts of which I am an executor. I had enough to do just looking after the properties owned by my wife and myself, acting as executor for Ida Bliss, for my mother-in-law, Mrs. Marcus Daly, Sr., for the trust estate of Marcus Daly II, and for a three-million-dollar trust created for charitable purposes in Kentucky by Mrs. James B. Haggin in memory of her husband. I am also head of a family corporation, of which my wife is a part owner, which farms the large Bitter Root Stock Farm in Montana.

In addition to the various responsibilities that I have briefly mentioned, I have had a heterogeneous collection of other activities, all of them interesting and some of them quite useful. Under the advice of Harold C. Skidmore of Shreveport I entered the lists of the seekers for oil in the Southwest with great success.

Among many dinners I recall speaking at a great dinner to James A. Farley in the Waldorf, where I referred to him as "that splendid citizen, that man of spotless honor, who never broke his word or deserted a friend"—a description that met with unusual applause.

During the winter of 1942–43 I enjoyed what must be the dream of every speaker and politician—and many who are neither—in the world. I had a regularly scheduled radio program. During the 1944 presidential campaign I was elected chairman of the New York State Democratic delegation to the national convention. This convention was fraught with historic drama. It seemed reasonable to think at first that Henry A. Wallace would carry off the vice-presidential nomination automatically. But when it became apparent that the forces behind Senator Harry S. Truman were strong and determined and that Wallace was not getting the administration support that had been expected, the tension and excitement made the occasion intensely dramatic.

CHAPTER XXXIV

As the time for the 1944 national election approached, I became active once more at the Democratic national headquarters in New York. No finance committee had been appointed, and Edwin W. Pauley, the party treasurer, had the arduous task of raising the money necessary for the campaign. I helped him as far as I was able.

My mementoes of this campaign include some correspondence with Franklin D. Roosevelt in which the details of fund raising are discussed in franker detail than in the ordinary public utterances on this subject. It also reveals Roosevelt in a more intimate and playful mood than most people were privileged to see him. Here it is in part:

September 30, 1944.

Dear Franklin:

. . . And I am asked to head a finance committee to deal with the sordid question of what will be used for money by H.Q. in this campaign. But sleeping on this I think it better to help quietly just as if I were in my old position rather than assume a position which might make Pauley, the treasurer, although he makes the request, feel that his plans and his prestige had been interfered with.

You see, in every campaign there has always been a finance

committee which was supposed to get in the money which was then held and spent by the treasurer. . . .

In this campaign no Finance Committee has up to now been appointed.

The present budget is at least $1,250,000–$750,000 for radio. Some of the radio for small stations must be cash down.

We can spend, by law, three millions if we get it.

However, you will undoubtedly be elected.

Yours ever,
(*signed*) James W. Gerard

P.S. I see you have been in conference with Frank Sinatra (the Voice) and one Toots Shor (is it male or female?). Perhaps the Voice will give a concert to help out and Toots (male or female) can take the tickets.

And the reply:

October 3, 1944.

Dear Jimmy:

That note of yours of September thirtieth is a joy.

I want to make it perfectly clear that Toots is the name of a man. If you saw him once you would have no question about it.

I suggest that in that new and eminent position of yours you get Frank Sinatra (The Voice) to sing to an assemblage made up of your PROSPECTS. He will make them swoon simultaneously and you can stand over the assemblage with a six-shooter in each hand. More than one way of financing a campaign!

With my warm regards,

Always sincerely,
(*signed*) F. D. R.

When my great-grandfather Gerard left New York in 1783 with the British troops and went to Fredericton, New Brunswick, he wrote a letter to his wife from his new abode. In it he said, "My dear Christina: I was sorry to have to leave suddenly without saying good-by to you and the dear children, but to change the subject, there is quite a real estate boom on here and last night they gave me a roast-beef dinner." All of which indicates that his Scotch and practical mind was in full operation. This letter also shows that my grand-father was alive when Louis XVI lost his head on the guillo-tine, an event which enabled Danton to declaim to the world, "The kings threaten us, we hurl at their feet, as gage of battle, the head of a king!" The thud of this head into the execu-tioner's basket inaugurated the era of modern history which is covered to date by the lives of my grandfather, my father, and myself.

The little thirteen colonies strung along the Atlantic sea-board were occupied for many years with their domestic problems, such as the great Louisiana purchase, the purchase of Florida, the area added by the acquisition of Texas, and the lands won as a result of the Mexican war.

We made a few excursions into foreign affairs such as the short war with England when the British burned the capitol at Washington, one with France of still shorter duration, and the pronouncement of President Monroe which has since been known as the Monroe Doctrine. Our own country was torn by the great Civil War which settled forever the ques-tion of geographical unity and the freeing of the slaves. Secretary Seward, for a mere pittance, acquired the magnifi-cent territory of Alaska, and the Northwest boundary was settled by agreement with England.

The sinking of the United States battleship *Maine* by mysterious explosion in the harbor of Havana ended an era. It projected us at last into all the intrigues, alliances, and wars which we had managed to avoid for so long while building up our own country and giving to our people the highest standard of living as yet enjoyed by any people on earth.

Speakers advocated that we create a mighty army, a great navy, a powerful air force, and that we should then sit safe behind three thousand miles of cool green water and mind our own business.

But this had become impossible. The Spanish War made us forever a participant in the hostilities and the age-old revenges of Europe, and we emerged from that war saddled with the custody of the Philippines and involved in all the problems of the Far East.

Our entrance into World War I was unavoidable. If we had stayed out of that war, the Germans would have attacked the Western Hemisphere, first probably by an invasion or revolution in Brazil. While I was Ambassador I learned that Germany was in the habit of sending a large sum of money every year to the three Brazilian states of Rio Grande do Sul, Paraná, and Santa Catharina to keep them in line as good Germans. Further, a German law provided that any Germans emigrating to Brazil should locate in those states, something which I commented upon when I testified for lend-lease before the Committee on Foreign Relations of the United States Senate just before World War II.

For many years British diplomacy was supreme and Britain occupied the place of power in Europe. But just before World War I the direction of the foreign policy of Great Britain fell into weak and hesitating hands. A very prominent Englishman told me that on the Friday before the march of the Germans into France he was at the house of Asquith, who said that he and Sir Edward Grey had been deviled by the French for a British declaration that she would enter the war if Germany invaded France. Such a declaration, even if a mere bluff carrying no evil consequence if it failed, might have prevented the start of World War I. But, as this English informant told me, there was hesitancy—a week end intervened, a bank holiday. Sir Edward Grey was said to have gone fishing. Finally, when the British were on the point of making the declaration, the German forces had already invaded France.

I have shown in these memoirs how at one time, when the war had degenerated into trench warfare and the first German submarine campaign had failed, the Germans were ready to make peace based on a return of all contending forces to their own lands. This was rejected by Colonel House and the British, the latter intent upon the absolute ruin of the German Empire.

I went abroad in 1922, and for several years thereafter I found that influential people in Great Britain, instead of promoting the friendship and leadership in foreign affairs of France and England, were saying "After all, France is our hereditary enemy and in the next war we hope to be on the side of the Germans."

Again, after Hitler came to power, this disinclination to join with the French was shown when the British made a separate naval treaty with Hitler without the knowledge of France. The culmination came and all the troubles and miseries of this modern world began when the British declined to join in a French proposal to resist the march of Hitler's troops into the Rhineland.

At the end of World War II we ourselves failed. We fell under the domination or the fascination of Stalin and the Russians, while they, contrary to the principles of the so-called Atlantic Charter, seized great territories and populations. Banners waved, orators spouted as we joined in creating the so-called United Nations, while the Russians laughed in their sleeves and strengthened their hold on the satellite states which they had brought into their orbit. At that time we possessed a mighty and victorious army on the soil of Europe, we had the greatest navy in the world, a powerful air force, and we alone possessed the secret of the atomic bomb. Nevertheless, instead of moving the Russians out of Germany, loosening their hold on Hungary, Romania, Bulgaria, Poland, Czechoslovakia, and Finland, our statesmen posed for their photographs on the platform of the United Nations meeting at San Francisco and seemed to think that the mere creation of the United Nations opened the way to paradise and peace.

A decade before this we had shown a far greater capacity for leadership and foresight when we proposed that the nations of the world unite in stopping the seizure of Manchuria by the Japanese. The failure to take this step made Pearl Harbor inevitable and predestined our entry into World War II.

I do not know the identity of the congenital idiot in our State Department who arranged that we should occupy part of Germany and a segment of Berlin with no road of communication between our two areas.

Of course, as I wrote in an article published by the *American Magazine* in July 1945, before the close of World War II, Germany should have been restored as a hereditary kingdom with all power in a parliament on the pattern of England. This would have constituted a bulwark against the advance of the Russian legions into the west.

And then came the greatest defeat in our history, the event which possibly marks our decline, when we refused to aid the Nationalists in China at a time when the present head of Communist China was a refugee in a cave. With little trouble and comparatively little expense we could have had the four hundred millions of China as a bulwark against the seizure by Russia of all the Far East. The outright armed aggression by Russia's satellite North Korea was directly attributable to our surrender of China without a fight.

As I survey the years of my lifetime I find a deep and bitter irony in the marvelous advances in science and technology which contrast so strangely with our backwardness in the art of living with one another. All of our advances in material well-being are threatened by a war of annihilation, a total war involving all mankind. This dread prospect is the result of the timidity, lack of foresight, and the disunity of the most highly civilized nations.

I had no love for Henry Stimson. As I have related, he refused me an opportunity to try to alleviate the tortures our prisoners of war were enduring in the prison camps of Europe and Asia. Nevertheless, in justice to him it must be said that it was the refusal of the nations in 1931 to heed his warning and halt the aggression of Japan in China which set the pattern of modern aggression and proved the prologue to the horrors of World War II, and, I fear, of World War III.

Our statesmen, after the "Day of Infamy" at Pearl Harbor brought war, never correctly appraised Russia. They seemed never really to understand that Russia, after first tying up with Hitler, became our ally not because of love for the West, but solely because Hitler treacherously invaded Russia in his lust for the Danube basin and the green fields of the Ukraine.

To my eternal regret, as I have written, I declined the proffer of the ambassadorship to Russia. I do not think that

I could have accomplished much of positive value, but at least I am sure I would not have succumbed to Russian blandishments and propaganda. Perhaps this alone might have preserved more of the fruits of the victories won by two great commanders, MacArthur and Eisenhower, whose invasion of Normandy must be considered one of the great military feats of all history.

It is problematical if any diplomatic course could have swerved the men in the Kremlin from the coldly calculated imperialism upon which they have embarked. Nevertheless there is one aspect of our relations with the Russians which never received the attention it deserved as we sought to understand the hostile suspicion we encounter at their hands.

After World War I, when the Soviets were fighting their revolutionary war, we invaded Russia, in concert with the British and Japanese, presumably to destroy the government just erected by Lenin and Trotsky. I happen to know that President Wilson at first did not favor this, but allowed himself to be persuaded by the British.

But our invasion of Russian territory from Archangel, our violation of their sovereignty, has naturally been violently resented by the Russians. Some of their hostile attitude today, I am convinced, is based upon the fear that we contemplate another invasion for the purpose of "destroying Communism everywhere." Whether the Kremlin really believes this or not, it is a powerful stimulant of animosity among the populace.

About June 1946 I organized a council of ex-ambassadors. All who were ex's at that time, with one exception, joined. I occasionally send them telegrams in order to get their sentiments and publish the same on various questions. For instance, they were nearly all agreed on the wisdom of the

Truman policy in Greece; they were practically unanimous in backing the Atlantic Pact, halting of the demolition of the plants in Germany, and the recognition of Franco by sending an Ambassador to Spain. But all did not share my views on giving aid to China. I sent the following telegram signed by those who did agree with me to the chairman of the Committee on Foreign Relations of the Senate and to the chairman of the Committee on Foreign Affairs of the House:

We the undersigned former Ambassadors of the United States believing that the vital interest of our country would be gravely menaced if China should fall under the domination of the Soviet Union urge you most strongly to give essential military equipment and economic and financial aid to the Chinese Government.

> F. Lammot Belin
> William C. Bullitt
> William M. Collier
> Josephus Daniels
> Wesley Frost
> James W. Gerard
> Boaz Long
> Lithgow Osborne
> William Phillips
> Robert P. Skinner
> William H. Standley
> Alexander W. Weddell

I regard the abandonment of China as the worst defeat that the United States has suffered in all its history. That surrender indicated, among other things, that we considered ourselves unable to counter the diabolical Russian technique of taking over a country with the aid of native traitors disguised as patriots. Our prestige in the Orient suffered a devastating blow.

We are today, against our inclinations, the leader of the non-communistic states—not of the world. I do not think that we have as yet appreciated the fact that Communism is a mental disease of great bodies of people—an attack by new ideas, or rather old ideas revamped, on the right of private property which is the sole basis of the so-called capitalistic state. Balzac wrote that "ideas devour epochs as men are devoured by their passions." And from Russia, always a socialistic state even under the czars, spreads this idea of totalitarian rule which makes slaves of all the people in its confines.

In a sense, Russia was a communism even under the czars. For instance, after the emancipation of the serfs in 1861, land was given to the village as a whole, the organization being known as the village mir. The elders of the village, confined entirely to the peasant class, distributed the land from time to time and even could send anyone they chose to Siberia. These village mirs were closed to all outside influence. Only a peasant might vote in a village assembly. The upper classes and the better educated, such as the lord of the manor, priest, and doctor, were not entitled to take part in arranging its affairs.

When the Soviet or Union of Unions came into being, Russia was easily turned to the Lenin brand of Communism.

The age-old push of Mother Russia to gain new countries or subject states added to the ideology of Communism has made Russia the world menace which it is today.

What is to be the result? A horrible war in which we with our crowded cities will be more vulnerable than Russia or a gradual development dividing the world? We pay now for our failure to take a strong stand when we alone possessed the power of the atomic bomb. We pay now for our abandonment of China. We pay now for hesitation, uncertainty, and appeasement.

A century and more ago Count Alexis de Tocqueville published his extraordinary book. In it he made the following prediction:

> There are at the present time two great nations in the world, the Russians and the Americans. The Anglo-American relies upon personal interest to accomplish his end and gives free scope to the unguided strength and common sense of the people. The Russian centers all the authority of society in a single arm. The principal instrument of the former is freedom, of the latter servitude. Their starting point is different and their courses are not the same. Yet each of them seems marked out by the will of heaven to sway the destinies of half the globe.

Is that to be the result? After a war or before?

In the meantime, our only indicated course is to arm the non-communist world, at the same time making the most strenuous efforts to break through the Iron Curtain with a propaganda to convince the Russian people that we at least have no wish to plunge the world into a war that may mean the end of civilization. And in even that there is danger. A restless Russia might tempt its rulers to use the age-old expedient of a government losing its grip on its people and try the adventure of war.

I am still active. In the 1950 campaign I was honorary chairman of the Finance Committee of the National Democratic Committee.

In November 1950 President Truman made me a member of the advisory committee in connection with Point 4 and aid to backward countries—a great chance to do much good.

In summing it all up, I conclude that it has been my good fortune to have a box seat from which to experience and observe the most exciting epoch of all history. I have watched the most grandiose schemes of human ambition rocket across the front pages and disappear into memories. The horsemen of destruction have ranged the earth, and at times their triumph has seemed imminent. And all the while, quietly and unobtrusively, the scientists and the artists and the statesmen and the men of good will have been at work building the sure foundations for a world in which cruelty and misery will not be man's inescapable companions.

There are those who fear that evil may be gaining preponderance; that our fumbling attempt to master the eternal secrets of nature may be the engine of our degeneration and downfall. I hold this view to be lamentably lacking in comprehension of the tenacity of human life, of man's strivings, and of the inconceivably complex scope of the divine purpose.

During my lifetime ten mighty empires have crumbled and crashed. They were the French Empire of Napoleon III, the Shereefian Empire of Morocco, the Empire of Brazil, the Chinese Empire, the Austrian Empire, the German Empire, the Turkish Empire, the Russian Empire, the Japanese Empire, and the British Empire. It is salutary to reflect that to the school children of today these great accumulations of power are distinguished only by a feat of memory from the old empire of the Pharaohs. Today the Danube flows as evenly as the Nile and the Euphrates, and so will it be tomorrow, while the inhabitants of their banks struggle up the painful road at whose summit is the knowledge of how to live in peace and contentment with themselves, each other, and their environment.

As David Hume observed, when we complain that there

are few wise men, we forget that the term is descriptive only of those who are far wiser than the average. When every youth is possessed of the scientific brains of an Einstein, the saintliness of a Gandhi, and the statesmanship of a Churchill, we shall still say there are few wise men, for only those few will tower above the crowd.

Therein I conceive to lie the hope of the world—in the gradual progress of the average, being sure that the exceptional will always appear. As always, the great strides forward will be led by these exceptional men, but wiser generations will learn to distinguish the truly noble leader from the ambitious mountebank and the power-mad tyrant.

For among the finer qualities of men is the ability to envision a wisdom and a virtue of a degree with which he has had no actual experience. And it has long been noted that man is the mimic of his dreams, often destroying them with his clumsy parodies, often frustrated by the chasm between his aspirations and his capacity, but forever replacing the bruised and battered failures with new generations blessed with eager enthusiasm for a new try.

I envy all who will be in the cast as the great and never-ending drama unfolds.

The skies above our sad world are dark and threatening, but the dawn cannot be halted and will come at last.

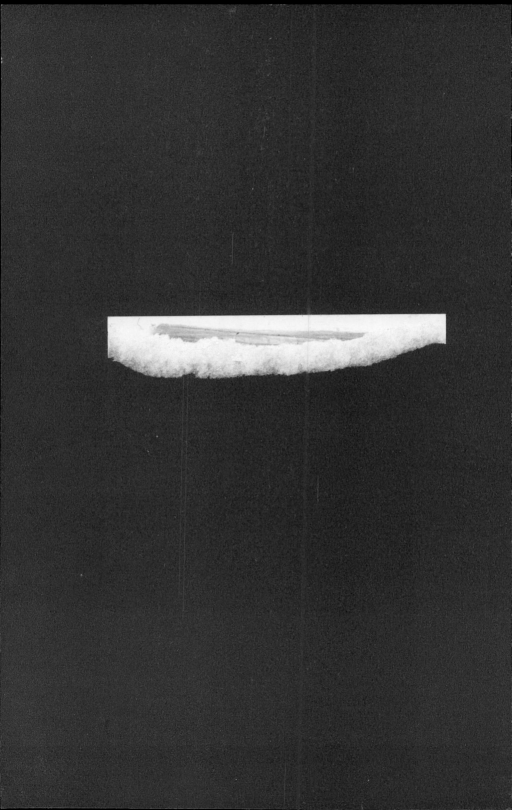